ROCK-A-BY BABY

PERSPECTIVES ON GENDER

Series Editor:
Myra Marx Feree, University of Connecticut

Pleasure, Power, and Technology:
Some Tales of Gender, Engineering,
and the Cooperative Workplace
Sally Hacker

Black Feminist Thought:
Knowledge, Consciousness, and the
Politics of Empowerment
Patricia Hill Collins

Understanding Sexual Violence:
A Study of Convicted Rapists
Diana Scully

Maid in the U.S.A.
Mary Romero

Feminisms and the Women's Movement:
Dynamics of Change in Social Movement
Ideology and Activism
Barbara Ryan

Black Women and White Women in the Professions:
Analysis of Job Segregation by Race and Gender,
1960–1980
Natalie J. Sokoloff

Gender Consciousness and Politics
Sue Tolleson Rinehart

Mothering:
Ideology, Experience, and Agency
Evelyn Nakano Glenn, Grace Chang,
and Linda Rennie Forcey (editors)

For Richer, For Poorer:
Mothers Confront Divorce
Demie Kurz

ROCK-A-BY BABY

Feminism,

Self-Help,

and Postpartum Depression

VERTA TAYLOR

ROUTLEDGE　　　NEW YORK AND LONDON

Published in 1996 by

Routledge
29 West 35th Street
New York, NY 10001

Published in Great Britain in 1996 by

Routledge
11 New Fetter Lane
London EC4P 4EE

© Routledge 1996

Printed in the United States of America on acid-free paper

Permissions:
Excerpt from "Eat for Two" by Natalie Merchant, © 1989 Christian Burial
Music.
"The Low Road" from Circles on the Water by Marge Piercy, © 1982.
Reprinted by permission of Alfred A. Knopf, Inc.
"Emotions" by Jeanette Honikman is printed courtesy of the author.

Library of Congress Cataloging-in-Publication Data

Taylor, Verta A.
Rock-a-by Baby : feminism, self-help, and postpartum depression /
Verta Taylor.
      p.   cm.
Includes bibliographical references.
ISBN 0-415-91291-1 (cl).   ISBN 0-415-91292-X (pb)
      1. Women—Social networks—United States. 2. Mothers—Social networks—
United States.   3. Mothers—Mental health—United States.   4. Postpartum
depression—United States. 5. Self-help groups—United States. 6. Feminism—
United States. I. Title.
      HQ1421.T39 1996   96-19519
      306.874'3—dc20   CIP

Design and typesetting by Leslie Sharpe with Hermann Feldhaus at Cave.

To Dagmar Celeste

CONTENTS

ACKNOWLEDGMENTS

IN RESEARCHING this topic and writing this book, many people have contributed to my work. First and foremost, I thank those who have allowed me to interview them: the women who shared their experiences of postpartum illness; the physicians, nurses, social workers, psychologists, and human service professionals who shared their frames of reference; and the members of Depression After Delivery (D.A.D.) and Postpartum Support International (PSI). I am especially grateful to Nancy Berchtold, founder of D.A.D., and Jane Honikman, founder of PSI, for opening their organizational and personal files to me. Without their guidance, insights, and friendship, and their deep personal commitment to the issue of postpartum illness, I could not have written this book. I also thank Karen Mumford, founder of the Ohio chapter of D.A.D., and Helen Cain Jackson, Chief of the Office of Prevention in the Ohio Department of Mental Health, for allowing me to attend the meetings of Ohio's Postpartum Depression Task Force and for sharing their memories and insights. For her courage in speaking out about her experiences, for her insistence on finding answers that might help other women, and for keeping the faith in the long and arduous struggle for women's equality, I dedicate this book to Dagmar Celeste.

The research was supported financially for a period of nearly ten years by three separate awards from the Ohio Department of Mental Health. I thank former director Pamela Hyde and especially Dee Roth, director of Program Evaluation and Research, for their steadfast commitment to and enthusiasm for this project. As I have worked with Dee over the past twenty years, I have developed tremendous respect for her technical skills, research ethics, administrative capabilities, and ability to survive the perilous shifting political landscape in Ohio. Further, I am grateful to the Ohio State University for providing various funds for the research, including a Seed Grant from the Office of Research, a sabbatical during which I conducted most of the fieldwork on the self-help movement, several grants from the College of Social and Behavioral Sciences, funding for two research assistants from the College of Humanities, and several awards directly from the Department of Sociology.

Completing a project of this magnitude would have been impossible without a number of research assistants. I am grateful to Lisa Ransdell, Kelly McCormick, Nancy Essex, Chris Smithies, Melinda Wolfe, and Claire Picone for conducting a portion of the first set of interviews; Phyllis Gorman, Susan Moseley, Sharon Carter, and Susann Rivera for handling administrative tasks on the research project; Stephanie Spears, who assisted with the analysis of the interview data, and Bridget Anderson, who helped with the analysis of the medical and popular sources; Alicia Hurtt, Nicole Raeburn, and Martha Schmidt for transcription assistance; and Nicole Raeburn and Molly Wallace for assisting with the bibliography and appendix.

I am deeply indebted to a number of scholars who read and provided thoughtful comments on the entire manuscript: Joan Huber, Myra Marx Ferree, Nicole Raeburn, Leila J. Rupp, Suzanne Staggenborg, Kate Weigand, Nancy Whittier, and Marieke Van Willigen. In addition I am grateful to those who read parts of the manuscript: Linda Blum, Florence Bonner, Dagmar Celeste, Kathy Charmaz, Hank Johnston, Michael Kimmel, Bert Klandermans, Judith Lorber, Patricia Yancey Martin, Susan

Osborn, Harry Potter, Lisa Ransdell, Laurel Richardson, Catherine Ross, Dee Roth, Michael Schwartz, and Barrie Thorne. I especially thank my editor at Routledge, Jayne Fargnoli, for recognizing the possibilities of this project and providing the impetus, encouragement, friendship, and enthusiasm necessary to complete the book. Everyone I have worked with at Routledge has been extraordinarily helpful and competent. I am grateful to Kim Herald and Karen Deaver for overseeing the manuscript through editing and production, and Jay Hodges for his determination to begin marketing the book before I had even finished writing the conclusion. Finally, my copy editor, Kathleen Silloway, facilitated and was a member of a postpartum support group in New York City. Her astute editing has made it more likely that those affected by postpartum illness will read my book.

On a more personal note, there are those who provided support so vital that, without them, I might never have been able to write this book. Myra Marx Ferree, my mentor, friend, and editor of the Perspectives on Gender Series at Routledge, has for many years helped me believe in myself and has encouraged my scholarship in more ways than she will ever know. Leslie Bomar, my college roommate and friend for nearly thirty years, provided the impetus for me to write a book that would appeal to a wider audience when I discovered that her own bout with postpartum depression was the reason I had not heard from her in nearly two years. My physician and friend Judith Lubbers spent endless hours helping me understand the medical perspective on women's health, sharing her own experiences of motherhood, and making sure that I stayed well enough to finish the book. Lisa Hurtubise was my massage therapist while I was working on this book. Not only did she treat the aches and pains that resulted from spending so many hours at the computer, but many of the themes in this book were the subject of our sessions. Several current graduate students—especially Nicole Raeburn, Marieke Van Willigen, Jo Reger, Kim Dill, Melinda Goldner, Willa Young, Beth Catlett, Linda Dobbs, Kim Dugan, and Andre Levi—not only influenced my thinking in important ways but also gave me the encouragement to continue, as they noted with sympathy and understanding the toll that completing this book was taking on me. And I thank those who managed to say and do exactly the right things just when I thought I couldn't work any harder: Nikki Raeburn, who called the manuscript a "page turner"; novelist Susan Osborn, who reassured me that I don't write like a sociologist; Ruth Peterson, who is the kind of friend with whom I share my agonies as well as my joys; Barbara Reskin, whose leadership of the department made such a difference; and Betty Menaghan, who, when I didn't make my September deadline, showed that she had never lost confidence by saying "the book will come, and we can celebrate." Betty Jo, Babs, Nikki, Kerri, and Trisha made sure I found time for fun when the pressure mounted to finish, and Sidney and Walter Rupp provided inspiration, lively conversation, and family vacations when I was weary. My mother, Alice Houston, and I grew even closer over the months as I struggled to complete this manuscript; she provided both the continual support I needed to finish and the laughter and vacations necessary to get me to take my work less seriously. I am also especially grateful to Nancy Whittier, who not only is an unparalleled intellectual colleague but who also assumed the burden of other projects so that I could finally complete this book; it is hard to believe that when I began this research she had not yet begun her graduate studies at Ohio State. Both she and Nikki Raeburn for some reason continued to answer their phones even though they knew it was likely to be me wanting to read them some new passage. And I can never thank Nikki enough for the millions of other things she has done—from watching our house to warning people to stay away from me when I had been up late writing—to make certain that I finished this book.

Most of all, special love and thanks to Leila Rupp, the woman with whom I share my life. She has read every page of this manuscript more times than I would like to remember, given me the self-confidence to be creative and imaginative and the will to go on through the most difficult of times, and for the past seventeen years has provided every kind of emotional, intellectual, and day-to-day support imaginable. Finally, I thank our precious Maltese, Emma, who spent as many hours asleep outside my study door as I did chained to my computer, but who also demanded that I stop now and then to appreciate the love and kindness of my family and friends.

PREFACE

S INCE THE inspiration for *Rock-a-by Baby* came from a sociological study, material contained in this book is of a scholarly nature. The topic of postpartum depression, however, has an audience that extends far beyond the bounds of academia. So in order to satisfy a variety of readers, scholarly documentation has been retained but placed at the end of the book, thereby making the text more accessible and readable for all concerned.

It has taken me a long time to write this book. Although the reasons are intellectual as well as personal, completing this project has led me to agree wholeheartedly with feminist Susan Krieger, who writes in *Social Science and the Self* that our arguments are always based to a certain extent on our own experiences. Researching the postpartum self-help movement admittedly has changed the way I think about the nature and significance of feminism. At the same time, the changes that took place in my life while I was completing this project have influenced the direction of the study almost as much as did the deliberate research strategies.

At first, it seemed as though this research chose me, instead of the reverse. When Dee Roth, director of the Office of Program Evaluation and Research of the Ohio Department of Mental Health, approached me about doing a sociological study of postpartum depression, the topic seemed too far afield from my ongoing interest in feminism and women's movements. True, Dee's office had funded my doctoral dissertation, which focused on the emergence of an indigenous network of mental health services when a tornado gouged a devastating path through Xenia, Ohio, on April 3, 1974. But when she approached me about the postpartum depression study, I had just coauthored a book on the American women's movement in the doldrum years of the 1940s and '50s. I had not worked on the sociology of mental health for nearly ten years. Learning that Dagmar Celeste, an ardent feminist and wife of Ohio Governor Richard Celeste, was behind the study sparked my interest. During her husband's political campaign, Dagmar had spoken frequently about the postpartum psychosis she had suffered after the birth of their sixth child, and she had made public her subsequent hospitalization. I suspected that the condition of postpartum illness might provide an opportunity to explore the broader sociopolitical context of women's mental health, particularly the connection between women's subordinate social status and their high rates of emotional distress.

As a sociologist, I wanted to understand the connection between the cultural myths and social requirements of motherhood and women's experiences of postpartum depression. But I soon discovered that there is an ongoing debate between the medical establishment and women's self-help groups over the very existence of postpartum illness. My focus shifted after I unearthed a groundswell of support for women who have experienced postpartum illness. I was first interested in whether women's internalization of the view that their main goal in life is to become wives and mothers leads them to frame their unhappiness in terms of postpartum depression. But as I listened to the themes in women's accounts of depression and recovery, I began to see how the experience of motherhood can provide a basis for questioning orthodox conceptions of femininity. Why are women organizing into self-help groups to reject the traditional notion of the selfless and devoted mother? What events have led women over the past decade to embrace psychiatric understandings and resources as a tool for social change? And what implications does organizing around the shared experiences of motherhood have for changing the larger system of gender relations? This book, as it turns out, is strongly linked to my earlier work on women's movements, which has focused on women's communities as sources of feminist protest and as sites where women negotiate new understandings of what it means to be a woman.

Over time, I also realized that this research is about my own experience of depression, which struck in the midst of the project. My dark cloud came after several months of debilitating pain that led me to have a total hysterectomy at the age of forty-one. Almost immediately, I began experiencing hot flashes, and within a matter of weeks after the surgery I became anxious, unable to concentrate, and incapable of sleep. Over the next three months, I was hospitalized two more times, once for complications resulting from the surgery and once in cardiac intensive care, as a result of the stress of recovery and a family history of early death from heart disease. Finally, a full-blown clinical depression set in, and I could not bear to eat, sleep, leave my house, or even read a book for nearly six months. During the same period, my stepfather was diagnosed with cancer, and he died four months later. Life seemed hopeless and not worth living until I finally agreed reluctantly—after three months of psychotherapy and only as a last resort to psychiatric hospitalization—to take the antidepressants my woman physician had prescribed. Within a matter of days, I was back on my feet and in six months found that I was able to stop taking the medication.

Until that time, the depression I had been studying had been more academic than real. As a feminist, I had been critical of the turn toward recovery and self-help taken by the modern women's movement since the 1980s. As a sociologist, I had long been skeptical that helping individuals could lead to change in the social processes and institutions I truly believe are responsible for people's suffering. And as a typical American, I had been dubious about turning to medication to solve my unhappiness. I vividly remember that about a year after I recovered from my depression, I gave a talk about my research on postpartum depression at a local hospital. What I had to say must have reflected the changes taking place in my thinking, for Dagmar Celeste, who happened to be in the audience, approached me and said, "I thought you understood our problem before. Now I can see you really understand what it is like to be depressed."

While this book is not in any way a memoir of my own experiences, a central tenet of feminist research is the recognition that the social location and standpoint of the author shapes one's observations and interpretations. Although I rely in this book on theories and arguments that come from the disciplines of sociology and women's studies to understand postpartum illness, I undoubtedly project a great deal of myself onto this topic. And there is another reason I begin with my own depression: it seems voyeuristic to lay bare the lives of the depressed women I have studied without articulating the meaning of depression in my own life.

Some readers may wonder why I have chosen to use the names of self-help activists in the text, especially since I often use their stories to elucidate generalizable patterns that are unrelated to the identities of the individuals whose stories I tell. The fact is that most of the self-help activists I interviewed are public figures who not only are accustomed to being quoted in the media but who also consider confidentiality an impediment to the movement's aim of bringing the problem of postpartum illness into the public domain. I have honored their requests to be named in this account of the postpartum self-help movement. In some instances, however, I did obtain information from women in confidence and assured these interviewees and survey respondents anonymity. In these cases, I have taken care not to use their real names and to disguise any identifiers. When describing these women's experiences, I have used pseudonyms and, in a few instances, have even changed minor identifying characteristics to protect their identities. I realize that some people are likely not to see themselves exactly as I have. But I hope that my interviewees will find my story, overall, faithful to their experiences.

If over the course of this research I have come to understand depression in a more personal way, I have also come to terms with my own decision not to bear and raise children. I have never been sure exactly how or when I came to the conclusion that I did not want to be a mother. But perhaps as a sign of how women's self-definitions revolve less around motherhood than they once did, the women I got to know while doing this study never questioned my decision. Nor did they challenge my ability to understand and write about their lives because I never have mothered a child.

INTRODUCTION

THE FEMINISM IN WOMEN'S SELF-HELP

ASK ALMOST any English-speaking American what lullabies she knows and the answer is likely to be "Rock-a-by, Baby." Sung to put babies to sleep, the words in this familiar lullaby convey an alarming image:

> Rock-a-by, baby, on the treetop,
> When the wind blows, the cradle will rock,
> When the bough breaks, the cradle will fall,
> And down will come baby, cradle and all.

How ironic that the classic American lullaby, by juxtaposing suggestions of care and harm, so thoroughly expresses the contradictions of motherhood. Is it any wonder that one of the women I interviewed for this book, overwhelmed by genuine unhappiness after the birth of her baby, found herself rocking her baby to sleep crooning, "I hate you, I hate you"?

Perhaps the ultimate expression of maternal contradictions can be found in the condition of postpartum depression. The clinical signs of postpartum depression are comparable to depressive episodes in general and include feelings of inadequacy, sadness and despair, anxiety and nervousness, appetite and sleep disturbances, an inability to concentrate, compulsive thoughts, loss of interest in sexual activities, and an absence of feelings for the baby. The birth of a baby is mythically believed to be joyful and exciting. Why is it, then, that both popular and medical writings have long acknowledged a link between childbirth and psychiatric illness? In her literary masterpiece, *The Yellow Wallpaper*, Charlotte Perkins Gilman narrates the story of a nineteenth-century woman who has been taken to the country by her physician husband to recover from an undefined illness following the birth of her first child. She feels trapped by the role assigned women and is further incapacitated by her husband's medical advice, which reflects conceptions of proper womanly behavior. Gilman's story recounts the emotional anguish of the narrator as she struggles to maintain her sanity while being haunted by the image of a woman imprisoned behind the sickly colored wallpaper in her bedroom. She spends her illness stripping the wallpaper in order to free the woman, an act that serves as a metaphor for Gilman's own struggle to break loose from the constraints of motherhood that are so closely intertwined with gender.

In the nineteenth century, there was a fairly universal consensus among physicians that psychiatric disorders associated with pregnancy and childbirth, referred to as "puerperal insanity," were common enough to account for about 10 percent of asylum admissions. The symptoms of this "disease"—aversion to the child and husband, meanness, obscenity, incessant talking, excitement, and sleeplessness—were virtually the opposite of the feminine traits of the period. Now it is tempting to view puerperal insanity solely as an attempt by the male-dominated medical establishment to reinforce gender inequality by defining and regulating behavior that violated orthodox conceptions of femininity as illness. The fact is that women, as patients seeking and demanding treatment, also played an active role in creating the disease, although they were by no means equal partners in the medicalization of their suffering. By translating women's desperation and rebellion against maternal constraints into symptoms of disease, the male medical establishment managed to silence women. As gynecologists in the early twentieth century gradually abandoned the view that women's diseased reproductive organs accounted for female insanity, and as the field of psychiatry advanced new and presumably more scientific theories of mental illness, puerperal insanity became a suspect classification and soon disappeared altogether from the medical literature. Indeed, since 1952, the American Psychiatric Association's *Diagnostic and Statistical Manual*, the official handbook of mental illness, has excluded psychiatric illness connected to childbirth as a distinct diagnostic category on the grounds that "there is disagreement about the importance of child-birth as the precipitating factor."

In the 1980s, the pendulum began to swing back toward the nine-teenth-century view of postpartum psychiatric illness. Studies uniformly reported a relatively high incidence of psychiatric disorders following childbirth, with short-lived episodes of the "baby blues" occurring in about 50 to 80 percent of women; moderate depression in 10 to 20 per-cent of women, and major depression, psychosis, and psychotic depression in roughly 1 to 2 percent of women. Concurrently, the popular discourse on pregnancy, childbirth, and motherhood on television talk shows, in dramas, popular fiction, women's magazines, and the self-help literature increasingly highlighted the sadness, ambivalence, guilt, anxiety, anger, depression, and mental illness associated with motherhood—conditions that had dropped out of the storyline during the pronatalist decades of the 1950s and '60s. The spotlight was placed on postpartum depression when Princess Diana, in her much touted November 1995 television interview, admitted suffering such severe "postnatal depression" that she not only could not get out of bed to perform her duties as "wife, mother, and Princess of Wales," but inflicted injuries on her own arms and legs.

It is not surprising that the negative side of motherhood came to the fore in the 1980s and '90s. After all, these were the decades when the concept of the modern woman successfully combining child care with employment gained a foothold. In fact, the labor force participation of white married women with children reached the high levels characteris-tic of African American women. By 1990, 53 percent of all mothers with a child younger than one year old worked outside the home, compared with only 31 percent in 1976. An even higher proportion of college grad-uates (68 percent) combined work and childrearing. For the first time, the majority of women struggled to balance work and family commitments. As a line from popular rap group Arrested Development put it, "Mama's always on stage."

Even as women enjoy greater opportunities in the work place, moth-erhood is becoming the focus of some of the most heated political controversies of the day—maternity policy, medical and family leave, abor-tion, adoption, welfare for single mothers, and the ethics of the new reproductive technologies. Mothers, traditionally revered in the public discourse, are now being portrayed as much more complex, even wicked, beings. One has only to think of the story of Susan Smith from South Carolina, who strapped her two children into her car and rolled it down a ramp into a lake, drowning both children, and who then used her history of depression, abuse, and abandonment to avoid the death sentence; or of headlines trumpeting the news of mothers who sacrifice their babies' lives for the pleasures of crack cocaine. From single welfare mothers accused of draining the national coffers to surrogate mothers demanding custody of babies promised to adoptive parents, suddenly mothers are being blamed for many of the ills facing society. Such a transformation in the discourse of motherhood is not only a result of media sensationalism. Certainly another contributing factor is the cultural divide—opened by the New Right's alliance with the Republican party—between conservative advocates of "traditional social values" and liberals who defend social programs that allow for a diversity of family forms.

The conflict over the appropriate roles for women is played out not only in the arenas of politics and social policy but also in vociferous debates among women themselves about the relative importance of their status as childbearers in determining their social identities. One of the major sites where this contest is taking shape and where women are forging new ways to mother is in the myriad of self-help groups throughout American society. The focus of these typically all-female groups can be as specific as childbirth education, breast feeding, or lesbian mothering, or as general as parenting and motherhood. Such groups not only promote a collective female consciousness that is reinforced by small group meetings, but they also frequently question traditional gender relationships within the family, sharing the conviction expressed by feminist philosopher Joyce Trebilcot that "mothering must now be defined and controlled by women." Although women's self-help groups have been largely overlooked in scholarly discussions of social movements, studying them is important in helping us to understand the significance of women's collective action for the reconstruction of the female role.

What is especially interesting about the modern dialogue over postpartum illness is that, unlike in the nineteenth century, the male-dominated medical establishment is not taking the lead in the campaign for medicalization. Rather, women patients and medical practitioners (physicians and nurses) are the main forces behind the national campaign that aims to raise public awareness of postpartum psychiatric conditions, to provide mutual support to women who suffer emotional distress associated with childbirth and the overwhelming responsibilities of caring for and raising a child, and to pressure medical and mental health institutions and the society at large to take seriously the emotional problems of new mothers.

Coming to terms with the contradictions of motherhood embodied in the experience of postpartum illness is the goal of what participants refer to as "the postpartum depression self-help movement," which consists of two separate but interacting national social movement organizations, Depression After Delivery (D.A.D.) and Postpartum Support International (PSI). Both groups were formed in the mid-1980s, coalescing out of the experiences of women who suffered serious postpartum psychiatric illness and were unable to find sources of treatment and support that confirmed their own self-diagnoses. Although the founders of both D.A.D. and PSI had long histories of feminist activism, it is significant that they launched their support groups during a period that scholars of the women's movement have characterized, following Judith Stacey, as "postfeminist."

For all sectors of the women's movement—national groups fighting for women's rights in the political arena, such as the National Organization for Women and the National Abortion Rights Action League, and loosely organized smaller groups struggling for gender equality outside the conventional political system—the 1980s were years of retrenchment. The decline of the movement was, in part, a response to the New Right, which contributed to the defeat of the Equal Rights Amendment in 1982 and mounted the attack on legalized abortion. Opposition to feminism hardened with the explicitly antifeminist policies of the Reagan administration and a virulent backlash against feminism in popular culture, both of which contributed to a general waning of public support for feminism. While it may have fragmented the broad feminist coalition that had emerged by the 1970s and caused some groups to retreat from political engagement, this shift to a more hostile national political climate did not spell the death of feminism. Rather, it transformed both the form and the strategies of women's movements. By the mid-1980s, feminism was beginning to spread to different constituencies of women who were applying the goals and strategies of the women's movement to a variety of "women's problems" that had not been central to the movement of the 1960s and '70s. As new generations of activists continued to be drawn to feminism in the 1980s, they found new arenas for political action as they struggled to define a feminism that would reflect the specific disadvantages of gender in their own lives.

The postpartum self-help movement gathered steam through widespread media attention that began when Nancy Berchtold, the founder of D.A.D. appeared on the *Phil Donahue Show* in connection with a book about postpartum depression written by journalist Carol Dix entitled

The New Mother Syndrome. Then in 1988, a nurse from Los Angeles—who had killed her nine-month-old son during a postpartum psychotic episode and was found not guilty by virtue of temporary insanity—began to appear with activists on nationally televised talk shows and news programs. Widespread media attention, especially to the possible link between postpartum illness and infanticide, helped Depression After Delivery to grow into a network of more than 250 support groups tied together in some cases by statewide or regional associations. Today the movement operates a "warm line" that links women with support groups located in most regions of the country, national and regional conferences, newsletters and publications, and a network of lay and professional leaders and experts whose perspectives on postpartum illness are sanctioned by the movement. Its membership consists mainly of women who have suffered major depression or psychosis connected to childbirth, a small number of husbands of women who have endured major depressions and psychoses requiring hospitalization or prolonged outpatient care, and a handful of medical and mental health professionals and researchers interested in the treatment and study of postpartum disorders. The movement has also attracted women, both imprisoned and acquitted, who have killed their children in connection with postpartum psychosis and are interested in legal reform as well as emotional support. Also in some localities, the parents and spouses of women who have committed suicide in the throes of postpartum mental illness have founded support groups.

The movement's three main strategies—consciousness-raising, direct service, and lobbying—have come directly out of the women's health movement of the 1970s and are deployed not only to provide emotional support to participants but also to work for long-term institutional changes in the medical and mental health systems, the law, family policy, and the society at large. Furthermore, like most self-help movements, its tactics are heavily cultural and revolve around disputed meanings—in this case the debate over whether postpartum illness should be treated as a bona fide medical condition—and contested identities, namely the changing meaning of motherhood. Scholars of the women's movement use the term "discursive politics" to underscore the extent to which feminism, in the contemporary context, is perhaps best understood as a shared discourse and identity to which women feel accountable, rather than a set of particular organizations. This is not to imply, of course, that feminists do not engage in action in the "real world" to effect change. From political scientist Mary Katzenstein's perspective, however, a great deal of the work of the women's movement does not take the form of conventional interest-group politics but involves "rewriting through language texts and symbolic acts their own understanding of themselves in relation to . . . society."

Over the past decade, self-help, recovery, and support groups that draw upon the discourse of feminism have gained increasing importance as sources of emotional support and settings in which women seek to redefine the female self. Self-help, or women joining together to solve common problems not being addressed by existing organizations and social practices, has always been integral to the women's movement, because such practices serve to anchor feminism in women's most elemental everyday experiences. In the women's movement of the 1970s, the feminist rallying cry that "the personal is political" justified self-help strategies as the foundation of a fundamentally separatist and radical feminism aimed at reclaiming power from male-dominated institutions. But by the 1990s, self-help had taken on quite a different cast. When Gloria Steinem, often looked upon as the standard bearer of second-wave feminism, published a best-selling self-help confessional of her journey to self-esteem entitled *Revolution from Within*, it came under sharp attack by feminists of varying stripes. Activists and scholars as diverse in their disciplinary training as historian Alice Echols and psychologists Celia Kitzinger and Rachel Perkins stamped women's self-help an apolitical variety of cultural feminism or identity politics. Critics have argued that by defining women's problems primarily in individual terms and offering psychological and medical frames for their resolution, self-help strategies divert attention away from the more significant political and economic barriers to women's equality. Self-help, they argue, encourages women to put a feminist veneer on such activities as recovering from addiction and abuse, getting in touch with one's inner child, and restoring one's self-esteem, while stressing private and therapeutic solutions over public and institutional challenges to the inequalities of gender, race, and class.

Some popular writers have gone so far as to suggest that self-help culture works against feminism's most fundamental tenets by promoting what Naomi Wolf calls "victim feminism" and what Wendy Kaminer and Carol Tavris label a "cult of victimhood." By this, they mean that women's self-help grossly exaggerates gender oppression and motivates women to retreat from the challenges of equality into an all-female world that valorizes traditional notions of femininity. Feminist critics cast an especially skeptical eye on twelve-step self-help programs which, they argue, promulgate ideas that reinforce women's subordination. The admission of personal powerlessness and the need for outside help of a spiritual nature, which is a central component of most twelve-step organizations modeled on Alcoholics Anonymous, can run counter to the feminist goal of empowering women. At the same time, the vast literature on code-pendence, spurred by the formation of Al-Anon in 1951 by wives of alcoholics, has helped set the tone for women to challenge conventional ideas about their place. There is undoubtedly some truth, along with a good deal of snobbery, behind critics' condemnation of self-help as exploitative, superficial, and perhaps even a dangerous throwback to tra-ditional feminine roles. But this is only the most obvious piece of a more difficult puzzle.

In this book, I take issue with the one-sided negative view of self-help that currently dominates the scholarly literature. The problem with most critical analyses is that they speak mainly to the voluminous popular self-help literature that occupies such a large amount of space in today's neighborhood bookstores, especially titles promoting those twelve-step principles. Or they target, as Naomi Wolf does in her book *Fire With Fire*, the form of self-help dished out on syndicated daytime talk shows, which increasingly serve as platforms for women to speak openly about such top-ics as domestic violence, child abuse, marital conflict, and sexual harassment.

In a recent national survey of support group participation in the United States, Robert Wuthnow found that nearly half (45 percent) of the adult female population claims to be involved in a support group. And women's support groups, according to pioneer self-help researcher Alfred Katz, make up a large proportion of the 500,000 to 750,000 contempo-rary self-help groups comprising at least 10 to 15 million members operating in the United States today. Both Wuthnow and Katz report, however, that therapy-oriented twelve-step groups—the subjects of the most virulent attacks by feminists—are not the most popular. Women form self-help groups not only to deal with problems pertaining to the abuse of alcohol and drugs, but also to come to grips with other prob-lems and personal stresses—parenting, sexual violence, eating disorders, illness, bereavement, marital and relationship problems, divorce, retire-ment, and looking after a sick child or relative. In every region of the country, whether in small towns or major metropolitan areas, local news-papers routinely announce the names and locations of support groups focusing on every problem imaginable. Hoping to expand participation in church activities, religious leaders increasingly capitalize on the popu-larity of self-help by organizing support groups that address a host of individual problems ranging from parenting and the loss of a spouse to the abuse of alcohol and an overemphasis on work. Missing from the cur-rent feminist debate over the self-help enterprise is an understanding of the many types of women's self-help movements that operate in the 1990s and the ways they have been informed by feminism.

There is a growing scholarly interest in understanding the significance of the burgeoning self-help industry for what it tells us, on the one hand, about the postmodern fragmentation of community and identity and, on the other, about modern forms of association that have emerged to fulfill individuals' need for a renewed sense of community, new self-definitions, and a spiritual dimension to their lives. For example, the popularity of support groups for new mothers is undoubtedly connected to the isolation of mothers in nuclear families, a growing problem in modern urbanized societies characterized by high geographic mobility and the weakening of extended families. The seemingly curious rise in therapeutic self-help groups can be attributed to a combination of two tendencies in modern societies: first, for people to turn to anonymous authorities for help with their emotional problems, and second, the changes taking place in American social policy toward mental health care in the 1980s that have reduced individuals' access to outpatient and inpatient care. Even as the broad-based community mental health system built in the 1960s was being eroded by the conservative political tide in Washington, medicine was taking advantage of the crisis in human services to further expand its domain into new problem areas. At the same time, feminism—whose adherents played a major role in the 1920s and '30s in developing the social services that have been central to the modern welfare state—turned hostile to the therapeutic impulse in the early 1970s and began establishing their own alternative social services.

By ignoring the larger social and political context in which self-help flowered, feminist scholars have only asked limited questions that overlook self-help's transformative potential. Even if women's self-help takes the individual to be the locus of change, it encourages the collective pursuit of personal problems that can be seen as a direct result of men's domination and women's subordination. It seems clear that part of the popularity and spread of the contemporary women's self-help genre can be explained because—as bell hooks argues in *Sisters of the Yam*, her self-help book for black women—it speaks so directly to the tensions in women's everyday lives brought about by gender inequality and its intersection with other forms of institutionalized oppression based on race, ethnicity, class, and sexuality. The study of women's self-help, then, provides a window into the workings of groups that have used social services to curb male domination.

The postpartum support group movement sits at the intersection of all these developments in American society: the ascendance of conservative politics, the struggle over the meaning and practice of motherhood, the transformation of feminism, the alienation of postmodern society, and the therapeutic turn. In this book, I chart the course of the postpartum self-help movement to explore the relationships between gender, the ideas and strategies of contemporary women's self-help movements, and feminism. Beyond explaining this movement, I intend to contribute to our understanding of the gendered nature of contemporary social movements and the significance of women's self-help movements for the reconstruction of gender.

THE FEMINIST RESEARCH

The seeds for this project were planted in the spring of 1982 when sociologist Dee Roth, director of the Office of Research and Evaluation of the Ohio Department of Mental Health, convened a meeting with feminist researchers in the social sciences on the Ohio State University campus. At this meeting, I learned that Dagmar Celeste, the wife of Ohio governor Richard Celeste, was eager for the department to sponsor a study of the social aspects of postpartum illness. Dagmar's interest stemmed from her own postpartum psychosis and depression, which led to a period of hospitalization and extended outpatient psychiatric treatment. Although the media had used Dagmar Celeste's history to question her emotional stability when her husband ran for office, her commitment to research on postpartum psychiatric illness was motivated more by her own feminist convictions than her husband's political aspirations. As a result, when the research director of the Ohio Department of Mental Health insisted that she would not sponsor a project without a guarantee there would be no interference with the research, the governor's office set only one condition: the study was to be carried out by a feminist researcher.

Thus began a project that has generated several different kinds of qualitative data and has taken me ten years to complete. Although the research did not start out as a study of a social movement, I have ended up conceptualizing the project in this way because, as a sociologist, I found this the most meaningful and valid way to think about the struggle currently taking place over postpartum illness. Moreover, the history of this research is intertwined with the emergence of the movement. Not only did Dagmar Celeste's activism on behalf of postpartum illness precipitate my interest in the topic, but the participatory methods I have used have substantiated Anthony Giddens's claims about the self-reflexivity of modern societies.

Throughout the study, I have sought the advice of self-help activists in designing the study, identifying interviewees, and interpreting results. Not only have I shared preliminary research reports with activists, but I have also frequently presented my findings at local and national conferences and in other public forums. From its inception, this project has also had the kind of action component typical of much feminist research: at the same time that I have studied the movement, I have sought to make the results of my work available to policy makers who can make changes to benefit women who have suffered postpartum illness. I have done this in several ways, ranging from serving for three years on the first board of directors of D.A.D. to presenting my research to health and human service professionals. And more times than I could ever count, I have referred individual women who have contacted me by telephone or letter to support groups.

At first, I was interested primarily in women's experiences of postpartum illness for what they tell us about the meanings of gender, motherhood, and the female self. The cornerstone of my initial research was fifty-two open-ended interviews, conducted primarily between 1985 and 1989 with women who suffered postpartum illness following the birth or adoption of a child. I chose this interview method because of its compatibility with my commitment, as a feminist scholar, to allow women to describe their experiences in their own terms, to develop more egalitarian relationships with interviewees, and to encourage interviewees to introduce new research questions based on their own lived experiences. These interviews were supplemented by fifty-six semi-structured interviews, conducted between 1985 and 1989 with medical and mental health providers, and by an analysis of the self-help and medical and scientific discourse on childbirth, postpartum illness, and motherhood published between 1975 and 1994. These data opened my eyes to the renegotiation of motherhood taking place through the discussion of postpartum illness in the popular advice literature, and to the challenge women are posing to the discourses and practices of medicine and mental health that do not accurately reflect women's own experiences of motherhood.

In the course of my research, a self-help movement focused on postpartum depression began to emerge in Ohio as part of a larger national campaign. This opened the door for me to begin thinking about women organizing around postpartum illness as a means of resisting and challenging the dominant construction of motherhood that is so pivotal to women's subordination. When my focus expanded to the postpartum depression self-help movement, the data gathering shifted to activists involved in the self-help campaign, the two major self-help organizations—Depression After Delivery (D.A.D.) and Postpartum Support International (PSI)—and the variety of forms of support that are the heart of women's self-help. In 1990 and 1991, I conducted semistructured tape-recorded interviews with twenty-nine participants (twenty-four women and five men) in the postpartum support group movement, including the leaders of both D.A.D. and PSI. To get a broader picture of the movement, in 1994 I mailed a survey to D.A.D.'s 220 telephone support contacts around the country.

In addition to these individual level data, I have relied upon three other sources of information, obtained through ethnographic methods, in hopes of preserving the context of women's self-help. First, D.A.D. and PSI generously opened their files to me, providing access to organizational documents, personal correspondence, surveys of their membership, copies of D.A.D.'s quarterly newsletter *Heartstrings* from 1987 to 1995, and files of thirty infanticide cases maintained at D.A.D. national headquarters. Second, I watched, taped, and obtained written transcripts of television talk shows and news programs that featured self-help activists. Finally, I got to know the women and men who inspired this book and whose lives are told between these covers through field work I conducted from 1988 to 1993. I attended local and regional conferences and training sessions, board meetings of national D.A.D., the annual conference of Postpartum Support International, quarterly meetings of Depression After Delivery Ohio; and spent endless hours on the telephone, eating meals, and socializing with members of these groups.

Often the boundary between my life and the field site seemed to disappear, as when I provided support to an activist and friend who had been hospitalized after a recurrence of postpartum psychosis. While I always presented myself as a researcher, I have been influenced by feminist writings that value openness, reciprocity, and empathy between the researcher and the person studied. I therefore spoke openly with interviewees about my own experience of depression, my feminism, and the fact that I am not a mother myself. And I have frequently sought the advice of participants in my interpretation of their experiences. Since the various sources of data I collected are used to address distinct questions, I describe them in greater detail in the chapters where I take up the analysis.

Since the beginning of this research, I have been fortunate to have had the support of the sponsoring agency in designing a project in accord with the emerging standards of feminist research. By this I mean that I have sought in this research to describe postpartum illness and women's self-help from women's own point of view, to provide an explanation of the postpartum self-help movement that links it to gender inequality, to use methods that give research subjects a more powerful role in the research process, and to empower women by incorporating a policy component into the research. At the end of the first two years of funding, the Ohio Department of Mental Health sponsored two statewide conferences to disseminate the preliminary results. The audience included policy makers in health, mental health, and human services, along with the women and men interviewed for the study. That the feminist approach to research had real meaning for participants came home to me when one woman attending a conference expressed her excitement by exclaiming, "You used my words!"

By moving from the experience of postpartum depression to the postpartum support group movement, I take up larger questions about the connections between gender inequality and women's self-help. Although the focus on a single case always raises the question of generalizability, I couch my conceptual contributions in such a way that others can explore their relevance to different women's self-help movements.

WOMEN'S MOVEMENTS AND THE RECONSTRUCTION OF GENDER

The central argument of this book is that women's self-help movements, for all their limitations, are central players in the redefinition of gender relations in American society. While I concentrate here on a more explicitly feminist strand of women's self-help, the most cursory examination of the best-selling mass market advice books for women published between 1970 and 1990 reveals that the discourse of feminism has seeped into the core of even the most popular writings. From arch-conservative Marabel Morgan's *The Total Woman* to Colette Dowling's *The Cinderella Complex*, and Robin Norwood's *Women Who Love Too Much*, and Melody Beattie's *Codependent No More*, the commercial transmutation of feminism guides women in their search for solutions to intimate life. Furthermore, television talk shows such as *Geraldo Rivera*, the *Jenny Jones Show*, *Sally Jessy Raphael*, *Maury Povich*, and *Ricki Lake*, have proliferated since Phil Donahue pioneered the format in the late 1960s and Oprah Winfrey went national in 1985. Unlike these earlier shows, which presented issues in a more straightforward discussion format, the newer talk shows encourage conflict and name calling and display what psychologist Jeanne Albronda Heaton and Nona Leigh Wilson have recently described as a "fixation on gender war." Increasingly, the more than twenty syndicated talk shows have served as a forum where women can confront men, who typically are presented in the worst possible light, as cheats, stalkers, adulterers, rapists, child molesters, sexual harassers, chauvinists, and murderers.

Looking at the many varieties of women's self-help through the lens of gender and social movements gives us insight into their larger significance. If there is a single point on which gender scholars agree, it is that notions of femininity and masculinity, the gender division of labor that assigns the primary responsibility for parenting to women rather than to men, the

13

institution of motherhood, and the numerous other structures and practices that reinforce male dominance—even the very idea of gender itself—are not expressions of natural differences between women and men. Rather, the gender order is socially constructed. Viewing gender as an institution means that the social construction of maleness and femaleness is simultaneously a process, a system of stratification, and a structure. In this process, individuals learn societal expectations regarding "gender-appropriate" behavior and enact them in daily interactions—what Candace West and Don Zimmerman refer to as the "doing of gender." As a stratification system, gender distinctions are socially constructed and then differentially valued by ranking men above women of the same race and class and rewarding them unequally. It is in this sense that Joan Scott refers to gender as "signifying power relations." Finally, as a structure, gender divides work in the home and in the wider economy, legitimates existing hierarchies of authority, organizes sexual expression and emotions, and structures every aspect of our lives because of its embeddedness in the family, the work place, the state, as well as in sexuality, language, and culture. While this view of gender hinges on the premise that gender inequality is fairly universal, gender is not necessarily synonymous with male domination and the devaluation of women; gender dominance can also involve the subordination of some groups of men.

Like others who have demonstrated the various manifestations of inequality, I view gender, race, class, ethnicity, and sexuality as what Patricia Hill Collins terms a "matrix of domination" that creates many different categories of women and men of varying social locations as a result of the multiple hierarchical stratification systems of different societies. While I researched as diverse a group of women as I could locate—including working-class, lesbian, African American, Latina, Asian American, and Native American women—the postpartum support group movement is dominated by white and middle-class women. Following the lead of scholars such as Wini Breines and Ruth Frankenberg, I have found it fruitful to acknowledge the racial specificity of the postpartum self-help movement and to use this to answer questions about the changing meaning of motherhood for these white middle-class women.

For some scholars, the biological and social roles of motherhood form the foundation of the gender order because they serve as the basis of the gender division of labor in the family that limits women's opportunities for paid work and their access to positions of power and authority. In this vein, early feminist writings accentuated the oppressive aspects of the role, openly questioning motherhood as a destiny for all women. While the 1980s saw an about-face, with feminists celebrating and valorizing motherhood, by the 1990s research expanded to emphasize the varied practices of mothering and its costs as well as its benefits. Black feminists, for instance, began to write about the significance of motherhood in minority communities and to describe a lack of ambivalence toward mothering uncharacteristic of white middle-class women. These writings posed a serious challenge to earlier models of motherhood based primarily on the experiences of white middle-class heterosexual mothers.

Looking at mothers as subjects, as the recent scholarship on mothering does, reflects the increased attention feminists are paying to the dynamic nature of gender and the significance of human agents in the making and remaking of femininity, masculinity, and existing gender arrangements. If, after all, gender is socially constructed, then surely the structures and practices that shore up the gender order, such as motherhood, must be subject to change or reconstruction. Yet despite the fairly universal adoption of social constructionist perspectives, only recently have feminist scholars turned from a preoccupation with explaining the maintenance and resilience of gender inequality to take note of processes of resistance, challenge, and change.

Current attempts to theorize gender change, which harken back to the sex roles tradition of the field, have shown a preference for mapping the way that individuals rebel against and reconstitute the meaning of masculinity and femininity. Contemporary writers think of gender as fluid and shifting and call attention to the way individuals perform gender in concrete social interactions, sometimes embracing, sometimes transgressing, and other times resisting gender norms. In her study of the creation of gender in children's play, Barrie Thorne describes, for example, how "sissies" and "tomboys" not only break down the gender divide but sometimes cross over to the groups and activities of the other gender. There is now a fairly large body of literature across the disciplines documenting various forms of individual opposition or resistance that women have used throughout history to strike at the chains of patriarchal oppression. Analysts have treated everything from black women's mothering for political ends, maternal child abuse, and infanticide to depression, psychosis, and physical illness as oppositional acts through which women turn the consequences of gender oppression to their own advantage. There are enormous differences, however, between individual and collective resistance; as William Gamson puts it, "Resisting is a very different process if one is part of a Resistance."

Placing more emphasis on the power relations that underlie the institutional and structural basis of gender, R. W. Connell's theory of gender links the institutional and interactional levels that maintain gender

15

distinctions and differences in power between women and men in a way that other, more individualistic approaches do not. In Connell's theory, which serves as the foundation for Judith Lorber's institutional approach, the structural and institutional basis of gender lies in the allocation of different types of work to women and men, in the pervasiveness of male domination, and in sexual practices that presuppose differences between women and men. The gender order nevertheless is created and maintained only through the everyday practices of individuals who give gender meaning through the constant and contentious process of engendering behavior as separate and unequal. But in practicing gender, individuals not only affirm and perpetuate the gender order, they also sometimes oppose and undermine dominant constructions of masculinity and femininity. It is social movements, however, rather than individuals, that perform the critical role of calling institutions to account for gender inequality and refashioning the gender code.

In this book I draw upon social movement theory to analyze how women's self-help movements challenge and change the gender order. I do this by putting together the theoretical pieces of gender and social movements not only to demonstrate how theories of social movements expand existing approaches to gender change, but also to show how attention to gender processes enlarges our understanding of women's collective action. The field of social movements, especially when compared with other areas of study, has been remarkably untouched by the gender revolution that has taken shape in the social sciences over the past decade. Research on social movements not geared specifically to women's concerns reveals that all movements are organized along gender lines in ways that previously have gone unrecognized. And analysts of the women's movements take the argument even further by suggesting that the mobilization, leadership patterns, strategies, and even the outcomes of social movements may be gendered. In this book I am interested in the way that women's self-help reflects the gender of its participants and in what these collective campaigns imply about the gendered nature of social movements in general.

SELF-HELP AS A SOCIAL MOVEMENT

Even if it is undeniable that women's self-help seeks to rework cultural assumptions about what it means to be a woman, there is a great deal of disagreement over whether self-help groups ought to be considered social movements. As is so often the case, the quarrel originates in competing strands of thought in the field of social movements. Applying the definition of social movements offered by classical collective behavior theorists, public health researcher Alfred Katz—a pioneer in document-ing the self-help trend in American society—points out that self-help groups have many of the standard features that traditionally define social movements: an ideology or set of beliefs and values that point out injus-tices in the system; a sense of "we" that derives from members' sense of being part of a group that shares some common characteristic or pur-pose; a structure or formal organization that involves a division of labor between leaders and followers and allows for continuity of members and mission; and a set of strategies and tactics that specify goals and processes of social change. Drawing upon collective behavior theorists' distinction between expressive movements (groups seeking mainly cultural and per-sonal transformation) and instrumental movements (groups struggling to win political and institutional change), Katz concludes that self-help groups cannot be considered social movements for the simple reason that they do not constitute a concerted force for political change. This posi-tion, which bears a striking resemblance to the dominant feminist stance on self-help described earlier, rests on a narrow definition of politics and overlooks entirely the political significance of self-help movements in modern societies.

New social movement theorists and scholars of modern culture espouse a fundamentally different view of self-help. Sociologist Robert Wuthnow, in *Sharing the Journey*—his landmark study of support groups in America—characterizes the vast array of support and self-help groups that have cropped up on the social landscape over the past decade as a major social movement in itself. The support group movement, accord-ing to Wuthnow, has the potential to change American society in fundamental ways through fostering distinctively postmodern forms of community to replace those that have evaporated as family structures have changed, neighborhoods have broken down, and large-scale institutions have come to dominate most areas of life in American society. Wuthnow, along with social theorists and philosophers associated with the European "new social movement" approach, such as Anthony Giddens, Alberto Melucci, Alaine Touraine, Jürgen Habermas, and Michel Foucault, see the growing popularity of movements concerned with the identity and self-actualization of their members as linked directly to larger social and cultural changes taking place within the postmodern societies of the United States and Western Europe. Self-help, according to this school of thought, represents not a withdrawal from political engagement but rather the displacement of protest from the economic and political realms to the arenas of medicine, mental health, law, religion, and education. In these arenas, peculiarly modern forms of power operate, reinforcing the fundamental social inequalities of gender, race, class, ethnicity, and sexual orientation. Anthony Giddens describes this as a shift from "emancipatory politics" to "life politics," because issues pertaining to the self, the body, and the life of individuals are becoming a major focus of modern movements.

In treating women's self-help as a social movement, this book might appear to be squarely in the camps of classical collective behavior theory and the more recent European "new social movement" perspective. Proponents of these two schools of thought have been interested in a much wider range of forms of collective action, including cultural and personal-change movements, than the resource mobilization model of social movements. In attempting to understand the rise of social movements, resource mobilization theorists downplay the grievances and beliefs of activists. Instead, they emphasize the way that group organization, the availability of resources—discretionary time, expertise, access to publicity, and connections to influential groups—and increased opportunities for collective action combine to trigger social movements. It is certainly the case that new social movement theory supplies better tools for understanding both the identity formation processes that figure so prominently in modern self-help and the political significance of the new cultural assumptions promoted by self-help campaigns for post-industrial societies. Furthermore, resource mobilization theory has shown a distinct preference for studying forms of protest that target governmental policies and practices and the political system.

In this book, however, I join recent theoretical work that aims to bridge the gaps between these various models of social movements. In order to understand the emergence of the postpartum support group movement, I find it necessary to draw from major premises of all three approaches to social movements. This means that, in tracing the origins of the self-help campaign, I begin with resource mobilization theory. This leads me to the story of the feminists who formed the first support groups and their strategic decisions to broaden their base by tapping into medical and mental health networks and resources. I then take a look at the opportunities for growth that opened up to the movement's founders in the changing climate of health care in American society in the 1980s. But because resource mobilization theory downplays the role of people's beliefs and convictions, I find that I need to draw from the insights of new social movement theory to understand the importance of community building and the collective redefinition of self that takes place in modern support groups. Finally, my analysis is guided by the work of classical collective behavior theorists, who recognized early on the connection between prevailing cultural ideas—in this case the popularity of the therapeutic world view—and the rhetoric used by groups struggling to change the status quo.

Applying this combination of theoretical perspectives, we can see how the characteristics of self-help place these forms of collective action squarely within the tradition of social movements. Self-help groups generally mobilize around some *shared experience*, characteristic, or problem that so resonates with participants' sense of "who they are" that it becomes a basis for building solidarity with others. If the personal and fleeting social relationships of modern societies, coupled with the declining influence of traditional institutions such as religion and kinship, can be seen as providing fewer reference points for personal identities, then self-help groups offer people firm ground in which to anchor personal identities. Whether as a "recovering alcoholic," a "survivor of incest," a "relationship addict," or a "breast-cancer survivor," participants in self-help are claiming the right to understand their lives in their own terms and to name themselves in ways that challenge conventional assumptions.

The core of self-help is its emphasis on *experiential knowledge*, or common-sense wisdom of people's problems as an alternative or supplement to professional knowledge. Modern social life is regulated more and more by the highly specialized, technical, and impersonal knowledges of science, medicine, mental health, the law, and other expert systems. These systems transmit technical knowledge that influences how we experience almost every aspect of our lives—the illnesses we suffer, the foods we eat, the medicines we take, the emotions we express, our recreational habits, even how we experience sexual desire. In modern self-help groups, people find a social space where they can develop their own explanations of, and solutions to problems based, at least in part, on everyday experience. It should come as no surprise, however, that the indigenous knowledge of some modern self-help groups can sometimes be as rational and scientific as the knowledge systems under attack. In recent years, for example, a phalanx of breast-cancer victims, inspired by the successes of the AIDS lobby, has pushed for better regulation of mammography standards, for mandatory insurance coverage for mammograms, and for more research into the still mysterious roots of breast cancer.

According to most definitions, another ingredient of self-help is *mutual support*. A sense of solidarity derives from the strong emotional bonds, empathy, unconditional acceptance, and support networks that form between people by virtue of helping each other understand and cope with problems overlooked by existing social institutions. In self-help, organizations are not the main actors. Rather, the movement is found in the ideas, discourse, identities, and life changes of participants. Few would deny that the community-building and positive identities offered by self-help groups, combined with the knowledge and skills associated with their "do it yourself" attitude, are a source of individual and collective empowerment. Support groups not only build social connections between participants, but also enhance participants' perceptions and feelings about themselves; their knowledge and self-confidence when dealing with medical, legal, and other professionals; and their mental and physical well-being.

From the standpoint of social movement analysts, a last feature of self-help is the most controversial. To the extent that self-help groups call attention to problems not being met by existing institutions, propose alternative conceptions of problems, support changes in the self-concepts and social identities of their members, and exert pressure on professional and public agencies to allocate resources for new solutions to problems, there can be little doubt that self-help promotes not only personal but *societal change*. And most definitions treat collective actors who aim to change some element of society through unconventional means and channels as social movements. But despite this fairly broad definition, not only have social movement researchers favored "conflictual" movements over "consensual" movements, but they have also concentrated on groups seeking "institutional change" rather than "personal change." As might be expected, self-help displays some of the same qualities of the modern institutions that it challenges, namely a heightened emphasis on the interests of the individual rather than the community and the accentuation of transient and partial rather than stable and integrated identities. It is these tendencies that lead critics to point the finger at self-help for further fragmenting modern societies and undercutting attempts to implement a broad-based program of fundamental change. In my analysis of women's self-help, however, I take a less pessimistic stance toward self-help, siding with new social movement writers who recognize that self-help frequently takes advantage of the rational and scientific discourses of modern society to open up new opportunities for self-development and community.

AN OUTLINE OF THE BOOK

Besides attempting to portray the dimensions of postpartum illness and the significance of the self-help campaign, this book is concerned with the connections among gender, self-help, and feminism. I am interested in how the emotions that go along with living as a woman in a male-dominated society figure into the self-help and recovery movements that have swept up so many women in recent years. I also consider the consequences of the marriage between feminism and self-help; my intent is to discover whether women who are drawn to self-help movements that base their claims chiefly on women's traditional reproductive and nurturing roles represent new and diverse constituencies being alerted to their disadvantages as women. Finally, I analyze the significance of gendered political participation for understanding the shape and direction of modern social movements.

Chapter 2 weaves the voices of depressed women into a discussion of the competing definitions of mothering presented in the medical, popular childbirth, and postpartum self-help literature. I address three questions. First, how does the dominant, mainly white, middle-class model of motherhood as a caring, nurturing, altruistic relationship compare to the actual emotions of new mothers? Second, to what extent can postpartum illness—which represents almost the antithesis of the cultural ideal for new mothers—be understood as a form of gender resistance that defies emotional norms by giving credence to women's expression of anger, anxiety, depression, and guilt in response to the burdens and sacrifices of motherhood? Third, how and why are women searching for medical and psychiatric solutions for a set of problems that are so clearly connected to broad social and collective processes altering the practice and meaning of motherhood in contemporary American society? By focusing on the influence of the postpartum self-help movement on women's interpretations of their maternal emotions, I outline an approach to women's mental health that emphasizes women's agency in the definition and medicalization of their problems.

Chapter 3 begins with the lives of the feminists who founded the first postpartum support groups and tells the story of the emergence of the self-help movement in the mid-1980s. I demonstrate that those drawn to contemporary women's self-help campaigns include veterans of the feminist movement and new constituencies coming to feminist insights through participation in support groups. Using resource mobilization and frame alignment perspectives on social movements, I trace the emergence of the postpartum support group movement to the feminist critique of the medical establishment and a general social climate supportive of "women's rights." Although the first support groups for women suffering postpartum illness were spawned from personal networks of women with a long history of feminist participation, activists relied upon talk shows, self-help reading, and other forms of media to recruit more widely. Using resources obtained from medical and mental health professionals and capitalizing on the larger self-help tide swept in by reductions in federal support for professional mental health care, women have managed to build a viable support network at the local, state, and national levels. By highlighting the movement-to-movement influence, my line of analysis differs from that of most critics, whose negative assessments of women's self-help are based on its failure to live up to the tenets of an author's particular variant of feminism.

In chapter 4, I take the postpartum support group movement as a site for answering questions about the relationship between the membership, culture, and strategies of contemporary women's self-help movements and those of the feminist movement of the 1960s and '70s. I am interested in whether the use of self-help as an organizing tool for feminism in the 1990s facilitates the development of the activist communities that scholars of social movements argue are essential to feminist mobilization. From the perspective of new social movement theory, I analyze the organizational styles, tactics, and ideas of the movement, which draw heavily on the personalized political strategies, collectivism, and ideological emphasis on women's differences from men that were advocated by early radical feminists. At the same time, women's self-help communities are built around new forms of mass communication, which means that the face-to-face support group is no longer the prototypical form of organization that it was in the 1960s and early '70s. In addition to the traditional support group, I explore telephone support, self-help reading, talk shows, and pen-pal networks as examples of new repertoires of collective action associated with modern self-help.

In chapter 5, I take up first a controversial question: To what extent does feminism remain a viable force in modern women's self-help? I delineate the collective identity, or shared self-definitions, that connect predominantly white and middle-class women in the communities of support formed within the postpartum movement. Joining forces with others who have suffered similar problems may mean that women are choosing a therapeutic explanation of their problems. But meeting with others also provides an opportunity for women to develop new collective self-understandings that link their emotional distress to the requirements of mothering and the inequities of gender. As a result, women's self-help both extends the reaches, and transforms the meaning of feminism. Next, I trace the impact of self-help activism on women's emotional well-being and on the gendered social institutions that are the target of self-help campaigns. Women participate in self-help primarily to enhance their sense of control in their dealings with health and mental health professionals and in their daily lives. Yet feminist critics have been less interested in the biographical consequences of self-help than in its failures on the political front. By looking at the effects that activism has had on health and mental health institutions, the law, and the popular media, I demonstrate that the postpartum depression movement has opened up a space for new definitions of motherhood that compete with traditional models by bringing women's emotional distress and suffering to the fore of public and political debates. My analysis, therefore, takes issue with those who hold that feminist therapy is a backlash against political feminism. Instead, I argue that self-help is a distinctively postmodern project that allows women to combine the tenets of feminism with the professional discourses of medicine, law, psychology, therapy, and the social sciences in the ongoing struggle to reconstitute the meaning of the female self.

In the concluding chapter, I explore what the postpartum support group movement tells us about the intersections of gender and social movements by looking at how women's self-help forces us to rethink existing theories of social movements. I analyze the effects of gender as a power relation on the preexisting networks from which the postpartum support group movement mobilized. How does the widespread belief—on which gender hierarchy rests—that "woman" can be equated with "mother" shape the agenda, strategies, culture, organization, and leadership of women's self-help movements? Finally, I address the impact of self-help on the reconstruction of gender relations in American society. Here I return to the contradictory nature of contemporary women's self-help movements, namely the way that they are both supportive and subversive of gender as an institution. The postpartum depression movement, on the one hand, challenges the meaning of motherhood in contemporary American society. On the other hand, the movement advances a therapeutic model that locates and classifies women's experiences as "illness," thus reaffirming the model of the self-sacrificing mother. The book concludes, then, by looking beyond this case to highlight new directions for social movement theory that become imperative when gender and its emotional dynamics move from the margins to the center of the field.

THE CRADLE FALLS

POSTPARTUM ILLNESS AND THE
CONTRADICTIONS OF MOTHERHOOD

O, Baby blankets and baby shoes,
baby slippers, baby spoons, walls of baby blue.
Dream child in my head
is a nightmare born in a borrowed bed.
Now I know lightning strikes again.
It struck me once, then struck me dead.
My folly grows inside of me.

     —Natalie Merchant of 10,000 Maniacs, "Eat for Two"

MARSHA WAS in her early twenties when she and Tom had their first child. She had been a full-time college student before marrying. When they moved to another community, where Tom took a position as an industrial engineer, Marsha began taking classes sporadically in between waitressing jobs. They had always planned to have children, but for Marsha pregnancy came sooner than she had anticipated. "Instead we conceived about thirty seconds after my last pill." On the third day after her son was born, while Marsha was attending a presentation in the hospital on how to bathe babies, she began to sob. "I cried so hard that the nurses had to wheel me back to my room. 'Oh, it's the third day, and a lot of people get the third–day blues,' the nurse told me. But it didn't end when the fourth day, the fourth week, or even the fourth month dawned."

After a year had passed, she was still feeling anxious and having other emotional difficulties, which angered her husband. Her nightmares had gotten so frequent that one time she found herself on the stairs, her baby in her arms. "I had dreamed of a fire or disaster and was trying to save him." Her relatives were no help either. "One said, 'You have a beautiful son, a good husband, a new home, what do you have to worry about?' How could I explain the feeling of doom I felt? My gyn–ob said, 'Shape up or ship out,' and I'm not making that up. The pediatrician said, 'Why are you so nervous? Your son is very healthy.'" Although many of her friends were nurses, none had children of their own or offered any words of advice.

Finally, Marsha went to a psychiatrist, who at her insistence prescribed sleeping pills and tranquilizers, referred her to group therapy, and suggested she go back to school. Marsha explains that "the therapy didn't cure me so much as give me some direction. I did go back to college and finally got my degree when Seth was three. But it was a bitter shock when I discovered I was pregnant again when I was two quarters short of my degree. I considered an abortion. My husband loathed me for even thinking of it for a second." When her daughter was born two days before Seth's fourth birthday, Marsha didn't experience another deep depression. By then she had developed a "safety net" of other mothers in their new neighborhood and was making plans for her own life that included completing a college degree in home economics with a major in child development and family relations. To this day, however, Marsha regrets that her long postpartum depression and anger negatively affected her son: "he bore the brunt of my emotional turmoil."

Diana is vice-president of a bank. She and her husband, who holds a high-level management position in a major retail business, waited until Diana was thirty-nine to have what turned out to be their only child, Melinda. During their first ten years of marriage, Diana and Sam took advantage of their freedom and financial resources, traveling extensively, attending the theater, and dining out regularly. She had always expected to have children, and her biological clock had started winding down about the same time that her older parents' health began to fail. Eagerly, Diana and Sam looked forward to the birth of their baby, and Diana arranged to have six weeks unpaid pregnancy leave. Diana's delivery was complicated by her age, and treatment for a serious infection following an unanticipated cesarian section kept her in the hospital for a week after delivery and left her drained and exhausted. Still, the last thing she expected was the debilitating depression that overtook her life in the weeks and months following her daughter's birth. Her crying began in the hospital, where she was reassured by her mother, herself a nurse, that it was the baby blues and would subside in a few days. But the feelings only got worse. "When I came home from the hospital I had these strange feelings. I would be here during the day and would just vegetate and sometimes I would just lose control and weep. I felt like I didn't have a friend in the world. Other times I was climbing the walls. But it was the crying that was so awful. I couldn't stop crying. I would be walking down the street and break down. Someone would call me on the phone and 'boo hoo.' I would call the doctor's office to make an appointment and break down crying." None of her friends had young children, so Diana didn't have anyone to talk to except her mother. "And she was still adjusting to Daddy's death and beginning to get sick—she had contracted hepatitis as a nurse—herself."

Diana attributes her depression, in part, to the death of her father a year before her daughter was born. "I was still grieving and hadn't gotten over that yet, and then Melinda was born and I realized my father would never get to see his granddaughter." Diana had never felt depressed before or experienced "such a sense of losing control." But she also had never been as isolated as she was in the first few weeks and months after her daughter was born. Diana was surprised to discover the toll that her pregnancy and the long period of adjustment to motherhood took on her emotional well-being. She explains, "I'm a professional, I'm used to having a life outside the home. Plus, I just didn't feel the maternal urges that were supposed to be there for a long time. Then there were the hormonal changes and sleep deprivation on top of the fact that you lose your life." When Diana finally found a woman physician who diagnosed what she was going through as postpartum depression, she refused the antidepressant medication the doctor prescribed. Although her husband Sam stood by her through her ordeal, Diana knows she could never live through "this kind of nightmare again, even though it means Melinda will grow up as an only child."

Ruth is twenty-eight, has been married twice, and is the mother of three children. After each was born, she immediately felt happy, but then "every time difficulties set in." In the case of the first baby, she believes her problems might have been related to the fact that her husband was a heroin addict and she also had been using drugs before the baby was born. Soon after she gave birth to David, she started to have constant mood swings: "I'd be up and the next minute I'd be down. I couldn't control them. I asked my doctor what it was and she said, 'It's depression, it'll go away with your hormones.'" About a year after David was born, her physician finally took her complaints seriously by prescribing Mellaril, which Ruth did not continue to take because of unpleasant side effects. When she returned to her part-time work as a pharmacist's assistant, Ruth felt better. But the birth of the second child, nearly six years later, triggered an even more severe depression.

Ruth remembers feeling fine in the hospital, but the first morning she woke up after she got home, "I felt like I was in a dream. Everything was confusing to me. The baby was crying, and I would break out in a sweat. I couldn't sleep, I kept tossing and turning and saying to my husband, 'What's wrong with me?'" Unable to eat for nearly two weeks, Ruth got progressively worse until finally she wanted to die. "I'd get bad thoughts, really morbid thoughts. Every time I'd pick up a knife, I'd think of something really bad. . . . I'd think of killing somebody, myself, the babies, I mean who would take care of them if they didn't have me? I wouldn't go near a knife so I wouldn't have those thoughts." Ruth pleaded with her husband to help. She saw her gynecologist, who admitted her to a hospital psychiatric unit and treated her with medication. Things didn't seem much better, however, after she was released. Looking back, she explains, "I got pregnant pretty soon after I married my second husband. Then we moved down here from Cleveland and I left my friends and my family. I'd just never been away from home and I started getting depressed about that. When I first found out I was pregnant the second time I can remember thinking, I love my husband now, but I thought since I don't know him well, what happens if things don't turn out, I'm going to be stuck?" When she continued to be plagued by depression and anxiety after being released from the hospital and her husband insisted she "snap out of this or our marriage will be on the rocks," Ruth learned to conceal her distress.

It is not surprising that a little more than two years later, when Ruth gave birth to a third child, her problems returned in full force. "It was like a nightmare. For a while I thought I was possessed, but I just kept fighting it. After all I've been through, I sometimes think that's all you can do is fight it, 'cause the pills don't help, they just make you feel like a zombie. When I went to the hospital that time I thought, boy, these people are really going to help me, but when I left I felt worse." Believing that her husband, her parents, and her doctors had failed her, Ruth remembers the thing that helped most was the validation of other women who suffered the same problems: "I thought I was the only one going through this until I read that article on Governor Dick Celeste's wife in the paper, and she sounded like she had just what I had." Although Ruth continues to be plagued with chronic depression and anxiety, she looks less to medical solutions for her problems, advising other women to "get out of the house as much as you can, get a babysitter, do things that you enjoy, and talk to other women." She has had a tubal ligation to prevent future pregnancies and openly admits that "though it may sound hard to believe, when I was growing up I never really wanted kids. I didn't even plan to have the ones I had. It just happened; before I had time to think about what I was getting into, I was a mother."

These are the voices of women treated for postpartum depression, women for whom symptoms of psychological distress came out of the blue. They had no previous history of depression or psychiatric treatment, and the accepted wisdom had led them to expect that giving birth to a baby would bring happiness and fulfillment. Yet these women's experiences, as much as they go against the grain, are typical of the problems described by most of the women I interviewed for this book. In *Of Woman Born*, feminist writer Adrienne Rich portrays the conflict between institutionalized motherhood and a woman's drive for self-preservation, which is the theme of these narratives, as "a primal agony." In terms of prevailing psychiatric standards, the feelings these women talk about are comparable to the clinical signs and symptoms of depression: feeling sad, lonely, anxious, hopeless, and worthless; crying; having trouble sleeping, being unable to get going; wishing one were dead; and having compulsive thoughts. At the same time, their stories bring to light the extent to which the depressive thoughts associated with postpartum illness articulate women's ambivalence toward motherhood and how they felt unable to fulfill an idealized but demanding and restrictive role. Traditionally, the kinds of problems these women describe have been depicted in the popular discourse as either the "baby blues" or more recently the "postpartum blues" as a way of connecting women's mood swings to the sharp hormonal fluctuations and other physiological changes that accompany childbirth. While there may very well be a physiological substratum to postpartum depression, as the voices of the above women suggest, postpartum psychiatric illness is a complex problem that has different signs and symptoms, and multiple causes.

In this chapter, I take the experiences of women who have suffered postpartum distress as the starting point. Attending closely to what these women have to say about their lives allows us to see how internalized expectations about motherhood and the feminine role are bound up in women's problems. And it also helps us to understand how societal changes that have affected women's lives, discussed in chapter 1, set the stage for a particular set of problems that have motivated mainly white and middle-class women to organize a support group movement to convince physicians, mental health providers, and society at large to take their problems seriously by defining them as a disease.

How are we to understand the fact that nearly thirty years after the modern women's movement set out to erase biological justifications for women's disadvantages, some women appear to be embracing psychiatric explanations of the distresses of motherhood? To apprehend this anomaly requires that we delve further into the way that the distress of new mothers is connected to the contours of their lives and to women's failure to find alternative solutions to their problems. In this chapter, I will look beneath the standard psychiatric symptoms of postpartum depression described in the research literature to explore the lived experience of postpartum depression. What are the feelings and signs of postpartum illness from the standpoint of women who have experienced it? How do women make sense of the feelings they have that deviate from the maternal ideal? Where do they turn for understanding and help for their problems? To what extent do the sources women rely upon advance competing definitions of motherhood that validate their experiences? These are the kinds of questions that can only be addressed through a sociological perspective on women's mental health.

SOCIOLOGICAL PERSPECTIVES ON WOMEN'S MENTAL HEALTH

To understand the nature and meaning of postpartum depression in women's lives, it is important to place the condition in the larger context of studies of women's mental health. One of the most consistent findings in the research literature is that women are about twice as likely as men to suffer, be diagnosed, and receive treatment for depression in general. In attempting to take apart this puzzle, a few medical and psychiatric researchers have postulated the influence of fluctuations in female hormones and other biochemicals in connection with pregnancy, childbirth, menstruation, and menopause. These hormonal shifts associated with the normal functioning of the female reproductive system are thought to be linked to changes in the neurotransmitters norepinephrine and serotonin, which regulate mood, and may explain why women experience higher levels of depression, anger, anxiety, and other symptoms of psychiatric illness. But even researchers who are sympathetic to neuroendocrinological explanations of gender differences in depression are quick to point out that the neuroendocrine response itself can be altered by the social context. Blaming biology, in other words, takes the focus off the social factors that contribute to women's problems.

Although I am aware of the increasing attention being paid to the possible biochemical influences on depression, in this book I am interested in the social processes that contribute to women's recognition and labeling of their problems as postpartum illness. Pregnancy, childbirth, and motherhood occur within a larger social milieu that structures the adult roles of women and men in particular ways and defines the personal and social meanings of mothering. Variations in women's family and employment roles, social supports, and women's class, racial, and ethnic backgrounds also shape the practice of mothering, further expanding the range of social influences on a woman's psychological well-being. For these reasons, simple biological explanations that correlate gender differences in depression solely with reproductive changes over the female life cycle cannot fully explain either postpartum depression or women's higher rates of depression in general, let alone the complex issues that determine how a particular set of personal problems gets constituted as mental illness.

Feminist sociologists and historians interested in explaining the impact of social factors on women's mental illness have approached the problem from one of three different vantage points: societal causes, the physician/medical institution, and the patient. Each of these perspectives is important but incomplete. The social causation approach, which dominates much current thinking and research on women's mental health in sociology, emphasizes the connection between the social disadvantages of being female and women's higher rates of depressive disorders and phobias. Studies in this tradition point to how gender inequality subjects women to subordinate roles such as marriage, childrearing, and gender-linked occupations; stressful life events such as rape, battering, and divorce; and disadvantaged circumstances such as poverty and powerlessness—all or any of which heighten their vulnerability to psychological distress and limit their ability to cope with stress.

For a long time, scholars believed that it was possible that women's higher rates of depression were not real but could be explained by women's greater willingness to express their feelings. A 1995 study by John Mirowsky and Catherine Ross helps to dispel this myth. From interviews with 1,282 women and 747 men, Mirowsky and Ross found that, although women are somewhat more likely to express emotions than men, they nevertheless do suffer more real symptoms of psychological distress. As far as motherhood goes, the stresses of trying to combine full-time employment with being a mother cross all racial, ethnic, and class groupings. The differences in being able to cope seem to arise, in part, from the social supports available. In working-class and African American families, where women have a long history of combining full-time employment with motherhood, there is extended family and community support traditionally available. The mainly white and middle-class women I interviewed for this study lack these supports and have had to devise their own coping strategies to handle the stress.

Concentrating on the social causes of women's distress forces us to come to terms with the impact of women's disadvantaged social status on their higher rates of depression. But this perspective sidesteps the question of meaning in mental illness by failing to ask why a particular set of symptoms is seen in a particular way at a particular time. Responding to this criticism, feminist scholars writing about women's mental health have concentrated on the power of male-dominated medical and mental health institutions to categorize women's routine violations of gender norms as mental illness. There are two basic theoretical traditions in sociology that start from the premise that the institutions that diagnose and categorize patients are as important to understanding mental illness as is the disease itself.

The first, the labeling theory, questions the very existence of mental illness and holds that the creation of psychiatric categories to describe everyday problems reflects and helps to maintain gender stereotypes and the imbalance of power between women and men. Edwin Schur, a major proponent of this approach, goes so far as to suggest that the tendency to treat women as emotionally disturbed as a way of dismissing what a woman says or does is so prevalent in our society that it serves as a real and ever-present threat to any woman who deviates from gender prescriptions. Elizabeth Lunbeck's analysis of the treatment of female psychopathy at the Boston Psychiatric Hospital in the early 1900s illustrates the way that mental illness definitions help maintain the gender status quo. According to Lunbeck, women who were committed to the hospital for "hypersexual behavior" in this period were mainly sexually active, working-class women who had chosen either to forego or delay marriage, or who were widowed or divorced. Their sexual freedom, which reflected women's increasing autonomy in the work place and family, challenged traditional ideas of femininity to such an extent that the male psychiatric establishment responded by characterizing them as suffering from a mental disorder. In the labeling framework, then, mental illness does not exist apart from psychiatric diagnosis, which serves, however unwittingly, to perpetuate the undervaluation of women by silencing and regulating those who challenge conventional gender norms.

As appealing as labeling accounts of "invented identities" might be for understanding the reemergence in the twentieth century of postpartum depression in the popular discourse, there is a fundamental problem with this line of analysis. Postpartum psychiatric disorders, like many conditions that afflict women, have received little attention in the medical and psychiatric literature. Since postpartum illness has not been listed in a single edition of the American Psychiatric Association's *Diagnostic and Statistical Manual of Mental Disorders*, it is unlikely that large numbers of women have found themselves the unwilling and passive victims of psychiatric definitions of postpartum depression and psychosis.

Considering the basic premise of labeling theory, the question automatically arises as to why people would be diagnosed as suffering from illnesses when, in reality, their problems may not constitute diseases that require treatment. Medicalization perspectives provide the answer. Closely aligned with the labeling theory, writers who pursue this second explanation point to the professional practices of medicine as a powerful institution that frames women's unhappiness, alienation, and discontent in strictly medical and psychiatric terms. Women's higher rates of mental illness, according to this perspective, result from the tendency of the male-dominated medical system to expand its domain by translating an ever-increasing number of women's problems into psychiatric illnesses, treating these problems within a medical and particularly a psychiatric framework, and maintaining professional control over knowledge and services related to these conditions. Medicalization theory tended to dominate early studies of women's health, because it provided an accurate reading of the history of the care of pregnant women in preparation for childbirth and motherhood. Ann Oakley demonstrates how the medical profession in western industrialized societies, by constituting pregnancy and childbirth as a disease and advocating increased standards of antenatal care, managed to expand its surveillance over women's health and increase the state's control over motherhood.

As useful as these approaches have been for understanding the way that medical expansion has figured into the medicalization and psychiatrization of everyday life, it is important to recognize that organized medicine is not always eager to embrace women's health problems, especially if they cannot be treated through profitable technologies. Furthermore, over the past three decades, the mental health enterprise has been transformed from a system of large public hospitals supplemented by outpatient clinics and private psychiatrists to one in which an array of providers (including psychiatrists, clinical psychologists, clinical social workers, marriage and family counselors, psychiatric nurses, clergy, support groups, and cocounselors) dispenses services mainly to people suffering less debilitating problems. Under today's diversified system of mental health care psychiatry is, in effect, losing its stronghold. To concentrate solely on the role that psychiatrists play in interpreting people's problems would provide an incomplete picture of the variety of sources women turn to for help in understanding and managing their distressing feelings. The popular self-help literature is an increasingly important resource where women find validation of their problems and possible solutions. To understand the variety of social actors who are engaged in the creation of mental illness, we must therefore consider the role that self-help movements are playing in the growing tendency of women to use mental illness terminology to define their problems.

A third perspective on women's mental health is more interested in the meaning of psychological distress to the patient. Carroll Smith-Rosenberg's analysis of women's hysteria suggests the ways that nineteenth-century middle-class women embraced the role of hysteric as an extreme way of coping with Victorian expectations of wives and mothers. By carrying the passive and submissive female role to extremes, women managed to assert themselves, reject sexual relations, and avoid domestic duties. Similarly, Joan Brumberg's historical analysis of anorexia nervosa traces the roots of this disorder to social definitions of femininity, expressed in the adage that "a woman can never be too rich or too thin." She uncovers the fact that women have used fasting, a form of self-destructive behavior different from dieting, since the Middle Ages not only to conform to societal values regarding the female body, but also as a means to resist the stresses of womanhood.

The social causation approach adds to our understanding of the social situation of people diagnosed as suffering psychiatric illness, and labeling and medicalization approaches force us to recognize the sexual politics of medical and mental health professionals and institutions. But scholars recently have moved away from these purely structural or victimization models that dominated early theories of women's health. Feminist writers have turned their attention, instead, to documenting the significance of women's agency for the recognition and definition of their own health and mental health problems. This newer research, informed by feminist poststructural theory, finds that women have been active participants—as physicians, nurses, researchers, and patients—not only in medicalizing their experiences but in creating gender biased medical institutions and practices.

Studies that take a poststructural line of analysis share many of the assumptions of the labeling and medicalization perspectives by emphasizing the way mental illness is produced by the gendered social organization, practices, and diagnostic classification systems of psychiatry and the mental health industry that strip women's emotions and feelings from the context of their lives and encourage women to define their biographies in terms of mental illness. But feminist writers in this tradition also recognize the contradictory effects of psychiatric and mental illness discourse about femininity: it can both reinforce women's subordination by concealing the collective sources of women's emotional problems and also serve as a resource to modify the female role and resist male domination. Through a process that Michel Foucault terms "reverse discourse," it is possible for women to reject the definitions of femininity encoded in the discourses of medicine and mental health by turning them around to their advantage. For example, a woman may define herself as an incest survivor, which means that, in effect, she is embracing mental illness as an explanation of her problems. Even so, therapy, as Anthony Giddens points out, need not always be the oppressive force in women's lives that labeling and medicalization approaches posit it to be. Rather, counselling can sometimes provide the knowledge and support women find necessary to refashion their lives, reconstruct new identities, and challenge the gender status quo that victimized them in the first place. What recent feminist and poststructuralist theories of women's mental illness fail to provide, however, is a framework that allows us to locate the meaning of mental illness within the context of women's everyday lives. How precisely do traditional ideas about the female role that are reflected in medicine and mental health get translated into the everyday lives of women? And how do women come to use mental illness as a site of resistance to gender rules?

Peggy Thoits's self-labeling perspective, which emphasizes the way that the mismatch between a person's feelings and societal expectations about how one is supposed to feel generates distress, provides a basis for understanding how women draw upon competing popular and professional discourses to give meaning to their symptoms. Self-labeling theory shares the key assumption of labeling theory that mental illness definitions are socially constructed through psychiatric categories that define certain signs and symptoms as mental illness. Concentrating on the role of self-labeling in the construction of postpartum illness is consistent with the fact that, for most people, mental health treatment is self-initiated and is not imposed either by physicians or family members. According to this approach, the key to understanding women's willingness to embrace psychiatric conceptions of their problems is in recognizing that new mothers make assessments of their own feelings and symptoms of distress based on their ideas about how mothers ought to feel. Even if women increasingly position themselves in various ways in relation to the maternal role, motherhood nevertheless remains a core identity for many women. The image of motherhood as the supreme act of caring and connection serves as a strong emotional imperative. And this dominant story line comes from many sources—not only from physicians, nurses, and other medical and mental health providers, but also from religious teachings, family members, other women, and the popular and self-help discourse on childbirth and mothering directed to women. To underscore the fact that ideological representations of femininity rarely correspond to actual femininities as they are lived, sociologist R.W. Connell uses the term "emphasized femininity" to describe the female roles and identities that are given most cultural and ideological support. Although the content of "emphasized femininity" is linked to the private realm of the home and sexuality, as Dorothy Smith has observed, it is promoted in mass media and marketing on a much greater scale than is found for any form of masculinity.

In analyzing women's accounts of postpartum illness, I rely on Peggy Thoits's self-labeling theory, which sees mental illness as emotional deviance to understand the way that women give meaning to the subjective experiences they associate with postpartum psychiatric illness. The main assumptions of the theory are two: that emotional disorders such as postpartum depression can best be understood as violations of what Arlie Hochschild in *The Managed Heart* has termed "feeling norms" and "expression rules"; and that it is the individual's own recognition of the discrepancy between her private emotions and the emotional states perceived as "normative" that triggers a woman's self-attributions of mental illness. This approach allows us to place postpartum illness squarely within the context of women's lives at the same time that it connects women's interpretations of their feelings to the competing definitions advanced by medicine, mental health, and self-help groups. Focusing on these different sources of influence on women provides insight into the reasons that medicine has failed even to admit to the need to treat postpartum disorders. It also illuminates the significant role that self-help, and its emphasis on women's own definitions of their problems, plays in women's medicalization of their own experiences.

TALKING WITH WOMEN ABOUT POSTPARTUM ILLNESS

I began by interviewing women who self-identified as having suffered "emotional problems" in the year following the birth or adoption of a child. My fifty-two interviews, conducted in Columbus, Ohio, between 1985 and 1989 explored the nature of women's postpartum emotions, their maternal expectations, the sources that influenced their attributions of disturbance, the techniques they used to manage their feelings, and other issues such as family structure, work histories, and patterns of social support. I posted notices at home birthing centers, day-care centers, mental health centers, physicians' offices, hospital maternity units, social service agencies, restaurants, a citywide baby fair, and in local newspapers in an attempt to reach a diverse group of women; I offered child care to facilitate the interviews. The 300 women who responded were generally somewhat older white women with higher levels of income and education than American mothers in general. The women I interviewed ranged in age from eighteen to forty-three, with a median age of twenty-eight. Ninety percent of the women were white, the remaining 10 percent African American, Mexican American, and American Indian. About a third of the women were high-school graduates, a third had some college, and the remaining one-third had B.A.'s or, in several instances, advanced degrees. A little over half (54 percent) of the women worked in a variety of blue-collar, pink-collar, clerical, and administrative and professional positions. Although annual family incomes ranged from a low of $5,000 to a high of over $100,000, the mean household income was $39,000, somewhat higher than the national family average of $35,000 in 1993. Most of the women were married at the time of the interview, although 11 percent were not. A little less than half of the women (43 percent) had only one child, while 41 percent had two, 12 percent had three, and 4 percent had four or more children. Along certain lines, the sample was diverse: it included women in traditional nuclear families, as well as single women, coupled lesbians, and adoptive mothers of both American and foreign-born children.

To gain insight into the emotional expectations surrounding new mothers, I also examined the popular and professional discourse on childbirth and mothering published between 1975 and 1994. Popular literature included women's magazines, best-selling books, and manuals on childbirth, parenting, and motherhood. I also read scientific and medical publications on postpartum psychiatric illness, including the most commonly used medical and nursing textbooks. These sources get at the formal emotional culture that sets the standards of the good mother. I also drew from interviews with fifty-six medical and mental health providers—including obstetricians and gynecologists, pediatricians, psychiatrists, nurses, social workers, psychologists, and clergy—to uncover discrepancies between actual medical and mental health practices and the conception of postpartum psychiatric illness as it is presented in formal medical discourse. Finally, I used organizational documents, newsletters, and personal files of two self-help organizations, Depression After Delivery (D.A.D.) and Postpartum Support International (PSI), to analyze the emotional culture of the postpartum self-help movement. These voices of women, of advice givers, of doctors, of mental health providers, and of self-help advocates all joined together in a complex jazz piece, sometimes discordant and sometimes melodious. I found that for most of these women the process of naming and reflecting on their experiences was closely tied to the competing representations of motherhood in popular culture, medicine, and psychology. Juxtaposing women's own experiences against the cultural myths allows us to see how the tensions in women's lives are important ingredients in their collective efforts to break apart the myths and their effects on women's mothering.

POSTPARTUM ILLNESS AS GENDER DEVIANCE: VIOLATING THE EMOTION NORMS OF MOTHERHOOD

Although the term "postpartum depression" is perhaps the most commonly used label to describe postpartum emotional disorders, I found that women do not apply this term to only one feeling. Nor do they generally use "depression" in a strict psychiatric sense. Rather, the term "postpartum depression" is often meant in popular and self-help discourse to convey a web of distressing emotions. Feminist scholars increasingly emphasize that motherhood is shaped by women's race, class, ethnicity, religion, sexual orientation, and other social differences, as well as by gender ideology and identity. My emphasis here is on the commonalities in the accounts provided by the predominantly white and middle-class women to whom the postpartum depression self-help movement is pitched and on the way their emotions are shaped by their awareness of the strong cultural imperatives— or "feeling rules"—that govern maternal emotion.

The feelings that new mothers find to be the most disturbing cluster around the four basic emotions of guilt, anxiety, depression, and anger. These feelings can be thought of as constituting the lived experience of postpartum mental illness. To illuminate the connection between women's emotional distress and the confusion the mothers experience when their feelings diverge from what they expected, my discussion relates these four emotions to the contradictory meanings, or the "emotion norms," of motherhood as described by the interviewees and as debated in popular, self-help, scientific, and medical writings on postpartum depression.

The women interviewed for this study make it clear that it was not the reactions of physicians, nurses, and medical providers that led them to assess their feelings as a sign of postpartum depression. Indeed, fewer than 20 percent of these women ever discussed their emotions with obstetrician-gynecologists, family practitioners, pediatricians, or other health-care providers. To the contrary, most of these women do not agree with prevailing medical opinions of postpartum illness, and many see themselves as victims of an unresponsive male-dominated medical system that failed to hear their "cries for help." Rather, they hear confirmation of their feelings in the voices of other women who, as part of a submerged network of self-help groups, share their personal experiences of postpartum depression through self-help reading, parenting and baby magazines, television talk shows, childbirth education classes, parent education courses, and mutual support groups. Nearly three-fourths of the women interviewed identified their main sources of socialization into motherhood as books, magazines, and pamphlets on pregnancy, childbirth, and parenting; interactions with close women friends; and formal childbirth education courses. The significance of self-help for women's definitions of postpartum depression is clear from one woman's story published in a D.A.D. newsletter:

> Until I attended the support group, I wasn't sure if I had postpartum depression. Now I know that I suffered it. Because of the encouragement of others in the group, I sought help with the right doctor, changed therapists to someone who understood and could deal with my guilt over PPD. Thanks to those who listened, cared, and offered support, I was able to accept myself as a loving mother who was suffering illness.

Although the feelings women refer to as postpartum depression vary considerably in intensity and duration, for most women they are very distressing and more than transitory. The women I interviewed spoke of their suffering in stark terms as "shattering" their lives, leading them to feel "trapped in a dark tunnel with no escape," going through "our own living hells," "living a nightmare," and experiencing a "tortured and slow death." Only about a third of the women reported that their emotional difficulties began in the first few days following the birth or adoption of a child and lasted for less than a month. On the contrary, the highest prevalence of postpartum depression occurred in the third month following the birth or adoption of a child and, on average, the distress lasted between two and six months. About one-fourth of the women interviewed experienced emotional disturbances for as long as six months to a year postpartum. Even those who described psychotic episodes and long histories of depression placed their emotional problems squarely in the context of motherhood. Stephanie, who suffered a major depression following the birth of a second child—nearly twenty years after having her first—went so far as to state that her "postpartum depression began the year the first baby was born and didn't end until he left home for college." Because most women do not expect negative emotions, it is typical for women to talk about having been robbed of the first several months of motherhood. As the above-quoted article put it, "Postpartum Illness Feels Like A Thief."

Guilt, Shame, and Mother-Infant Bonding

For about half of the women interviewed, the feeling that signaled the onset of postpartum depression was guilt, described as "at times overwhelming"—brought on by the fact that their feelings for their newborn or adopted child did not match what they expected. So many women reported a sense of detachment from their babies and feeling guilty and ashamed as a result that it is safe to say that the experience of Shirley, who suffered a year-long depression that began almost immediately following the birth of her first child, is fairly typical:

> I had in mind this cooing, laughing baby, someone I could love and have that special kind of close relationship with that you can't have unless you're a mother . . . so I was a bit let down when in the hospital I was handed this sleeping infant who didn't seem to care whether I was there or not. It just wasn't what I expected. Here was this baby I was supposed to love, and I just didn't feel a thing. I literally went numb. I can't tell you how guilty I felt.

Linda, whose depression was so severe following the birth of her daughter that she nearly refused to have a second child, tells a similar story:

> I read every book there was, including horrible little old pamphlets. But nobody ever told me there is a chance you might not like her. I got her as this clean unrecognizable bundle plopped on my stomach at the hospital. And when I recognized that I felt absolutely nothing for her, I fell into deep depression.

As these accounts illustrate, a major source of women's guilt and shame is failure, for whatever reason, to experience immediate and intense bonding with the newborn child. Women who were unable for any reason to nurse the baby soon after birth, or those who experienced difficulty with nursing, were likely to feel as though they had failed to experience the "rush of mother love" they expected. Anne, whose depression began right after her first baby was born and lasted for six to nine months, explained:

> Nursing is supposed to be this instinctive thing. Well, I couldn't nurse her, and I felt I had failed. Maybe I was too anxious to do all the right things. Then I found out you had to be taught how to nurse, that the baby had to be shown too. So what's all this about it being natural? I honestly think that nursing was half of my problem.

Guilt sometimes was associated with separation from the child brought on by having to return to work in the early months following the birth or adoption, as well as by separation linked to psychiatric hospitalization. Whatever the origins of women's feelings, guilt and shame were almost always taken by them to be signs of postpartum depression.

That so many women expect, as one popular advice book on pregnancy and childbirth puts it, "to bathe in the glow of maternal love" is undoubtedly linked to the idea of maternal infant bonding that says that there are innate physiological and emotional processes that commit a mother to her newborn infant in the first few moments following the baby's birth. Despite a demonstrated lack of validity, the concept of bonding took hold in medicine and the social sciences during the 1970s and early '80s. Contemporary medical writings on postpartum depression do not by and large subscribe to the assumptions of biological motherhood inherent in the bonding theory. Nevertheless, the idea of a maternal instinct has firmly implanted a biological justification for maternal caring in the popular view. Biological determinist perspectives on mothering have also been a recurring theme throughout the history of modern feminism. Whereas some feminists have held biological reproduction to be the fundamental origin of women's subordination, others claim special maternal powers for women based on women's role in bearing, breastfeeding, and rearing children.

It is not surprising, then, that the popular discourse on pregnancy and childbirth, which is written primarily by women, contains contradictory messages. For example, the following passage from *A Good Birth, A Safe Birth*—an advice book for new mothers popular in the 1980s—contrasts postpartum depression to what William Arney terms the instinctive "falling in love with your child" implied by the concept of bonding:

> Some of the new mother's emotions bother both herself and those closest to her. . . . These symptoms are usually labeled "postpartum depression." On the other hand, when the new mother thrills at feeding and holding her baby, and when her tears are tears of joy, these actions are labeled "maternal."

In *What to Expect the First Year*, one of a series of best-selling books on pregnancy and parenting written by Arlene Eisenberg, Heidi E. Murkhoff, and Sandee E. Hathaway, women are given permission to feel not only "incompetent" but unloving toward their newborn babies. Eisenberg recounts her ambivalence toward her own child in the book's preface:

> Not only weren't my feelings on cradling my brand-new daughter, still damp from amniotic fluid and ruddy with blood, less glowing than I'd expected, they were more ambivalent than I'd ever imagined. Why didn't I feel close to her?

Why didn't she seem to feel close to me? And why—oh, why—didn't she stop crying? More faults surfaced as I lifted my gown and aimed Emma's swollen face at my breast. Instinct seemed sorely lacking on both sides.

In the training materials distributed to its telephone volunteers, Depression After Delivery does its part to counter the myth of instant bonding by encouraging volunteers to reassure women concerned about failing to bond with their babies "not to feel guilty about how they are feeling toward their child." At the same time, by communicating to women that "when the PPD begins to lift and the symptoms begin to lessen, loving feelings will begin to come," Depression After Delivery nevertheless holds maternal attachment to be synonymous with normal motherhood. The emphasis in the self-help and advice literature, then, is on a gradual "falling in love" that occurs between mother and child. Tracy Hotchner, in her popular book *Pregnancy and Childbirth*, compares motherhood to a "prearranged marriage" and urges women who are not "automatically infused with a joyous desire to love and nurture a new baby" to "ease into it slowly." The overriding theme, however, is that a mother's detachment from her child should "not be judged harshly but rather seen as an indication that she may be ill and unable to function."

Sociologists of emotions generally think of shame and guilt as among the most fundamental of emotions because they serve as powerful negative motivations for behavior and imply a degree of personal insufficiency that raises serious questions about the adequacy of the self. For many of the women I interviewed, the shame and guilt experienced when the "overwhelming rush of love and instant maternal bonding" they expected did not "come right away" had such a corrosive effect that, as one woman wrote, it "steals away their sense of motherhood." As Hotchner notes, by identifying guilt and shame as components of postpartum depression, women are permitted the latitude of expressing what are seen as normal feelings brought on by women's fears of being an unfit mother. The advice contained in *This Isn't What I Expected*, a guide to recovery from postpartum depression written by two women (one a physician and another a social worker), both members of Depression After Delivery, clarifies the importance of using collective strategies to manage guilt:

> *The key to overcoming shame is to risk reaching out to someone and talking about whatever is making you feel so badly. It sounds very simple, yet it is very hard to do. Once you can talk about it, you can begin to free yourself of the shame attached to your feelings.*

The discourse of the postpartum depression movement, then, encourages women to "off-load much of the guilt" they have accepted by turning away from "the traditional and socially acceptable standards" about being a "good mother and wife" that induce guilt and feelings of inadequacy.

Anxiety, Fear, and Mother-Care

All of the women interviewed expressed some degree of anxiety and fear connected to mothering. Initially, women were inclined to link their feelings to the burdens of caring for an infant and, especially for first-time mothers, to inexperience and uneasiness about how to meet the child's needs. To the extent that care and nurturance are central to the definition of motherhood, an inability to care for the child strikes at the very core of maternal identity. Sally, a successful dentist in private practice, recalled being so worried about whether she was "taking care of the baby properly" that on some days she telephoned her closest friend as often as ten times a day for advice:

> I was so anxious that I would do things like, I couldn't bathe the baby. I couldn't give her a bath because I was afraid I would drown her. I didn't want to change her diaper because something made me afraid I would stick her with the pin. Everything I did with that baby I was afraid to do. I was so paranoid sometimes that I was even afraid to feed her.

While anxiety almost always began with concern over the child's well-being, for several women these feelings gave way to full-fledged panic attacks and obsessive thoughts of harming or killing their babies. One woman had visions of drowning her baby in the bathtub, another thought about cooking her baby in the oven, another woman envisioned dropping her baby off a freeway overpass, another was preoccupied with thoughts of killing her baby with a kitchen knife, and one woman was haunted by "these goofy thoughts of cutting off the baby's nose." Although few women who consider harming their children carry through, the psychiatric literature reports that around one-fourth of maternal child murders are connected to acute psychosis. Another nearly one-half of mothers who kill their children murder "out of love," when they realize their own suicide would leave the child virtually abandoned.

There was a marked tendency for some women's anxiety to generalize beyond the baby to themselves. The five women I interviewed who were diagnosed by clinicians as suffering from postpartum psychosis experienced acute feelings of anxiety. In her keynote address to a 1987 Postpartum

Depression Conference in Columbus, Ohio, Dagmar Celeste, hospitalized for postpartum psychosis six months after the birth of her sixth child, recounted the onset of her condition. Her fear and anxiety became so intense that the world at large suddenly became frightening and dangerous:

> *It was a crisp winter day . . . I sat down on a chair in the baby's room . . . letting my mind drift while watching the mobile gently turn over the sleeping baby's head, and all hell broke loose. The frozen river outside invaded the peaceful family bathroom; the usually clumsy and lethargic donkey jumped the fence as if possessed; and the dog who would ordinarily not hurt a fly stood in front of the window, teeth bared and furiously growling. The mobile above the baby's bed started to follow me around the house, and the phone began to ring. . . . My speech turned into riddles and rhymes, my body could not sit, I was terrified, and I felt like my soul was in immediate danger.*

Dagmar Celeste attributes her psychosis to the combined stress of having another baby at the same time that she was juggling the demands of caring for five children, completing a college degree, and campaigning for her husband, who was defeated in a bid for lieutenant governor. Only a few women in my study reported the extreme level of anxiety, irrational fears, mania, and delusions she describes. But a majority of the women I interviewed saw their excessive worry and irritability as the inevitable result of trying to combine and balance in various ways the demands of what Arlie Hochschild and Anne Machung have termed a "second shift" of child care, housework, and a marriage or partnership with paid employment.

At the heart of women's concerns about providing good mothering is the division of labor in American society that designates women as being primarily responsible for the care and nurturing of children, even though the societal circumstances under which this pattern developed have changed. This patriarchal model of childrearing, as Barbara Katz Rothman terms it, does not accurately characterize the mothering patterns of women of color, immigrant women, some working-class women, and lesbians. Despite this, the dominant line reflected in the obstetrics and gynecology literature is that, even if women are urged to receive "a certain amount of 'special' help, either from their husbands, or from another woman, often the maternal grandmother or aunt of the new baby," child care ultimately remains the province of women. These days, medical articles—many now written by women—take as the standard the liberal feminist image of the "supermom" who combines marriage and childcare with employment. Indeed, the popular advice literature on pregnancy and childbirth tends to parallel the medical overemphasis on the plight of the supermom, thereby ignoring the experiences of other groups of mothers. From this standpoint, mothering is defined primarily as a voluntary decision and a learned skill acquired through medical consultation, formal childbirth education, and popular writings by childrearing experts. With so many choices available to a woman and presumably so many resources at her disposal, the new mother who experiences anxiety, fear, and ambivalence over her caring labor, although no longer a biological misfit, is nevertheless someone who has failed at "accommodating the female role."

The postpartum self-help movement offers women an alternative to both the traditional and the new views of maternal caring. In its support groups, literature, and media campaigns to raise public awareness, the movement gives voice to women whose feelings defy the expectations of maternal caring. At conferences and in the newsletters of D.A.D., women speak frankly and openly about their ambivalence toward motherhood by discussing not wanting to have another child, advocating the use of antidepressants to prevent postpartum illness, contemplating suicide as a way out; some even give testimony to killing their babies while suffering postpartum illness. Because the feelings women associate with postpartum illness challenge the view that a mother's love uniquely equips women to care for children, the movement advocates "father-care" and "other-care." Husbands of women suffering postpartum depression are encouraged to participate in housework, assume responsibilities for child care, and "adapt to the changes they see in their wives" by providing friendship and understanding.

In some communities postpartum support groups are closely intertwined with the childbirth education movement. Childbirth educators do not treat parenthood as instinctive but as a learned skill that can be performed by women or men, and they emphasize that both women and men are unprepared for the task because "there is rarely an apprenticeship for parenthood." Due to the leadership of a lesbian mother in Pennsylvania, an African American woman in Ohio, and a Mexican American woman in Santa Barbara, at least some individual activists are struggling to expand the notion of mothering to include the distinct forms of community caring and nonexclusive mothering of women of color, working class, and lesbian mothers. In *Mothering the New Mother*, a self-help book recommended by Depression After Delivery, Sally Placksin acknowledges that the decline of extended families and close-knit communities, coupled with women's obligations to be "working in an office—maybe even our own office—ten hours a day," have made the idea of the "traditional baby seem too intrusive for many new families." To compensate, she recommends a type of support provided to new mothers in some traditional cultures: the paid postpartum doula or caregiver who comes into the home to nurture and instruct both the mother and the father about parenting.

The emotional requirement that mothers love and care for their infants is so central to the meaning of motherhood that it is not surprising that women find it distressing to feel anxious and fearful about caretaking. Women consistently describe the labor of caring as producing a sense of "not being in control of one's life," and studies uniformly report that feelings of powerlessness and lack of control are associated with high levels of emotional distress. In the publications and discourse of the postpartum depression movement, anxiety and fear are taken to be clear signs that a woman is "experiencing ppd." In fact, Carol, whose words I used at the beginning of this book, provides an example of how self-attributions of postpartum depression can in certain instances be comforting. Carol had two young children in addition to a three-month-old infant, and recalls the day she knew that she was suffering from postpartum depression. She "lost control" because the baby would not stop crying, "smacking each of the children once" and rocking the baby while repeating, "I hate you, I hate you." By reassuring women that feelings such as these "do not mean that a new mother doesn't love her baby, or is ambivalent about motherhood," the postpartum depression movement permits women to express the anxiety associated with parenting. Presenting postpartum illness as a metaphor for less-than-successful motherhood, especially the failure to demonstrate intense and unswerving love for the child, means, however, that the link between motherhood and caring remains unchallenged. The postpartum support group movement is, nevertheless, a major proponent of a new model of parenting that insists that fathers and mothers share equally in the care of their children and in the anxiety that goes along with a role that is so closely scrutinized.

Depression and Maternal Satisfaction

Women who think of themselves as suffering postpartum depression describe feelings of sadness, hopelessness, worthlessness, and loss in the weeks and months following the birth or adoption of a child when they discover that for them motherhood is not the ultimate road to happiness and fulfillment. A clear majority of the women interviewed marked the beginning of their depressions with unexplained episodes of crying that started sometime in the first two weeks after birth and lasted on average about two months. Many described excessive crying to the point that they "lost control" and were unable to take care of either themselves or their child. Gina attributed her crying to "disappointment." Ever since she could remember, she had wanted to have children. When she finally had her baby, she was "devastated" to find that she "didn't feel the sense of achievement she anticipated." This made it difficult for her "to present the image of the happy, glowing mother to the world."

For about one-fourth of the women interviewed, sadness and tearfulness did not subside in the first few months but gave way to major depression that lasted for as long as six months to a year. Depression is a complex and many faceted condition with physical manifestations (such as sleep disturbances, changes in appetite, physical ailments, weight gain or loss, and fatigue) and affective dimensions (such as feeling sad, demoralized, lonely, hopeless, worthless, and wishing to be dead). Women's descriptions of postpartum depression include both elements.

The major theme that emerges from women's accounts of depression is the loss of self that women associate with motherhood. The most common source of loss reported by women who experienced postpartum depression was leaving a job after the birth or adoption of a child. Connie, who quit her job as a secretary for an insurance agency, became "depressed about being stuck at home, and being useless, and her taking all of my attention." Susan, a school psychologist who took several months of maternity leave before returning to work full-time, felt she had made such a mistake that she actually wanted to get rid of her baby: "I resented him, I wanted to get up in the morning and take a shower and eat my breakfast and go to work like I used to . . . nothing was the same." Margo, an African American woman who took extended maternity leave from her job as a social worker in a family services agency where she worked with black families suddenly found herself feeling "self-centered." She lost her identity as an "othermother" of the black community working on behalf of race uplift and became so depressed that she contemplated getting into her car and driving it "100 miles an hour into a brick wall."

Women describe other kinds of loss of self as well. Jessica, an eighteen-year-old mother who chose to raise a child as a single parent while working part-time and attending college, talks about the loss of her youth:

> I'm a mother now and even though I thought I would be different, I feel old like my Mom. I felt like some of my youthfulness left. If I want to go somewhere and do anything, I've got to think about having a babysitter or getting my Mom or my brother to take care of her. I've got to think about coming back in an hour or two to feed her. I can't go on dates, to the mall, the movies, or do any of the things my other friends are doing. I feel restricted and tied down.

Another single woman, Lynne, a university professor who wanted a child so badly that she traveled to El Salvador to adopt an eight-year-old girl, describes a "dark cloud" that fell over her life the first year as she began to question her earlier commitment to her career. Her depression made her aware that before having a daughter she had been "only half a person."

The loss described by more traditional women was in a sense more fundamental, as it stemmed from the way that the societal shift in "the very core of what it means to be a woman" has eroded their status as full-time housewives. As traditional women try to find fulfillment in a glorified image of motherhood acquired through religious teachings, their own family backgrounds, their husband's expectations, childbirth and parenting manuals, or their own fantasies, they often suffer serious and prolonged depression. Jane, who waited until she completed her bachelor's degree to have her first child, planned not to begin work or graduate school until her children were in school. Despite her high expectations for motherhood, she experienced a major depression that led to hospitalization after the birth of her first child. She attributes the depression, at least in part, to disappointment with full-time motherhood:

> That was the way I was raised, to have my mother there for me all the time. That was the way things were supposed to be. We were going to have kids. And I was going to stay at home and my husband would be a successful college professor. We were going to have everything. . . . I never expected that it would all just come crashing down.

Alice, who described a "deep, dark unhappiness" that came over her after having a baby explained:

> When you have so much invested in one role like women do in motherhood and you're having negative feelings about it, it goes to the core of questioning your sexuality and your very identity as a woman.

Even if the sociological literature demonstrates that pregnancy, childbearing, and childrearing increasingly have different meanings for women, in medical writings motherhood continues to serve as the primary reference point for female identity, as illustrated by the following passage from a widely used textbook in obstetrics and gynecology:

> Acceptance of mothering as a natural element of every woman's biologic endowment is a normal part of psychosexual development. This implies a willingness

*to accept the giving role as well as the physical discomfort and other sacrifices
that pregnancy and motherhood impose on every woman.*

True, since the 1980s, the medical literature has modified its approach
somewhat to promote the image of the middle-class working mother
who combines maternal satisfaction with paid employment. But medicine continues to advance an "ultimate fulfillment" account that treats
motherhood as a precondition for adulthood and sets up the expectation
that, for a woman, true happiness cannot be gained without motherhood,
even if it is almost always combined with paid employment.

For some physicians, contentment begins as early as pregnancy. Cynthia
recalls being told by a male gynecologist that she "glowed" while she was
pregnant because of what he diagnosed as a "madonna complex." He also
used this condition to explain the fact that, although she ordinarily was
afraid to stay alone at night when her husband was out of town, she was
comfortable doing so when she was pregnant.

The belief in maternal satisfaction, reinforced by the medical establishment, veils the negative side of motherhood. A growing research
literature that reports high rates of depression among mothers of young
children is almost entirely omitted from medical discourse. For example, the widely respected and most commonly used text for the
education of obstetricians and gynecologists, *Williams Obstetrics*, contains only one paragraph on women's emotional and psychological
response to childbirth. When the emotional distress of mothers is discussed at all in the medical and psychiatric literature, the feelings of
irritability, moodiness, weeping, tiredness, fatigue, anxiety, vulnerability,
and antagonism toward one's partner reported by between one-half and
two-thirds of all women are normalized under the label "baby blues" to
distinguish them from more serious but less frequent psychiatric illnesses
that might require attention.

The dominant medical view maintains that major depression, manic
depression, and psychosis suffered in the postpartum period are not distinct conditions except in timing and are "most likely a variant of primary
affective illness and not separate disorders." Ironically, a recent review of
psychiatric syndromes linked to women's reproductive function published
in the *Journal of the American Medical Association* offers a feminist explanation: it states that the medical labeling of postpartum psychiatric
conditions may reflect "culturally biased attitudes toward women."

In the 1990s, however, medicine has started to retreat from its one-
sided view of motherhood. Postpartum psychiatric conditions are
beginning to reappear in medical texts at the same time that some

medical schools, hospitals, and professional organizations are bowing to pressure from patients and self-help groups to include discussions of post-partum disorders in medical education, to sponsor conferences on the subject, and to provide education and treatment. This change in view can be seen as the result of a concerted campaign by two groups of women to define their emotional experiences for themselves and to stake a claim to medical benefits and resources. The first is women physicians and nurses who, joined by a handful of receptive male physicians, have drawn from their own and patients' experiences to challenge the dominant medical view. If the role that women health care providers have played in filling in the gaps in knowledge about postpartum illness is an indication of larger trends, it would appear that women physicians are taking the lead in questioning why the knowledge and practices of the medical estab-lishment have neglected and distorted women's health issues.

It is not surprising that, in pursuing this agenda, women physicians often find themselves allied with self-help movements. Cheryl, a family practi-tioner, admitted, for example, getting most of her information about postpartum depression not from medical journals but from women's own accounts published in childbirth, parenting, women's, and baby magazines. Increasingly, medical accounts of postpartum depression are written by women, and they note "the possible adverse effects of the 'rosy' picture of pregnancy, childbirth, and early parenthood which is painted in many ante-natal classes and in most books and magazines for expectant mothers." In addition, women physicians are more willing to discount dominant med-ical discourse about the female body by considering hormonal explanations of postpartum illness. British gynecologist Katharina Dalton, for example, links postpartum illness to a progesterone deficiency, and the women doc-tors interviewed for this study were more likely than male physicians to advocate progesterone therapy or antidepressants to treat the biochemical basis of postpartum depression.

The second means by which women have been active in embracing medical diagnoses to explain their abnormal feelings is through collec-tive attempts to carve out a territory where women can define their emotional experiences for themselves, recognize their own medical and psychiatric experts, and find sources of support and treatment. In this way, even if motherhood still tends to be regarded as the pinnacle of fem-ininity in the popular literature on pregnancy and childbirth, the depression and unhappiness associated with motherhood are not swept entirely under the rug. More often than not, firsthand accounts of post-partum depression and psychosis published in popular sources as well as professional outlets are likely to be written by activists associated with the postpartum self-help movement. Indicative of the ongoing struggle between professional and lay definitions that plagues most contemporary self-help campaigns, popular and childbirth education writings pay considerable attention to hormonal and other biochemical explanations of postpartum illness, which have had little impact on the mainstream medical establishment. For example, *What to Expect When You're Expecting* warns that roughly half of all new mothers are "miserable during one of the happiest times of their lives." The authors link postpartum depression to the precipitous drop in the levels of estrogen and progesterone that takes place following childbirth. They nevertheless provide a litany of other explanations, including the new mother's shift in status, the overwhelming responsibilities of motherhood, the loss of freedom associated with motherhood, feelings of disappointment with the baby, feelings of inadequacy, exhaustion, hospitalization, and the new mother's unhappiness with her appearance.

The discourse of the postpartum support movement poses the most serious challenge to "the myth of blissful parenthood that is ingrained in our society" and confirms women's feelings of sadness, unhappiness, hopelessness and loss that can accompany the changes brought on by motherhood. Whereas medical accounts focus principally on the normalized condition of the "blues," the postpartum self-help movement treats these fairly common feelings as "the little sister" of the "severe illnesses." Activists publicize the personal tragedies of women and families who have suffered and survived postpartum depression. Their tactics include face-to-face encounters with physicians and health administrators; appearances at local, regional, and national medical and mental health conferences; aggressive letter-writing campaigns; and more than three dozen media appearances on nationally syndicated talk shows and news programs. Participants in the postpartum support group movement have published their own self-help books such as *This Isn't What I Expected* by Karen Kleiman and Valerie D. Raskin, and *Postpartum Survival Guide* by Ann Dunnewald and Diane G. Sanford to warn women of the likelihood of experiencing postpartum disorders and the necessity of treating these problems in a straightforward manner. Through these alternative discourses, self-help activists have opened up a space for public discussion about postpartum psychiatric conditions and provided women with a label for their unusual emotions. The paradox is that, even if the postpartum depression movement holds that maternal satisfaction is not inevitable, its actions reaffirm the cultural myths by promising to restore to women—through support groups, medication, therapy, hospitalization, or whatever it takes—the happiness, joy, and fulfillment of motherhood.

Writing in celebration of Mother's Day, one of the movement's founders illustrates the contradictory nature of such claims:

> Those of us who had the tough start to motherhood we call postpartum depression may rejoice on Mother's Day even more than most. We made it through. We can FEEL again . . . and we will never take JOY for granted. We've gone through personal tragedies and emerged, at first shaken, but later stronger. We've survived.

Sociologists generally agree that, although depression is experienced as a personal problem, it can also be understood as a type of social distress that originates in the larger social problems of inequality, alienation, and powerlessness that affect certain groups of people. Dana Crowley Jack's psychological perspective that views depression as a consequence of the self-silencing women engaging in and conforming to traditional feminine roles shares an important dimension with Theodore Kemper's sociological analysis of depression as status deprivation. The common thread running through each of these explanations is the way that motherhood and women's nurturing, relational, and caregiving activities figure into the imbalance of power between women and men and become a basis for women's devaluation and ultimately their unhappiness.

Anger and Maternal Self-Sacrifice

The feeling that women almost universally treat as a sign of postpartum psychiatric illness is anger. Historically, the expression of anger by women has been seen as violating gender norms to such a degree that it has almost always been equated with mental and physical illness. Sociologists understand anger to be a distressing emotion provoked by inequity or a sense of unfairness and associate it with depression. Unlike depression, however, which turns on the self, anger targets those held responsible for the inequity. For the new mother, feeling angry at the very persons she expects to love represents the ultimate failure to feel and act in a motherly and wifely fashion. Women's accounts of postpartum illness reveal strong feelings of hostility and anger directed at their husbands or partners, children, the male-dominated medical establishment, and medical and popular representations that glorify motherhood and deny women's subordination.

If there is a single discovery that triggers women's anger, it is the stark realization that motherhood requires that a woman put her feelings at the service of others by enhancing her child's and her husband's or partner's well-being, even at the expense of her own. It is not surprising that when women discover the extent to which good mothering is synonymous with altruism and self-sacrifice, they become angry with those seen as responsible for constraining their lives. Well over half of the women I interviewed expressed anger, hostility, and resentment toward their husbands or partners for failing to share child care and household responsibilities. The anger articulated by Christine, whose depression persisted for seventeen months after the birth of a third child and was exacerbated by serious marital and financial difficulties, is fairly typical. Even though it was financially necessary for her to work, her husband had traditional ideas about marital roles—ideas that were typical of about one-third of the husbands and partners of the women I interviewed who experienced postpartum illness. She began to resent him so bitterly for not sharing household responsibilities that she looked forward to the time when she had the financial independence to seek a divorce:

> *I was angry a lot because my husband is not real supportive. He was just there. He was not any help as far as fathers go. He's old fashioned. It's okay if you want to work and everything, but the kids are your responsibility.*

The majority of women indicated that their husbands or partners subscribed to less traditional gender strategies, but even husbands and partners willing to share child care frequently took little responsibility for the other tasks necessary to keep the household running. It is not unusual for women who were satisfied with their marriages before having a baby to become so angry with husbands—whose lives changed very little as a result of parenting—that they begin to "distance" themselves from the relationship.

More stigmatized, however, are the feelings of anger, resentment, and hostility women direct at their children; one-fifth of the women harbored thoughts of harming their babies. Kim, a twenty-one-year-old intensive care nurse who was so depressed that she was unable to go out of the house for three weeks following the baby's birth, resented her child so much that she dreamed of giving him up for adoption. Janet, who like most of the women I interviewed never acted on her feelings, became desperate. Prior to her first pregnancy, she had been a successful graduate student working to complete her doctoral dissertation. Her husband already had completed his doctoral degree and taken an academic position at a university where the future looked bright for him. The demands of being a mother and wife, in the meantime, required so much of Janet's time and energy that she fell behind on her dissertation and decided to let her career temporarily take a back seat to his. One night as she was washing the dishes, while her husband relaxed in the living room, the baby began to cry:

> I recall picking up a butcher's knife to wash it. And for one moment, I considered the possibility that if I went into the baby's room and killed her, my life would return to the way it was before.

Women also direct anger at male obstetrician-gynecologists who downplay their suffering by refusing to treat postpartum depression and postpartum psychosis as illness or who give advice that reinforces gender stereotypes by espousing the view that good mothers sacrifice their own happiness to childrearing. Diana, the woman who held a high-level management position and waited until her late-thirties, when her career and marriage were well-established, to have a child, talked about being oppressed by the medical establishment. After a medically complicated delivery that resulted in an unanticipated cesarian section, she suffered such serious depression that she was forced to take an additional three months of sick leave following six weeks of unpaid pregnancy leave. Her anger was provoked by the fact that her obstetrician-gynecologist "dismissed" her concern over the loss of an independent identity, which she held responsible for her "unrelenting depression." Worse yet, she objected to his advice, which reflected and helped maintain gender stereotypes by setting up expectations about "proper motherly behavior":

> I started crying at the doctor's, saying I was lonely, I needed work, and I needed structure. He said, "This is normal. This will pass. Don't focus so much on yourself. What you have to think of is the baby. In time, you will adjust your priorities and forget that you ever felt the way you do now."

Working-class, lesbian, and women of color articulate anger over the dominant cultural representation of motherhood constructed around only two possible images—either that of the middle-class, stay-at-home heterosexual mother, or the "briefcase-toting supermom" who combines marriage, motherhood, and career. These images, they believe, deny their specific experiences of motherhood. Maggie, a lesbian mother whose partner is sharing the responsibility of raising their son, explained that for her motherhood had not been an "oppressive" act of unselfish altruism. Her comments were consistent with the findings of other studies of lesbian mothers; she described mothering as a "strategy for undermining the cultural opposition between motherhood and lesbianism." Margo, a middle-class African American mother, expressed anger over the negative media portrayal of black mothers as either "emasculating matriarchs or drug-addicted teenage welfare mothers who abandon their kids," highlighting that the societal expectations to which black women are subject may be even more stringent than for white mothers.

The medical discourse on postpartum illness treats the kind of anger women describe almost exclusively as a matter of individual abnormality. Little or no attention is paid to the wrongs or injustices that might be causing women's anger. It is not uncommon in medical writings for the burdens of child care and domestic work to be trivialized and women's requests for assistance in these areas to be seen as a sign that they are suffering postpartum illness. Without any explanation of the context and causes of women's anger, the references to mothers' "aggressive thoughts," "homicidal thoughts," feelings of "violence to the infant," "thoughts of harming the baby," and "anger toward the baby" found in medical texts seem almost baffling to the inexperienced health care provider. Yet women's inappropriate anger is so central to the medical definition of postpartum illness that feelings of hostility toward the infant are the most commonly discussed rationale for medical and psychiatric intervention.

It is in the popular discourse on childbirth and pregnancy that women find the most acknowledgment for their anger, which is treated not only as natural but sane. In this venue, the advice new mothers get is not unlike the advice women receive in general about the expression of anger in relationships. As Francesca Cancian and Steven Gordon point out, since the 1960s and '70s there has been a major change in emotional norms, a change these authors connect to the wave of social and political protest of the period. As a result, women have been advised in more and more popular books and on talk shows to express their angry feelings and to challenge the authority of men over women. The frustrating situations likely to provoke the new mother's anger expand to include not only hostility toward the baby, but toward "the doctors, the nurses, her husband . . . society in general . . . and anyone who was supposed to take care of the baby and didn't." In *Pregnancy and Childbirth*, Tracy Hotchner advises:

> *Allow yourself to have negative feelings about the baby. There will be ways in which you feel put-upon by the burdens of baby care. It's alright not only to have those feelings but to voice them. A baby turns your life upside down and you're more than entitled to resent that.*

Even if the popular discourse on postpartum mental illness offers women a deviant label for their anger, it does not represent motherhood as selfless and sacrificial or women's anger as irrational and unexpected. *Jane Fonda's New Pregnancy Workout and Total Birth Program* urges the woman "not to feel selfish buying clothes for herself instead of toys and equipment for the baby." A baby needs its mother in a "good mood" more than it needs material things and a mother who has been "pushed into unnecessary sacrifices."

The writings of the postpartum self-help movement acknowledge anger as one of the major "clues" to recognizing postpartum illness. The discourse of the movement goes further, however, than the popular literature on pregnancy and childbirth to link women's anger to gender inequality. Like most contemporary self-help movements, the postpartum support movement holds the male-dominated medical establishment responsible for the sexist treatment of women's health conditions. Male physicians are routinely criticized in the movement's publications and confronted in open forums, informal meetings, and medical consultations for dismissing women's suffering by telling women to "relax and things will clear up in no time" and refusing to treat postpartum depression and psychosis as the illness that it is. Activists compile lists of sympathetic medical and mental health professionals who treat postpartum conditions and disseminate this information to women who request help over a volunteer-staffed "warm-line." The movement strikes out at the sexual division of labor in the household that saddles women with the responsibility for child care and maintaining the home, linking postpartum depression to women's subordinate status. Jane Honikman, the founder of Postpartum Support International begins her public speeches with the following statement:

> *The position of women in any civilization is an index of the advancement of that civilization: this position is gauged best by the emotional support and care given her during pregnancy, at birth, and following the arrival of her child.*

Dagmar Celeste, an outspoken feminist with a bachelor's degree in women's studies, defines her public expression of anger in response to being hospitalized for postpartum psychosis as a deliberate challenge to "patriarchal definitions of mothering." She sees her public speaking and the activism of other women who are "breaking the silence" surrounding postpartum depression and postpartum psychosis as "defying the definition of femininity" perpetuated by the medical establishment and the society at large. She goes on to explain the movements' strategies by pointing to the ways self-help activists are struggling to reevaluate motherhood by exposing its "darker side," thereby "upsetting the entire gender system." In its public and private discourse, the postpartum support movement encourages women to trade their guilt, shame, and depression for anger over the injustices of motherhood and pride in having "survived" a condition to which countless mothers have lost their lives through suicide and infanticide.

Anger is a common response to social inequality, and it is the feeling that most clearly indicates the rebellious nature of postpartum depression. In contrast to guilt and depression, which hold the self responsible, anger positions women's suffering in relation to gender subordination and holds male domination accountable for women's being defined solely in relation to others, as well as for the segregation of roles and loss of an independent identity that can occur when women become mothers. For that reason, anger not only challenges the emotional rules but also has the potential to change them. The overt expression of anger and the refusal to accept the traditional, circumscribed roles of mother and wife leave little doubt that postpartum illness can be understood as a form of rebellion and resistance against male-dominated motherhood.

CONCLUSION

Postpartum illness is both individual and social. Since motherhood is, by its very nature, relational, and women's vulnerability to depression lies in large measure in the requirements of the maternal role, we cannot separate women's individual distress from the social arrangements and cultural fabric that channel women into subservient roles. The signs and symptoms of postpartum depression described by the women I interviewed sound familiar to anyone who has ever suffered the downward spiral of depression, as well as to the therapist who has treated debilitating depressions. Yet by attending closely to the voices of these women, we are able to understand that their symptoms have distinctive meaning. Placing their feelings in the context of their lives brings to life postpartum illness so that we can begin to recognize the extent to which the condition is tied to the white middle-class model of motherhood—that of a caring relationship almost entirely in women's hands. Even if ideas about a "correct" maternal role are giving way as the practice of motherhood shifts and becomes more diverse, the emotional demands of motherhood have not succumbed as readily to change. These women's stories make it evident that, at least for some women, the emotional experiences of motherhood are almost the antithesis of the dominant model. Guilt, anxiety, depression, and anger are hardly the feelings society associates with mothering. Rather, they are emotions that sociologists of mental health generally treat as barometers of psychological distress.

It is beyond the scope of this book to estimate the prevalence of the feelings women describe here. The fact that the "baby blues" and "postpartum depression" are so much a part of the popular discourse suggests that the feelings these terms evoke are probably not confined to a mere handful of women. Studies that have attempted to determine the frequency of these more transitory emotions agree that between 60 and 80 percent of U.S. mothers have negative feelings sometime in the first ten days to two weeks after they give birth. But even the more severe and persistent depression and anxiety described by nearly a fourth of the women I interviewed appear to be more common than we might ordinarily expect, with researchers reporting that from 10 percent to as high as 26 percent of all new mothers suffer major depression.

Apart from the nineteenth century, when the interests of an expanding medical profession were served by bringing postpartum disorders under its province, the medical establishment in the United States historically has withstood women's attempts to interpret and treat their maternal emotions as a disease. As we have seen, medicine ironically justifies its stance on the basis of an increasingly sociological view of postpartum illness, which stands in stark contradiction to psychiatry's general tendency after the 1930s and '40s to treat what Freud called the "psychopathology of everyday life." This failure to acknowledge postpartum illness undoubtedly also can be traced to the growing influence on the medical profession of the liberal feminist perspective that emphasizes the similarities, rather than the differences, between women and men.

Although medical and psychiatric discourse are sympathetic to women's search for answers to their unhappiness in the home and family, psychiatry's failure to bestow significance on women's problems has led women to take up arms in the battle for the medicalization of their own experiences. The contrast between the powerful role that biological explanations play in discussions of postpartum illness in the self-help and popular discourse and the broad social and cultural solutions proposed in these same writings is striking. This paradox illustrates the tendency for a woman's body to serve as what Michel Foucault has described as both an object and target of power. That is, the disease classifications and the routine practices of medicine and psychiatry reflect strong ideas about femininity that influence women's conscious and unconscious attitudes about their bodily emotional experiences. It is not surprising, therefore, that medical definitions and authority carry over into the oppositional ideas and strategies women use to redefine and take control of their own experiences.

Examining the different representations of postpartum illness in the medical, psychiatric, and popular self-help literature tells us more, however, than what the competing discourses women turn to have to say about their problems. It allows us to attend to the ways that women's own sense of motherhood becomes engaged with dominant and competing cultural definitions and to examine the process by which women use postpartum psychiatric illness to accept, negotiate, and resist the codes of femininity. But collective resistance is only possible when women are able to recognize that their feelings and experiences are common and when they can forge solidarity with others who have suffered the same problems. Not only are women physicians making their presence felt in the field of medicine by proposing competing ideas and practices, but women's self-help movements are becoming major players in the contest over who shall control the definition of women's health problems. To understand the challenge that postpartum illness poses to dominant representations of motherhood requires that we recognize the sometimes covert but always powerful role that feminism has played in the construction of postpartum illness. And that turns our attention to the emergence of the postpartum support group movement.

SEIZE THE DAY

THE EMERGENCE OF A SELF-HELP MOVEMENT

*I'm always impressed by the creative
agitation of women. Really I think
that if we can stay angry for the next
few years, we may work ourselves out of
a job. Because we will beat postpartum
psychiatric illness.*

—Jeanne Driscoll, "My Personal Journey"

F THERE is a single event that defines the transformation of a small
group of women struggling to come to terms with their own personal agonies into a full-fledged social movement, it happened the morning
of May 20, 1986, when Glenn Comitz appeared as featured guest on the
Phil Donahue Show. Glenn's wife, Sharon, was serving eight to twenty years
at the Muncy State Correctional Institution in Pennsylvania for killing their
one-month-old son, Garret, on January 3, 1985. Sharon had initially
reported that Garret had been kidnapped at a shopping center. But the next
morning, when the boy was found dead in a stream six miles from the family home and witnesses testified that they had seen Sharon driving in that

direction, the police charged her with murder. Under hypnosis she eventually remembered dropping her baby off a bridge into the creek. She subsequently confessed but maintained her innocence on the grounds that she was mentally ill and suffering psychotic symptoms of postpartum depression. In fact, this had not been Sharon's first bout. Shortly after the birth of their daughter seven years earlier, Sharon and Glenn had had to rush to the hospital with the baby in respiratory distress, and Sharon reported at the time having been awakened by a nightmare in which she was trying to suffocate her daughter. Following this incident, Sharon was admitted to the psychiatric unit of the local hospital for two weeks and then treated with antidepressants for two months until her depression lifted. Fearing she might experience a recurrence of depression, Sharon had been under psychiatric care as early as six months into her second pregnancy. Her physician prescribed antidepressant medication as soon as Garret was born, and she appeared to be doing fairly well for the first month. The day that she dropped Garret in the creek was the first time she had been left alone with the baby. Several psychiatrists who examined Sharon reported that during the forty-five minutes that it took to drive to the creek and drop her baby into the water, she had suffered a psychotic dissociation.

In addition to Comitz, the show featured Carol Dix, a journalist, survivor of postpartum depression, and author of a recent book *The New Mother Syndrome*; Barbara Perry, a professor of psychiatry and former researcher for the National Institute of Mental Health; and a woman identified only by her first name, Laura, who told her own story. Laura had suffered such severe postpartum depression following the birth of her then three-and-a-half-year-old son that she vowed not to have any more children. Describing herself as someone who had romanticized motherhood, Laura explained that when she found out she was pregnant she "read Dr. Spock from cover to cover" and dreamed of being an "earth mother" who did "everything right." Then following an extremely painful natural childbirth, Laura unexpectedly found herself depressed. After two weeks without sleep, she began to hallucinate, imagining herself "throwing the baby down the incinerator chute." Laura attributed her recovery to the care of two psychiatrists, a psychologist, and a live-in nurse. When members of the studio audience and home viewers began to recount their own experiences, Sharon's and Laura's stories did not seem all that unique. Several women admitted suffering depression, bouts of anxiety, and even psychosis following childbirth. One caller remembered a major depression that lasted for six weeks after her second son was born and climaxed one night eating dinner with her husband when she "broke a drinking glass and slashed both of her wrists at the dinner table."

Donahue emphasized the medical nature of women's problems, beginning the show with the statement that, "It is in the literature that women who suffer postpartum depression can in fact be moved to commit what society is calling a crime." But he also echoed his guests' concern about widespread "political ignorance" of postpartum psychiatric illness to highlight the social and political dimensions of this problem. What most viewers who saw this program did not know is that Donahue's guests were part of a submerged network of activists mobilizing to provide self-help to women and to demand that the medical establishment recognize their problems as a distinctive medical and psychiatric condition.

The *Phil Donahue Show* set off an explosion of media attention. During the following August, postpartum depression was featured on The *Oprah Winfrey Show*. By 1990, activists had made thirty-four appearances on nationally syndicated television programs and news broadcasts including the *CBS Morning Show*, *Good Morning America*, the *Today Show*, *20/20*, *Hour Magazine*, *Larry King Live*, and the *CBS Evening News*, and on local and national talk shows including *Geraldo*, the *Joan Rivers Show*, the *Morton Downey Jr. Show*, and *Sally Jessy Raphael*. The media attention catapulted postpartum depression into the limelight.

If there is a single point on which scholars of social movements agree, it is that the mere existence of a problem, no matter how widespread or serious, does not in and of itself explain why people band together to pursue collective solutions. Instead, there are several ingredients that must gel for a social movement to emerge. First, there is the element of *opportunity*, or the prevailing climate of support or opposition in the political, cultural, and social institutions targeted for change. The second requirement is some rudimentary form of *organization*. People must find ways of acting collectively to mobilize resources, develop strategies, and construct new self-definitions whether in an informal network or a formal association. The construction of a *collective identity* that conveys a group's own definition of themselves and explains the basis of their commonalities is the third ingredient of all social movements that do not confine themselves simply to institutional change. Finally, to convince others of the importance of their goals, social movements must frame their issues and goals so as to appeal to the concerns and interests of wider groups in the society. Sociologists David Snow and Robert Benford have coined the term *collective action frames* to describe the shared ideas and beliefs activists generate to justify their goals and to mobilize support.

When all of these factors come together to produce a social movement, it is tempting to see this as signaling the emergence of a new and pressing problem. In reality, the issues people define as problems and the social movements that arise to address them usually have much longer histories than meet the eye. In tracing the development of the postpartum support group movement, I take a perspective that emphasizes the continuities that link different movements. I start with the assumption that the antecedents of today's women's self-help movements are to be found in what Doug McAdam describes as a much broader set of "movement families." This means that we must look for origins in other social movements that supplied resources, tactics, justification, and networks; and also in the waning of what Sidney Tarrow terms the "cycle of protest" of the 1960s and '70s, during which many different kinds of social movements thrived.

When it began in the mid–1980s, the postpartum self-help campaign was "just a support group." Nevertheless, in a few short years one support group launched by a single woman blossomed into a national network of groups throughout the United States. This chapter tells the story of how it emerged and took shape. To understand why the problem of postpartum depression resonated with the lives of women, it is necessary to follow the path from the feminist movement of the 1960s and '70s to the postpartum support group movement that mobilized a mainly white, middle-class constituency of women in the 1980s and '90s. I begin by considering the long history of self-help in the women's movement and by discussing how this has shaped a distinctively feminist tradition of self-help.

SELF-HELP AS THE TAPROOT OF FEMINISM

From groups in the free black community in the pre–Civil War period to white middle-class women's literary clubs in the late nineteenth century, women of all stripes have come together to improve their own lives and to meet the needs of their communities. But it was not until the 1970s, during the crest of the second wave of the women's movement, that we began to see women's self-help groups with the kind of political dimension that characterizes modern feminist self-help.

Self-help was the modus operandi of hundreds, perhaps even thousands, of loosely structured groups that sprang up among mostly young, college-age women in the late 1960s and early '70s. Such groups were part of the direct action or radical feminist strand of the modern women's movement, which began a gradual decline in the 1980s during the antifeminist backlash that peaked during the presidency of Ronald Reagan. Although early feminist self-help actions addressed a wide range of concerns—from providing child care and teaching women how to service and repair their cars to delivering services to women victimized by sexual harassment, rape, and battering—it was in the women's health movement that self-help took center stage. The story of the development of the women's health movement reveals the five basic characteristics of feminist self-help: self-knowledge, awareness of gender oppression, women's culture, empowerment, and transformation of gender relations.

An important early event in the emergence of the women's health movement was the founding in 1971 of the Los Angeles Feminist Women's Health Center (FWHC), a gynecological clinic controlled and staffed by women. Although abortion reform served as the catalyst, numerous other issues drew women to the movement, including the sexist treatment of women by male physicians in gynecological examinations, alarm over mounting reports of the dangers of oral contraceptives and other medications such as the synthetic estrogen DES, dissatisfaction with childbirth practices in the male-dominated field of obstetrics, concern over women's high rates of pelvic surgery, and the sterilization abuse of black women in the south. For Carol Downer, one of the founders of the FWHC, self-help was not just one of many feminist strategies, it was feminism. Feminists were bitter about the lack of medical knowledge about women's health, and they also saw the passive model of health care as an affront to women's self-determination. In Downer's words, "The only way these things could survive was in ignorance, that as long as women stayed mystified about their bodies and alienated from each other then, of course, these things could happen."

Like most feminist self-help groups, the Los Angeles center began in a consciousness-raising group where two women simply wanted, at first, to learn more about their bodies. They hoped to be able to self-diagnose and treat routine gynecological problems such as vaginal infections, recognize the early signs of pregnancy, perform safe and inexpensive abortions, and educate women about natural childbirth. After discovering that using a flashlight, mirror, and physician's speculum, a woman could examine her own vagina and cervix, these two pioneers began demonstrating the technique to other women. Here was the *self-knowledge* or common sense wisdom that galvanized the women's health movement.

An earlier 1969 Women's Liberation Conference in Boston on the topic "Women and Their Bodies," in which participants expressed frustration and anger toward physicians and the health care system, had led to the formation of a consciousness-raising group to discuss, research, and teach about women's health issues. Calling itself the Boston Women's Health Book Collective, this group challenged what activists believed to be mythical and unscientific assumptions about women's bodies and health propagated by a male-dominated and profit-oriented medical establishment. Perhaps the best way to convey the radical challenge to professional medical knowledge posed by feminist self-help is to take a close look at how it was practiced in this group, whose efforts led to the publication of the best-selling health manual for women, *Our Bodies, Ourselves.*

> *Each took a topic such as birth control, natural child birth, masturbation, VD, abortion, postpartum-depression or rape. They went to other women, they talked to nurses and doctors. They did research in medical texts and journals, where vital information is ordinarily kept inaccessible to the public. None had expertise in doing research or experience in any health-related field. However, they did trust they could find reliable information and learn the necessary research skills as they went. Each woman shared what she had learned in discussion with the rest of the group. From the very beginning, personal experience was integral to their analysis as it enabled them to develop a critique of the information and health care they were getting.*

As this account illustrates, in the early years of the women's health movement, participants were drawn together mainly by a common awareness of the way that the physical and emotional health of women is shaped by gender oppression. Activists envisaged self-help as a way to learn more about their own bodies, but their vision went beyond self-care and a critique of the assumptions and practices of the medical establishment to pose a challenge to gender relations as a whole. Extending this critique, the women's health movement began to recognize the many ways that women's diversity—race and ethnicity, class, gender, and sexual orientation—affects health as well. Whereas middle-class white feminists, for example, were interested in obtaining affordable access to legal abortion, black, Puerto Rican, and Native American women were more likely to be concerned with forced sterilization. Such differences among women led eventually to the formation of numerous self-help groups that focused on specialized concerns such as natural childbirth, menopause, abortion, fertility problems, and breast self-examination. These were geared to specific populations of women such as African American women, Native American women, and lesbians. For example, nearly a decade after the emergence of the first feminist self-help groups, the National Black Women's Health Project formed to address distinct health problems such as high blood pressure and diabetes, and health centers began to recognize the diverse needs of Latina, Native American, Asian American women, poor, immigrant, lesbian, and disabled women.

Alternative women-only organizations validated a distinctive *women's culture* as a way of providing mutual support. Separatism, a central theme in the nineteenth-century women's movement, reemerged in the early to mid-1970s in lesbian feminist groups such as The Furies, which recast lesbianism as a political strategy that was the logical outcome of feminism, or the quintessential expression of the feminist belief that the "personal is political." This belief served as a basis for the growth of the separatist women's communities comprised of lesbian and heterosexual feminists that by the 1990s flourished in major urban areas throughout the United States and in smaller communities with major colleges and universities. A woman-to-woman approach appealed to women's health activists challenging the professional authority of the male-dominated medical establishment. By 1973, participatory health had emerged in the form of over a thousand women-run health centers around the United States. Feminist health centers stressed prevention, self-help, and patient-centered, affordable care as an alternative to mainstream medicine oriented toward intervention, physician control, male-centered medical thinking, and profit-making. The need for separate women's health care was rationalized, for the most part, by the cultural feminist belief in women's fundamental difference from men, the unique values of women, and the importance of homosocial bonds between women.

By the mid- to late 1970s, the emphasis on political advocacy and institutional change that drove early feminist self-help groups concerned with issues such as rape, battering, and incest was beginning to give way to a more therapeutic approach. In a 1972 book that became a feminist classic, Phyllis Chesler set the stage for the growth of the feminist psychotherapy self-help movement by demonstrating how the standard psychiatric classifications of disorders, illnesses, and symptoms; the use of individual therapeutic practices; and the institutional treatment of women mirrored the sexism of the larger society. Feminist therapy, which has grown to become a recognized specialty in psychiatry and mental health, started out pretty much the same way as did the self-help movement focused on women's health, as an offshoot of consciousness-raising groups. What is unique to feminist therapy, when compared to other forms of psychotherapy, is its concern with understanding and treating the way that women's inner well-being is affected by the social and political structures of gender, race, class, and sexual inequality that, on the one hand, subject women to daily assaults on their self-esteem and, on the other, undermine through feminine socialization their capacity to assert themselves.

If women's learned helplessness was the condition that feminist therapy addressed, then the *empowerment* that results from participating in what Gloria Steinem nearly two decades later would call "the revolution from within" is the medicine of women's self-help. Two developments in the

1970s gave new meaning to the notion of empowerment in modern feminist self-help. The first was the phenomenal growth and presence of Al-Anon, launched by wives of alcoholics to deal with the dysfunctional effects of alcohol on families; and of Adult Children of Alcoholics (ACOA), formed to address the "codependency," i.e., excessive caretaking and assuming responsibility for others characteristic of people who grow up in alcoholic families. Codependency is generally understood to be a distinctively female mental health problem linked to women's caregiving roles in traditional families and other institutions; as such, it is undoubtedly responsible for the fact that since the 1970s women have come to constitute nearly 80 percent of ACOA's membership. Empowerment in the context of ACOA means reconstructing female identity so that it is no longer primarily organized around traditionally feminine relational concerns. For that reason, the modern recovery movement contains a critique of the family and women's traditional subservient roles that most feminists would agree are the linchpin of gender inequality. In the context of feminism, then, empowerment entails an awareness of the connection between the social distress, self-doubts, and self-hatred of women and the imbalances of power between women and men manifested in social institutions as varied as the family, religion, medicine, the work place, and the state.

A second development in modern self-help has opened the door, however, for a more individual route to empowerment that skirts the support groups traditionally associated with feminism. Feminist writers consider the present crop of self-help books to have begun in 1963 with Betty Friedan's *The Feminine Mystique*. Since then, a whole new genre of therapeutically induced self-help books has proliferated on nearly every topic imaginable, lining the shelves of local bookstores and supermarkets, dominating best-seller lists, and capturing the attention of the mass media as the topic of talk shows, news programs, and newspaper and magazine columns. Women pounced on books such as Robin Norwood's *Women Who Love Too Much* and Melodie Beattie's *Codependent No More* and turned to talk-show hosts such as Phil Donahue and Oprah Winfrey for validation of their experiences and for the inspiration to change. Mental health professionals jumped onto the self-help bandwagon, as a new generation of feminist therapists brought the diagnostic language and tools of psychiatry to bear on women's emotional injuries, unfortunately extricating women's problems from their social and political contexts. Depression, for example, long the disease of women, became more interesting as a chemical imbalance than as an expression of the unhappiness and disadvantages suffered by women in a male-dominated society. Such developments were not surprising given the ongoing feminization of psychiatry, which brought feminist perspectives to bear on clinical practice but failed to transform either mainstream psychoanalytic thinking or the medical model of depression.

The agenda of feminist self-help began as the *transformation of gender relations*, whose site of change is taken to be the self and whose impact is felt mainly in the lives of individual women. Many of the original feminist self-help groups that focused specifically on women's health concerns have either disbanded or become mainstream providers of services to women. In their place have arisen scores of new self-help campaigns to address the myriad of problems of later generations of women, the most popular of which focus on overeating, breast cancer, and childhood sexual abuse. Self-help support groups can be found, however, on almost any topic.

But to what extent can contemporary women's self-help, bound up as it is with the therapeutic world view, be understood as an offshoot and a contemporary manifestation of feminism? Because time has a way of changing the flavor and composition of all movements that survive for any period, to address this question we begin with the first stirrings of the postpartum self-help movement and trace its evolution to the present.

THE FEMINIST ORIGINS OF THE
POSTPARTUM SUPPORT GROUP MOVEMENT

The Boston Women's Health Book Collective that formed in 1969 was, as far as I've been able to determine, the first self-help group to consider the problem of postpartum depression. Paralleling its approach to all areas of women's health, the collective placed postpartum psychiatric illness in the context of a broader critique of the medical establishment that denied women accurate information about their bodies.

In an interview, Jane Mansbridge, a collective member, recalled a woman she described as "very thin, almost waify, and not very vivacious who kept bringing up postpartum depression." A mother herself, Mansbridge realized in retrospect that "if this woman was suffering from postpartum depression, that might be why she was as she was." Mansbridge remembered thinking, like most other members of the mainly college-age group, that "postpartum depression didn't seem very interesting or important and that this woman was probably off on her own hysterical little thing, that this problem just didn't seem central to the women's movement." But she quickly added that "the way the women's movement functioned in its early stages was that the problems it dealt with came entirely out of women's own experiences, so this woman, nevertheless, ended up writing a section on postpartum depression for the book."

The book—*Our Bodies, Ourselves*, which began as nothing more than a collection of mimeographed pages stapled together—has since been published in four editions and translated into more than a dozen languages. It became the basis for courses on women and their bodies taught in universities and community centers throughout the United States and has sold over three million copies. Given the lack of medical attention to postpartum psychiatric illness in the late 1960s, it is not surprising that the passage on postpartum depression in *Our Bodies, Ourselves* was one of the first sources of inspiration for a subsequent generation of women who, in the mid-1980s, would launch a self-help movement focused specifically on postpartum psychiatric disorders. But the actions of the women who spearheaded this campaign were influenced in even more fundamental ways by the women's movement that preceded them. They mobilized by drawing on the activist networks, ideas, and tactics of the women's movement, benefitting from what David Meyer and Nancy Whittier have labelled the "spillover effects." As we shall see, the postpartum movement's goals eventually dovetailed with those of the growing self-help industry and the interests of sympathetic medical and mental health professionals, who also shaped the character of the movement.

Mobilizing Through Submerged Networks of Feminists

Researchers interested in understanding how people decide to engage in collective action to reform society generally agree that small face-to-face groups are the incubators of social movements. The formation of the National Organization for Women in 1966, the mainstay of modern feminism, illustrates this point. Most of the founders either belonged to one of the state-wide commissions launched by John Kennedy's President's Commission on the Status of Women, or were part of the close-knit feminist community surrounding the National Woman's Party, which had lobbied for women's rights since its inception in 1916 during the women's suffrage campaign. The fact is that participants in most social movements tend to come either from the same friendship groups or belong to the same organizations. But the significance of social networks for understanding the emergence of a social movement is to be found not only in how they cement bonds between participants but also in the symbols, discourses, stories, practices and other shared meanings that evoke the ties between people. In recent years, social movement scholars have used the concept of *collective action frames* to depict the ideas and interpretive frameworks that justify and inspire people to action. Collective actions frames make specific claims about the identities or shared attributes of a set of actors, and they suggest the collective causes of individuals' problems and set forth solutions. Once we recognize that the postpartum support group movement emerged among networks of feminists with clear connections to the women's movement of the late 1960s and early 1970s, then we can understand more fully why the movement took shape as it did. Quite simply, feminism served as what Ann Swidler described as the "cultural toolkit" for building the movement.

The first support group for women suffering postpartum distress began in Santa Barbara, California, in 1977. Jane Honikman led the efforts on behalf of a wide range of women's health issues, including pregnancy and natural childbirth, breastfeeding, and women's mental health. Honikman herself had suffered recurring bouts of depression since 1967, when she gave up a child for adoption after discovering that she was pregnant while an exchange student living in Copenhagen. Honikman ended up marrying the child's father a little less than a year later, but she continued to struggle for years with unresolved guilt over giving up their first child.

A 1960s generation idealist who graduated from Whittier College with a sociology degree, Honikman participated in the civil rights, feminist, women's health, and natural childbirth movements of the 1960s and '70s. Her activism in connection with mothering began in the mid-1970s when, as a mother of two, she organized a parent support group through her local American Association of University Women (AAUW) branch. Most of the participants were young women who had chosen to be full-time mothers but who perceived a lack of support for their roles from the mainstream women's movement and society at large. Honikman places the group squarely in the tradition of the "consciousness raising that was going on in the early seventies," because it mobilized women's anger at the societal forces responsible for "ignoring motherhood" and sparked the formation of several community projects to address childbirth and parenting, namely the Santa Barbara Birth Resource Center and a Parent Education Program. But she also credits the group with pulling her out of serious depressions following the birth of her children. She recalls how unprepared she was for the emotions she felt after having both her second and third babies:

> I swallowed my feelings of inadequacy, isolation, and fear and smiled as I coped. I wondered why I wasn't feeling terrific about the one job I had wanted so badly. Finally, I discovered that other women were having similar thoughts and experiencing these difficulties. We talked and shared, and started the non-judgmental, supportive listening group for ourselves.

69

It was not until 1987, nearly a decade later, that Jane Honikman, after meeting other activists and professionals concerned about postpartum psychiatric illness, used what had begun as a broad self-help campaign focused on parent education and support to launch an international organization devoted solely to postpartum psychiatric disorders. As a feminist steeped in the political culture of participatory democracy that propelled the movements of the 1960s and '70s, Honikman's early approach to self-help was shaped by the nonhierarchical ideals, woman-to-woman approach, and critical stance of the women's health movement toward the gender bias of the medical establishment. The way in which Honikman drew upon feminism to mobilize other women illustrates the process that Snow and his colleagues have called "frame bridging." That is, early on she sought out other feminists who were predisposed to her cause and provided them with the information necessary to persuade them to join the movement.

Connecting women's emotional distress to the structure and changing meaning of motherhood, Honikman's first support group mobilized around *a feminist frame* that linked maternal depression to the sexual division of labor in the family that gives women primary responsibility for rearing and nurturing children but places them at a distinct disadvantage in the public world. Members of this first support group were responding to what they believed was a devaluation of "the traditional woman" both by the society at large and by what Honikman termed "the feminist women's movement." When I interviewed Jane Honikman, she was eager to point out that early editions of *Our Bodies, Ourselves* emphasized not only physical and psychological stresses as explanations of postpartum depression but the socially defined nature of postpartum emotional disturbances as well. A passage from the first edition illustrates: "What little research has been done on postpartum is heavy with male bias and conventional attitudes about motherhood."

Honikman had been influenced from the start by the feminist analysis of postpartum depression developed by the Boston Women's Health Book Collective, which she credits with "having started the whole movement." The comments of another member of Honikman's first support group illustrate the extent to which participants saw their organizing as a way to expand the reaches of feminism: "I assumed that the feminist movement would follow me through, that just because I had a baby didn't mean I would be left out."

As the cultural climate shifted increasingly in the 1980s toward therapeutic solutions to individual problems, Honikman's "eyes were opened to the world of psychiatry and its role in motherhood" when in 1984 she attended her first meeting of the Marcé Society. An international research organization located in Edinburgh, Scotland, focused exclusively on advancing knowledge and treatment of mental illness related to child-bearing, the Marcé Society paved the way for Honikman to meet professionals who shared her concerns, such as Dr. James Hamilton, Professor of Psychiatry at the Stanford University School of Medicine. Dr. Hamilton authored the first medical book on postpartum psychiatric conditions in 1962 and would eventually be annointed "the father of post-partum depression" by self-help activists.

In 1987 Jane Honikman established Postpartum Support International (PSI), using her own personal funds. The organization began with thirty-four members, mostly feminists from Honikman's own support group and the women's health and parent education networks she had built in the Santa Barbara area. It also brought women who had experienced postpartum depression into contact with professionals interested in the problem from a more medical and psychiatric standpoint.

Through Carol Dix, a journalist who was doing research for a later best-selling book on postpartum illness, *The New Mother Syndrome*, Honikman became aware of efforts to launch support groups on the East Coast. Honikman invited these activists to attend a meeting hosted in Santa Barbara in June 1987, billed as the First National Conference of Postpartum Support International. By 1992, PSI, which is run out of Jane Honikman's home in Santa Barbara, had grown to encompass 200 members. The organization—a mix of professionals, volunteers, and activists headed by a formal board of directors—is funded primarily through member dues. In addition to public education, PSI's major national (even international) activity is to sponsor an annual two-and-a-half day conference that meets in the United States or Canada and brings together between 100 and 150 professional and lay activists from around the country and abroad. Honikman's original women's support group that sparked the formation of PSI has, in the meantime, been such a significant source of support and caring for her and its members that it still meets weekly for breakfast. A current member attributes the group's survival, in part, to Jane's "charisma" and "passionate commitment to feminism" and looks back on her own participation in the birth resource project and parent education program as a way to use the knowledge she gained from her women's stud-ies courses in college to become "politically active as a feminist."

Using the Mass Media to Found Self-Help Organizations

Participants who enter a movement at different time periods often form distinct political generations. That is, they define themselves, the issues

11

they are struggling against, the constituencies they hope to reach, and the changes they hope to accomplish in specific ways. In her study of the evolution of radical feminist identity from the late 1960s to the present, Nancy Whittier attributed changes in the meaning and strategies of feminism over time to differences in the various "micro-cohorts" of women who entered the movement. She demonstrated that women drawn to feminism at different points in the movement's history developed a unique political culture, shared a common world view, forged distinct strategies and tactics, and ultimately defined the meaning of feminism in radically different ways. Not only does this process help us to understand how the women's movement could change so substantially over time, but it also provides a key to some of the conflicts that have plagued feminist organizations over the years as the meaning of feminism has shifted to suit the changing political and social context.

Whittier's ideas about generational cohorts provide insight into the alterations to the postpartum support group movement as a later cohort of women struggled to found a national self-help movement. Around the same time that Jane Honikman met Carol Dix, a younger generation of women on the East Coast planted seeds for a larger and more grassroots organization called Depression After Delivery (D.A.D.). Its founder Nancy Berchtold admits some dissatisfaction with the name, which she had to create on short notice for an article about her support group printed in a local newspaper. An ardent feminist who left the Catholic Church because of its male-dominated hierarchical structure to become a Quaker, Berchtold envisaged the organization as "centered on women." As a result, she confesses "hating" the D.A.D. acronym. But she is eager to add that another outspoken feminist and founding member of D.A.D. reassures her that she shouldn't mind calling the movement the "Dad group." If it weren't for men refusing to help women raise children and refusing to take responsibility for the problems caused by women having to do all of the nurturing and caring, then we wouldn't be going through this in the first place." Ironically, as the movement expanded to include support groups for fathers married to women who have suffered postpartum illness, the D.A.D. acronym became a rallying point for holding men responsible for their share of the parenting. The Summer/Fall 1992 issue of *Heartstrings*, the newsletter of Depression After Delivery, pictured D.A.D. Vice President Joe Bound in San Diego displaying his tee shirt and redefining the group's acronym to mean "Dads Against Diapers—It's Not a Job, It's A Doody!"

D.A.D. sprang in 1985 from a support group of six women in Hamilton, New Jersey, just outside of Philadelphia. The group came together as a result of an article Nancy Berchtold placed in a local newspaper. A twenty-nine-year-old teacher, Berchtold was exhilarated when her daughter was born in December of 1983 and remembers thinking "I had the baby of my dreams." But by the time Allison was two weeks old, Berchtold was tormented by strange thoughts and soon afterward experienced a psychotic break. She thought she was a piece in a puzzle and that once the puzzle was solved she would die. Terrified and unable to sleep, she stayed up all night. When her husband finally woke up and asked what was wrong, she began screaming that Allison was dead. He rushed Berchtold to the hospital, where she was diagnosed with postpartum psychosis and hospitalized for two weeks, just long enough to get stabilized on medication.

After she was discharged, a deep and severe depression set in, and Berchtold was under the care of a psychiatrist for six months while other members of her family took care of the baby. She found support during her recovery by talking with two other women who had also been hospitalized for postpartum psychiatric illness, one of whom she met through a coworker of her husband and another through her Quaker meeting. It was only after meeting these women who had been hospitalized with the same diagnosis and discovering they felt the same things she had—guilt, loss of self-esteem, anxiety, and depression—that Berchtold decided to start a support group for women with postpartum disorders. In discussing the feelings that led her to launch a group, Berchtold stressed the connection between her own psychiatric problems and the isolation of motherhood as a social role. Before she had her baby, she had worked full-time as an art teacher in a junior high school:

> Following the two weeks I was hospitalized with the psychotic episode, there were a couple of months of real bad times, and then another six months on medication. I was off all medication about ten months postpartum, so it took ten months on meds for me to finally feel myself again. And also, I was a new mother. You know I had a whole new different identity, and my support system wasn't there. I had no support system. The people that I called my friends were all teachers and were all back doing their jobs. And I was stuck home with the baby, not feeling 100 percent, and wondering how had life dealt me these cards? And it was women talking to women, and mothers talking mothering issues that became my support group when I was going through this "oh god, I'm so alone." And in the group that was just normal stuff. I mean, I think a lot of new mothers feel that way.

Berchtold had never been diagnosed with mental illness prior to her episode, although psychiatric illness was not new to her family. Her sister previously had been institutionalized with manic depression, and both her mother and husband had suffered serious episodes of depression.

Like most of the movements's early founders, Berchtold had been a civil rights and community activist, volunteering for the homeless and poor inner-city children. Feminism remains, however, her most salient political identity. Motivated by the conviction that there is a unique women's perspective on health care that is the foundation of the feminist self-help tradition, Berchtold envisaged D.A.D. as a woman-centered nonprofessional group that would provide acceptance and support:

> *I started with being angry that other women were suffering alone, and I vowed to just raise my voice up high so that other women will know that you get better, you get through this, you survive this. It really basically was to support other women who were going through it.*

Like many women whose first participation in a feminist project occurred in the 1980s, Berchtold's approach to postpartum psychiatric illness also drew from the larger philosophy of self-help and recovery permeating the social movement sector at the time. Unable to find out much about her condition either from medical professionals or the medical literature, she felt "betrayed by the medical profession . . . and vowed to do something." Through consultation and training provided by the New Jersey Self-Help Clearinghouse affiliated with nearby St. Clare's Hospital, Berchtold acquired the skills and know-how to launch what is today a national network of local and state support group affiliates of D.A.D.

Unlike earlier women's health activists mobilizing in the wake of the influential antipsychiatry movement of the early 1960s, Berchtold did not hold a strong "anti-professional" orientation. Instead, she saw sympathetic health and mental health professionals as lending credibility to the movement and, even more important, as an alternative source of care for women. Unable to find a single physician familiar with her condition, she convinced psychiatrist Rick Fernandez, the husband of a close personal friend, to join D.A.D. Fernandez describes the way Berchtold's tenacity drew him into her cause:

> *She called one day, and she was pretty much recovered. She was still on antidepressants for her depression . . . but was interested in what I knew about postpartum depression. I really didn't know that much about postpartum disorders. I read the classic text on it—psychiatric—and I read her from there what I knew. And then she said she wanted to do something, she was interested in studying this. I don't know if she called it a self-help group then, a*

support group, I don't know what. Some sort of group for women who were suffering from this. I thought it was an o.k. idea except for the fact that she was a teacher and that a lot of people were going to be showing up for more than just support. Particularly since the disorder isn't really all that known. And there were some women who were suicidal. I didn't really ask to become a postpartum expert. I just got involved in treating these women clinically.

As it turned out the women who came to the first groups were, as Dr. Fernandez put it, "severely impaired women." Many had been suffering for two years or more, "couldn't find any answers, and finally heard there was a glimmer of light somewhere." A pro-feminist man who had always been interested in women's health issues and continues to serve as a formal and informal medical advisor to Berchtold and other D.A.D. members, Fernandez was willing to experiment with group and self-help treatment, as well as the standard clinical approaches. As a result, he has found that his practice is now comprised mostly of women who have suffered postpartum psychiatric illness. Because of his association with the postpartum self-help movement, Fernandez has teamed up with a psychologist, family therapist, and psychiatric nurse to establish the Center for Postpartum Depression serving the Philadelphia and Princeton, New Jersey, areas.

Even though Berchtold was eager to find sympathetic clinical professionals who were willing to lend their expertise to the problem, ultimately her aim was to build an indigenous base of support for women and their families. Starting with a $6,000 contribution from the husband of a friend who had committed suicide by hanging herself in a psychiatric hospital where she was being treated for postpartum depression and a $7,500 grant from the New Jersey Self-Help Clearinghouse, Berchtold set up a "warm line" in her home, established a clearinghouse on postpartum disorders geared toward new mothers and professionals, and began disseminating information to local hospitals. In 1986, D.A.D. began attracting media attention as Berchtold and other women told their stories through newspapers, women's magazines, and nationally syndicated television talk shows and tabloids, beginning with the fateful *Phil Donahue Show*. While access to these programs came, in part, from Carol Dix's promotion of *The New Mother Syndrome*, it was also facilitated by the media's interest in publicizing the small number of cases in which women diagnosed with postpartum psychosis had been charged with and had, in some instances, been convicted of killing their children. One of those women—Angela Thompson, along with her husband Jeff—played an important role in bringing attention to the movement.

Angela Thompson's story is not atypical for the genre of postpartum psychosis–induced infanticide, except in its legal outcome. In September of 1993, Jeff Thompson came home to find his wife, a registered nurse, agitated and shaken. She announced that their son, Michael, was dead. Believing Michael the devil and her husband Christ, Angela admitted that she had killed Michael as an act of faith to "expunge the world of the devil." She went on to tell her husband that "within three days" she expected him to "raise Michael from the dead." Jeff claimed that earlier that morning, when he had left the house for work, Angela had seemed fine, other than being a little preoccupied with the day's tasks. Although she had suffered psychosis following the birth of their first child (Allyson, then three years old), Angela had thus far shown no signs of similar problems following this birth. Jeff found Michael's body next to the house in a box covered with a towel and sprinkled with moth balls, which Angela had thought were rosary beads.

Initially the police charged Angela with first-degree murder. She was treated for one month in a psychiatric hospital and vividly recalls the "tremendous guilt and grief" she experienced when she "woke up from this delusion." She couldn't understand how she, as "someone who had always wanted to have children, to rear children, could do something like this" and remembers reacting by pounding her fists on the wall in disbelief screaming "my son, my son, how could I have done this?" A little over a year later, she saw Glenn Comitz on the *Phil Donahue Show*, and this program opened her eyes to that fact that she "was not alone." Angela contacted Depression After Delivery and Jane Honikman, who put her in touch with Dr. James Hamilton, by then retired from Stanford. He provided information about postpartum psychosis and made her aware of the Infanticide Act of 1938 in England, which provides that a woman in the first year after giving birth can be charged only with manslaughter, not murder, in the killing of her child.

The charges against Angela Thompson were eventually reduced to manslaughter and felony child abuse, and Angela was acquitted by reason of insanity. Although she was ordered into treatment for an additional six years, Angela and Jeff gave birth to another daughter five years later. Beginning with the *Phil Donahue Show* on February 17, 1988, almost two years after D.A.D.'s initial appearance, Angela and Jeff Thompson went public with their experience in the hope that they could get the word out about postpartum psychosis and postpartum mental illness. They made dozens of media appearances over the next year with members of Depression After Delivery and other self-help activists on such visible programs as the *Sally Jessy Raphael Show* and the *Oprah Winfrey Show*.

Publicity surrounding Angela Thompson's case drew psychologists Susan and Robert Hickman into the battle to help women charged with killing their children. Susan had experienced a serious depression in the 1970s after the birth of her child. When a close friend who suffered postpartum psychosis asked for help to get through a subsequent pregnancy, the Hickmans decided to start a free support group through a local San Diego Unitarian church in 1984. The first two members to attend were their friend and another woman Susan invited when she observed her holding her baby and crying in the grocery store. In 1986, Susan Hickman stepped in to help in the defense of Lorenza Penguelly who was charged with drowning her five-month-old baby in the San Diego Bay. In a court-ordered psychiatric interview after her arrest for murder, Penguelly explained that she took her daughter Sharai to downtown San Diego to give her away. When she found no takers, she tossed the baby into the bay thinking she was sending her to heaven. Reflecting on the outcome of the case, Susan Hickman noted the inequities of the criminal justice system:

> *Once you know about postpartum psychosis, it just jumps out at you. When I read about her case in the paper, I just knew it was a case of postpartum psychosis. When I started going through the records I found out she had been diagnosed with postpartum psychosis following the birth of her first child. But sadly that didn't end up saving this woman in the legal system. As a poor disadvantaged woman, she didn't get the same kind of positive outcome as Angela.*

Rather than take a chance on a conviction for second degree murder, Lorenza Penguelly's lawyers convinced her to plead guilty to voluntary manslaughter.

The media's fascination with infanticide allowed D.A.D. to capitalize on the publicity and played a critical role in the movement's growth by attracting the kind of public attention necessary to increase grassroots participation. Nancy Berchtold herself appeared twenty-eight times on nationally televised talk shows and tabloids between 1986 and 1991, and D.A.D. representatives were involved in another six nationally televised appearances. During this same period, articles appeared in countless local newspapers as well as in women's, parenting, baby, and even general-interest magazines. A March 30, 1990, column by Ann Landers included a letter from a woman unable to find satisfactory treatment for a depression linked to childbirth and mentioned D.A.D. as a resource. As a result, nearly 2,000 requests for information deluged the organization, only a little less than the total annual number of inquiries received in the previous two years. Hundreds of women wrote D.A.D. telling their own stories of depression, psychosis, and medical mistreatment. Between 1986 and 1988, support groups affiliated with D.A.D. formed in California, Massachusetts, New Jersey, Pennsylvania, Utah, Washington state, and the Washington, DC area. In my survey of national support group leaders and telephone contacts for D.A.D., I was not surprised to discover that the most frequently mentioned initial source of information about the postpartum self-help movement was television talk shows.

Media reports about postpartum illness focused on its widespread incidence and, without exception, relied upon the testimony of activists and professionals associated with the movement to direct attention to the medical establishment's failure to recognize and treat postpartum conditions. Activists presented their mission as "teaching health care providers what postpartum psychiatric illness is" with the hope that they can "be knowledgeable and know how to intervene and provide adequate treatment for postpartum psychiatric illness." The women who founded the first support groups in Santa Barbara had used feminist arguments to mobilize participants by linking postpartum illness to the requirements of motherhood and women's disadvantaged status. This later wave of activists discovered that the therapeutic discourse of self-help that stresses medical and psychological explanations rather than gender politics resonated with many women's experiences. But D.A.D.'s increasing use of a *psychiatric illness* frame to educate the public and mobilize support by no means should be taken as a sign that activists lack a broader interpretation of the myriad of social factors that figure into women's suffering. If the conference programs of D.A.D. and PSI mainly list medical and psychiatric professionals who advocate standard therapeutic and pharmacological treatments, it is also clear the explanations offered by medical professionals connected to the movement more often than not link postpartum illness to a broader set of social and psychological factors.

In 1991, Ann Landers mentioned D.A.D. for the second time in her syndicated column, and requests for information so exceeded the organization's capability to respond that Berchtold found it necessary to move D.A.D.'s operations from her home to a one-room office in Morrisville, Pennsylvania. A part-time administrative assistant, a single mother formerly active in the local chapter of the National Organization for Women (NOW), was hired to staff the office and answer a "warm line" three days a week. Two other women have held this position since D.A.D.'s first office manager resigned to pursue another career. By 1992, D.A.D. had over seventy affiliated support groups in forty-five states and had provided support to over 13,000 individual women through its "warm line" and to hundreds more through written correspondence. It operates nationally through 250 volunteers who staff telephone services and 105 designated support group leaders in forty-eight states. It has a board of directors of twenty activists and professionals, most of whom have themselves suffered postpartum illness. Funded primarily by donations, memberships, the sale of information packets, and fees charged to professionals listed in its clearinghouse materials, D.A.D. operates on a small budget. Despite attempts to formalize, president and founder Nancy Berchtold ran the organization through informal democratic decision making, frequently making the analogy to the "Quaker style Meeting." But as one of her coworkers emphasized in an interview with me, Berchtold had the administrative skills to go along with her commitment and compassion:

> *I just see her as incredibly dedicated and hardworking. I know when she goes to conferences she is like the guru, and everyone comes to Nancy. But from my day-to-day perspective, it is just damn hard work and she does it. Because of her dedication to helping others, and she has helped so many people, then others feel compelled to help others, and then kind of join in on that power of helping.*

In 1994 Berchtold assumed the role of past president by passing the gavel to Michele Kelly. A member of D.A.D.'s telephone network since 1988, Kelly founded and cofacilitates a support group at her local hospital in Kingston, Pennsylvania, and is currently in private practice as a counselor specializing in women's issues. She attributes her own recovery from postpartum depression to D.A.D.'s telephone network, support groups, and professional referral. Nancy Berchtold continues on as volunteer Executive Director and editor of *Heartstrings* and continues to make media appearances on behalf of D.A.D. As recently as September 1995, *Family Circle* featured her in its column, "Women Who Make A Difference."

Mobilizing through Health and Human Service Professionals

Until D.A.D. was founded, the women who initiated the postpartum support group campaign were primarily "outsiders" to the health and mental health systems, women whose ideas and repertoires of action had been born, tested, and refined during the 1960s and '70s cycle of protest when social movements flourished around a variety of concerns. This picture of the movement challenges much of the research that has tended to situate activist movements in medicine and mental health primarily as "professionalized" social movements, originating from the effective entrepreneurship and interests of "insiders" using their influence to capitalize on people's ongoing dissatisfaction.

These two outlooks parallel two competing views in the literature on social movements. An "insider" model would lead us to expect that self-help movements arise from within the ranks of the established health and human service professions. Contrasting with this is an "outsider" model that emphasizes the significance of lay and patient groups that draw strength mainly from the dissatisfaction, indigenous resources, and support they are able to mobilize from within their own ranks. In the case of the postpartum self-help movement, the distinction between grassroots activists and professionals is not that easily drawn. Feminist health and human service professionals and feminists working in other areas of women's policy—women that Hester Eisenstein would refer to as "femocrats"—have used their positions to open up opportunities for the movement to grow.

About the same time that Nancy Berchtold was forming D.A.D., a third locale of activism sprang up in Ohio. The Ohio organization, which in 1992 adopted the name Ohio Depression After Delivery, is the most highly professionalized and formalized network. It functions through support groups operating in six regions of the state and is coordinated by a statewide task force of activists, health and human service professionals, and researchers. Staff assistance from the Ohio Department of Mental Health through the Director of the Office of Prevention, who also heads the state's Depression Awareness Recognition and Treatment (DART) program, was critical in getting the movement off the ground. In addition to offering professional resources and a stable organization, the movement in Ohio has also managed to mobilize an invigorated grassroots strength. Despite the strong influence of professionals and state bureaucrats, the Ohio movement has not turned its back on feminism. Its success, in fact, can be traced to the firm alliances between feminists both as "insiders" and "outsiders" to the system.

The self-help movement in Ohio was organized by two women whose efforts came together in 1987. In the spring of 1986, Karen Mumford, from Cincinnati, was just coming out of a depression that had started the previous year after the birth of her second child when she saw Carol Dix discussing *The New Mother Syndrome* on the *Phil Donahue Show*. During the program Dix mentioned D.A.D., and Mumford telephoned Berchtold for information. Berchtold's dogged determination and charisma proved contagious. By the time Mumford hung up, she had been convinced to serve as the Ohio telephone contact for D.A.D. and was making plans to start a support group. With the sponsorship of a local hospital, the assistance of a sympathetic woman psychiatrist treating several women in the Cincinnati area, and the backing of her own physician, Mumford announced her intention to start a support group through a feature story that appeared in a local newspaper. Over sixty women telephoned the hospital in response to the article. Although Mumford envisaged the group as mutual support where women "with a common experience hooked up with each other, supported each other, and shared ideas with each other on how to cope," the hospital increasingly tried to take control by mandating physician involvement. To insure that the program would remain "community based," Mumford moved her operations to the local YWCA, where she was employed part time to work with toddler groups.

Unlike the founders of the other groups, Mumford had little history of prior participation in the women's movement. She had been a member of a feminist premenstrual syndrome (PMS) support group, which she looks back on as having been "very antimental health." The driving force behind the PMS group was the intention to empower women to gain control over their own bodies, but members resisted medical domination to the point that they were unwilling to use medications or make physician referrals. The PMS group's refusal to take advantage of medical resources convinced Mumford of the need for a "multi-disciplinary approach to postpartum depression" that would make use of the receptivity of at least some physicians to women's health concerns. At the same time, Mumford considered postpartum depression a larger social and "community problem" that "should not be just my responsibility, or the responsibility of other mothers."

Mumford brought a different kind of "cultural capital" to the movement. With a bachelor's degree in early childhood education, she had been employed as a teacher at a psychiatric center for children, where she served as a member of a multi-disciplinary treatment team comprised of psychiatrists, psychologists, social workers, speech pathologists, and educators. Despite such involvement with medical professionals, she shares the skepticism of most self-help activists and remains critical of medical and professional paradigms that fail to take into account "what the people who've been there know and the holes they recognize in the system." Nevertheless, in launching her campaign around postpartum depression, Mumford cultivated relationships with a wide range of professionals and policy makers, including psychiatrists, obstetrician-gynecologists, nurses, social workers, psychologists, childbirth educators, researchers, and policy makers in health and mental health. She sought not merely to provide an alternative or lay source of support for women who suffered postpartum psychiatric illness but also to challenge medical, mental health, and human service institutions to transform in ways that would make them more responsive to women's concerns.

If Karen Mumford was the spark that ignited the flame, Dagmar Celeste supplied the fuel that kept the movement going in Ohio. When the article detailing Karen Mumford's campaign on behalf of maternal mental health appeared in the Cincinnati *Enquirer*, Dagmar Celeste was first lady of Ohio. She had been hospitalized almost ten years earlier following a psychotic episode she experienced in connection with the birth of her sixth and youngest child. Since her husband, Richard Celeste, had been elected governor, she had often recalled in public forums the crisp winter day six months after Stephen was born when, at home caring for the new baby and playing games with her three other young children, her "speech turned into riddles and rhymes, [her] body could not sit, stand or lie still, and [her] mind was racing at ever-increasing speed while [her] soul was terrified." Following the psychotic episode, Celeste endured what she describes as a depression even "more painful than the psychotic break." Hospitalized for two months, she was treated for several years by a woman psychiatrist through a combination of psychotherapy and anti-depressant and antianxiety medications. Celeste had come to define what happened to her as postpartum depression.

Of all of the movement's founders, there is no one whose biography reads more like that of a 1960s activist than Dagmar Celeste. An avid participant in the women's movement since the 1960s, she and her husband had lent their energies to the civil rights, student, and anti-Vietnam War movements, and Dagmar had returned to college to earn a bachelor's degree in women's studies in the mid-1980s. Following the defeat of the Equal Rights Amendment, Dagmar did not abandon the cause of women's rights but continued to carry the torch of feminism forward as women organized to link their oppression to a broader set of issues, such as sexual abuse, drug and alcohol addiction, racism, anti-Semitism, heterosexism, war and violence, environmental destruction, global domination, and the androcentric theology and structure of traditional religion. When Richard Celeste was first elected Lieutenant Governor in 1974 and the family moved to the state capital in Columbus, they rented their Cleveland home to a feminist group for use as the first battered women's shelter in Ohio and the third in the nation. Elected to his first term as governor in 1982, Dick carried his commitment to women's issues into the governor's mansion, while Dagmar maintained strong ties not only to feminists but to other progressive groups in Ohio and on the national scene.

Dagmar Celeste's personal staff and circle of advisors consisted of feminists of varying stripes, including a former director of Women's Studies at Ohio State University, as well as activists from the National Organization for Women; and from the antirape, recovery, battered women's, lesbian feminist, AIDS, and women's health movements. Feminist scholars from Ohio universities briefed her staff and assisted in drafting speeches and developing policy initiatives. I served as a member of this group, consulting with Dagmar's staff in the preparation of speeches about postpartum illness. Directors of several state agencies were staunch feminists who maintained ties to the women's movement. The head of the Ohio Department of Mental Health, the agency with the second largest budget of any in the state, was a nationally recognized feminist lawyer by the time she assumed the directorship; but in the 1970s she had been a major player in the radical branch of the women's movement in central Ohio, when she helped to found the local Women's Music Union to sponsor feminist concerts and cultural events.

From the time that Richard Celeste took office, Dagmar used her influence and the resources available to her as first lady to campaign through public forums and the mass media for women's issues, calling especially for greater attention to postpartum illness. Every time she spoke publicly about her own postpartum psychosis and depression and subsequent hospitalization, dozens of women came forward by writing and calling her office. A magnetic, determined, outspoken, yet caring and nurturing woman, Dagmar Celeste threw her weight around to get others to take postpartum illness seriously. Physicians and health professionals no doubt felt compelled to listen because they were, after all, being summoned to meetings at the governor's residence. But Dagmar Celeste drew just as heavily on her personal and political ties to the wider feminist community to broaden the circle of activists. Feminists like myself, who had long admired Celeste's courage and commitment on behalf of women and other excluded groups, were brought into the effort as a result.

From the outset, Dagmar Celeste tied her own psychosis and depression to a broader critique of motherhood as a circumscribed role and devalued status. She frequently linked women's internal states to the external structures of gender inequality that place women at a disadvantage in relation to men by defining depression as "the normal state of femaleness." Further, as an outspoken critic of medical domination and its tendency to treat depression and other emotional problems with "miracle drugs," she accused the medical establishment of "playing God with the mind" while ignoring the importance of the "support of family and friends" for recovery. But if Celeste had a single goal in speaking out about her own postpartum psychosis it was to "raise women's consciousness" by giving them "permission to reclaim this experience."

Working through the Director of the Ohio Department of Mental Health, she convinced the department to fund a sociological study of postpartum depression to be carried out by a team of feminist researchers associated with the Ohio State University Center for Women's Studies and Department of Sociology. An advocate of feminist research that recognizes self-authority as well as the knowledge of experts and professionals, Celeste wanted two assurances: that the study would focus on social factors and that it would have policy impact. Upon completion of the first phase of research in 1987, the results were disseminated at two statewide conferences funded by the Ohio Department of Mental Health and directed at health professionals, policy makers, and lay audiences of potential activists.

It was at one of these conferences that Karen Mumford came into contact with Dagmar Celeste. In 1989 the postpartum depression movement in Ohio began to take shape as Mumford joined efforts with Celeste, who has never lost sight of the conviction that mutual support and caring are the cornerstone of feminism. Celeste's goal from the outset was to create a statewide system of small groups of women to support each other personally and act politically to break the silence surrounding "motherhood and madness."

In August 1989, a meeting of about thirty activists and professional volunteers convened at the governor's residence to launch a statewide network of support groups. This led to the formation of a Postpartum Depression Task Force. Over the course of the next year, the task force met almost monthly, with between fifteen and twenty members in attendance, including Karen Mumford, Dagmar Celeste and members of her staff, and lay and professional volunteers representing the network of support groups that had spread to most regions of the state. Staff from the Ohio Department of Mental Health, the Ohio Department of Health, the Women's Health Program of the Bureau of Maternal and Child Health, local hospitals, and researchers from nearby universities joined with activists, thus extending the reaches of the movement. In addition, the staff of the Ohio Department of Mental Health provided a training program for support group leaders. The fairly small amount of funding required to launch the campaign—a total of about $5,000, excluding the costs of the research project and the two conferences that totalled nearly $80,000—came from the Ohio Department of Mental Health, Ohio Department of Health, and the Women's Health Program of the Bureau of Maternal and Child Health. In effect, these femocrats, who headed key divisions and agencies in state government, joined hands with feminists outside of public service to put postpartum illness on the health and human services agenda.

With the Ohio movement on firm ground, in the spring of 1990 Dagmar Celeste and her staff handed over coordination of the Postpartum Depression Task Force to Karen Mumford and Helen Caine Jackson, Chief of the Office of Prevention of the Ohio Department of Mental Health. Jackson has a master's degree in social work, a background in counseling and training, strong managerial skills, and high national visibility in prevention and health promotion; she brought the kinds of organizational and technical skills necessary for the movement to gain legitimacy with health and mental health professionals. At the same time, as an African American woman with a long history of civil rights activism and strong ties to the black community, she has sought to expand the grassroots base of the movement by reaching out to women of color affected by postpartum illness. Also in 1992, the Task Force, comprised of most of its original fifteen to twenty members plus new support group leaders and a few women medical and mental health professionals recently recruited to the movement, took the name Ohio Depression After Delivery. Although it functions as a coordinating body, Ohio D.A.D. is continuing to expand as a grassroots organization as well. Monthly support group meetings throughout the state attract between four and eleven women per session. In 1992, Lilli-Ann Buffin, founder of a support group from Wooster, Ohio, joined Mumford and Jackson as a codirector of D.A.D. to prepare for the transition in leadership caused by Mumford's return to graduate school. The following year Lilli-Ann Buffin took the reins of a thriving and expanding Ohio D.A.D.

ACTING COLLECTIVELY:
COORDINATION AND CONFLICT IN THE MOVEMENT

The three social movement organizations just described, as well as the numerous local, regional, and state networks that formed over the past decade to focus on postpartum psychiatric disorders, followed a similar pattern. In each case, a woman who experienced the onset of a major depression or psychotic illness in the weeks and months following the birth of a child sought treatment for her condition and found established health and mental health providers unwilling to acknowledge a link between motherhood and her psychological distress. Virtually all of the founders of the core organizations already defined themselves as feminists. In two instances, the networks from which the movement's founders drew to mobilize built, at least initially, on common participation in the women's movement. But as activists struggled to reach a broader base of women beyond their own support groups and to obtain access to the resources necessary to help women, they found it necessary to build alliances with each other as well as with professionals sympathetic to their cause.

Scholars who have studied self-help movements emphasize that even though the relationships between professionals and self-help groups tend to be strained and can sometimes even be antagonistic, there is considerable variation in the stance that such groups take toward professionals. Massachusetts Depression After Delivery, for example, is probably one of the most highly professionalized of the postpartum support group networks I studied. Support groups in six regions of the state depend heavily upon hospital resources for publicity and meeting space, and the statewide network has one of the most extensive lists of medical referrals for women suffering postpartum illness of any in the country. In contrast, the "Emotional You" support groups run by Jane Honikman and affiliated with the Parent Education Program in Santa Barbara continue to be propelled by the same kind of grassroots organizing, indigenous community resources, and close friendships that were the impetus behind Honikman's first support group.

Even though the movement as a whole retains the highly personalized and decentralized structure compatible with the experiential knowledge and emotional support that are the foundation of self-help, the separate support groups and networks are linked through several mechanisms. First are international, national, regional, and local conferences that bring together professionals and activists. For example, the Annual Conference of Postpartum Support International—like most of the conferences—depends heavily on funding from hospitals, medical centers, and pharmaceutical companies as part of their continuing medical education efforts. Of course this means that the program is organized around professional presentations on the latest advances in medical research and treatment. At the same time, self-help activists share the limelight, and these gatherings provide an opportunity for activists to challenge the views of experts, debate strategies for medical and legal change, and renew the strong ties of friendship and support that exist among participants.

Of the women attending, most come without their husbands or partners, although a few women bring them to share the camaraderie and caring that flows freely at these gatherings, and a handful of men who are activists also attend. Describing national and regional conferences as "love fests," a founder of a support group in the Washington, DC area admitted that she is drawn to these events because she feels "loved and safe and empowered."

Regional and local conferences are also an important means of spreading the self-help movement's views of postpartum illness, which differ from the dominant medical line, in hopes of changing professionals' attitudes. In Ohio, for instance, conferences have been critical to the process of achieving the kind of "consensus mobilization" (or collective redefinition of a problem) that Bert Klandermans considers to be necessary for the growth and spread of a social movement. For example, Dagmar Celeste held several events at the governor's residence, one to bring local activists into contact with national groups, another to enlist physician backing for the network of support groups forming in the state, and a third, cosponsored by the Governor's Office, Ohio Public Defender Commission, and the Ohio Department of Rehabilitation and Correction, to consider the matter of criminal liability in cases where women are charged with murdering their children. With technical support from Children's Hospital and the Department of Obstetrics and Gynecology of Ohio State University, the governor's office and staff of the Ohio Department of Mental Health managed to organize a fourth conference, held at Children's Hospital in Columbus. This last event brought self-help activists face-to-face with researchers and health and mental health professionals with the aim of winning them over to the movement's position.

Depression After Delivery also serves as a link among the various separate support groups through its newsletter *Heartstrings* and the interactions it facilitates between local and regional groups that have chosen to affiliate with the national office to form a larger D.A.D. support network. In addition to disseminating information packets about postpartum illness to women and professionals, D.A.D. provides guidelines about how to begin a support group and how to give telephone support to women.

Because sharing the journey is so central to the mission of self-help, strong ties of love and friendship among participants are another source of connection between organizations. It is not uncommon for core activists in the movement to describe each other as "family." And one woman, harkening back to the feminist movement of the early 1970s, characterized other members of her support group as her "sisters," going so far as to say that "if the women's movement had really been this 'prowoman,' I might never have given up my NOW membership." Joe Bound, who has been active in D.A.D. practically from the start, admits that, even though "being a man in a woman's organization can sometimes make you feel like the outsider, everybody's so close" that it is easy to stay involved.

This is not to imply, however, that the usual conflict that plagues social movements is nonexistent in the postpartum support group movement. As we might expect, because the separate organizations represent different feminist generations and are home to strong feelings of admiration and fierce loyalty that have developed around charismatic leaders, the movement has been troubled by some of the same kinds of interpersonal animosities as have other feminist organizations. Tension and competition for leadership between Jane Honikman and Nancy Berchtold is thus a continual threat to the loosely coupled coalition of groups that can be considered to form a national postpartum self-help movement.

Strategic disputes, too, can be sources of conflict, as in the case of the 1991 PSI conference in Pittsburgh. Dagmar Celeste gave an explicitly feminist keynote address that linked postpartum depression to the lack of structural supports for mothers in a male-dominated society and to what she believes to be the fundamental "devaluation of motherhood." In the same speech, she was also critical of the tendency of contemporary women's self-help movements primarily to advocate medical approaches to women's health and to turn their back on the societal causes of women's problems. In response, a male activist in the audience engaged Celeste in a public confrontation, introducing his remarks with the reminder that "as one of the men in the group," he did not find "male domination an adequate explanation of postpartum psychiatric illness." At the same time, women, who constituted the majority of those present, praised Celeste, one woman stating that the movement's contribution to her own recovery from postpartum depression had made crystal clear the "therapeutic role of political work." The response of another woman laid bare the dissension within the movement over medicalizing the emotional distress of new mothers. She lashed out against the day's sessions advocating the use of antidepressants by shouting that "I am deeply disturbed by the idea that women can't manage without medication."

SHIFTING OPPORTUNITIES AND
THE RISE OF THERAPEUTIC FEMINISM

Students of social movements recognize that we need to investigate more closely what happens to social movements when they encounter a hostile and nonreceptive political climate. In my earlier research with Leila Rupp on the U.S. women's rights movement of the 1940s and '50s, I described one such possibility. A movement can go into abeyance, allowing a visionary core of activists to survive and carry on the struggle on a more limited scale by focusing mainly on internal processes of culture-building and identity. But this is not the only option. Sometimes defeat in the political arena can spur activists to search for new openings. This is what happened in the 1980s. After the failure of the Equal Rights Amendment in 1982, many women sought new avenues of protest. The Republican party's sharp turn to the right with the election of Ronald

Reagan brought further blows to feminism, beginning with an attack on reproductive rights, followed by a backlash against affirmative action, and culminating in the culture war of the 1990s focused, in part, on the changing roles of women. Of course, some feminists stayed the course. Lobbying groups, such as the Women's Equity Action League, for example, continued to pursue issues such as family leave, pregnancy discrimination, and reproductive freedom, but they moderated their goals and tactics. And the National Abortion Rights Action League and the National Organization for Women wielded both direct action and lobbying strategies. But many women moved their struggle to what Paul Burstein would describe as different "policy domains."

While changes in political parties, government institutions, and the ideologies, strategies, and policy styles of political leaders and government officials are central to the emergence and development of social movements, these are not the only societal factors that constrain or facilitate collective action. If we limit our attention only to the way movements respond to political realignments, policy changes, and electoral processes, we overlook significant social and cultural transformations that shaped the character of social movements in the 1980s, when we began to witness a turning away from the reformist and cultural revolutionary themes of the 1960s back toward the conservatism and privatism of the 1950s. This change in cultural mood brought with it a cycle of protest in which movements were more concerned with quality-of-life issues and self-definition than with influencing state policies and winning political power.

This may very well be the larger climate within which women's self-help has grown. When feminists were closed out of the political arena, they seized upon new opportunities for organizing that opened up in the 1980s when public attention and conflict over the role and costs of health care increased in American society. This debate led to significant policy reforms, such as the introduction of managed care and standardized treatment regimens and reimbursements for the most common diagnoses, designed to increase the numbers of people obtaining health services and to reduce health care costs. Since women comprise the majority of health care consumers in the United States, it is little wonder that medicine and health care provided fertile ground for feminists. Not only did medicine supply the resources to mobilize, but it also supplied psychological categories that displaced the more political categories of radical feminism that had proven so divisive.

The 1980s will be remembered by many for dismantling much of the social welfare system engineered in the wake of the New Deal. By the 1980s, mental health policy reflected the view of conservatives that the "welfare state" had grown bloated and ineffective and that individual health benefits were beginning to exceed even the private sector's ability to pay. As a result, individuals began having to accept a greater portion of the burden for their own health services, and mental health care was the hardest hit. Yet it was not just those who look to the state to pay for the costs of mental health care who were affected. Employers and insurance carriers cut back on reimbursements to private practitioners who serve mainly the working and middle classes. In 1989, only 21 percent of large U.S. companies offered the same level of mental health benefits as they had in 1980. Seeking to limit drastically the use of mental health services, the conservative political agenda brought numerous changes that altered the shape of mental health care in American society and fueled the flames of modern self-help.

As federal allocations for mental health care plummeted during the presidency of Ronald Reagan, self-care increasingly became a viable alternative to professional mental health care. Reagan's 1983 appointment of Dr. C. Everett Koop (a pediatric surgeon and advocate of self-help) as surgeon general furthered general acceptance of self-help as a strategy of medical and mental health care. Under Koop, the National Institute of Mental Health (NIMH) and the National Mental Health Consumer's Association (NMHCA) began issuing formal guidelines for the establishment of self-help groups and distributed them through regional state-funded self-help clearinghouses like the New Jersey Self-Help Clearinghouse. It would not be overstating the case to say that by the 1980s, mutual support, which had its origins in the anti-professional and direct action strategies of the social movements of the 1960s and '70s, was being coopted by government and insurance companies seeking to cut social expenditures, as well as by professional health and mental health providers as a supplementary source of care. Presently, there are more than fifty self-help clearinghouses in twenty states and the District of Columbia that keep track of self-help groups in their areas, maintain twenty-four-hour toll-free numbers, offer information about how to start a group, and compile and disseminate bibliographies on self-help and mutual aid strategies. Indeed, when it came time to establish a network of support groups geared to women's distress following childbirth, Depression After Delivery founder Nancy Berchtold turned to the New Jersey Self-Help Clearinghouse for assistance.

It is not surprising that the 1980s was a decade of tremendous medical expansion, as medicine responded not only to the pressure to serve more people with less funding, but also stepped in to pick up the pieces of the declining social welfare system. Total expenditures for health care costs nearly doubled in the period so that by 1991, the United States devoted 12.3 percent of its gross national product to health care. By 1995, health care spending, according to most analysts, accounted for one-seventh of the nation's annual output. Yet by 1991 the federal government had reduced its role in providing care to individuals to the point that it insured only about 40 percent of the poor under the Medicaid program, compared to 65 percent in 1980. It is perhaps ironic that as hospitals in a distended and expensive American medical system found themselves competing for the business of patients able to pay for their health care, women's health was one of the winners.

Despite the fact that women are the major consumers of health care and more women are beginning to practice medicine, male-centered approaches to the definition and study of health problems continue to exclude and to ignore pertinent issues in women's health and mental health. In response to the feminist critique of the inequities in women's health care and the medicalization of childbirth and reproductive health issues, major medical centers began to establish special programs in women's health that focused on a wide range of medical and mental health concerns besides just reproductive health. But the motive for establishing these services has often been less altruistic than it seemed. One physician I interviewed went so far as to admit that the major medical center in which he chairs the Department of Obstetrics and Gynecology promotes its maternity care widely in hopes that "the husbands of women patients will return to their hospitals to have their heart bypasses." A special advertising section for the Ohio State University Medical Center featured in the September 11, 1995, issue of *Time* magazine features support groups dealing with breast cancer and postpartum depression. Nevertheless, women's health centers have turned out to be major sites of organizing for women's self-help groups. They are structured to reach out into the community and to provide a meeting place, staff, funding, publicity, and many of the other kinds of resources on which self-help groups are built. As might be expected, as women's self-help groups increasingly have fallen into the clutches of professional medical and mental health providers, their impetus to challenge the expertise of professionals has sometimes taken a back seat to the goal of marshalling the knowledge and resources of experts to understand, treat, and prevent women's problems as symptoms and diseases.

The postpartum self-help movement followed the same road toward professionalization and medicalization taken by many women's health groups. By the time that Nancy Berchtold turned over the gavel to Michele Kelly in 1994, D.A.D.'s alliances with health and mental health professionals were as strong as PSI's, and PSI originally considered itself to be the designated professional arm of the movement. Activists in all regions of the country also struggle to increase awareness of postpartum issues through presentations at local medical schools. In addition to featuring the personal stories of women who have suffered postpartum illness, in recent years D.A.D.'s newsletter, *Heartstrings*, contains more articles that take an explicitly medical approach to postpartum illness. In the Winter/Spring 1995 issue, for example, psychiatrist David Goldstein, Director of the Mood Disorders Program at Georgetown University in Washington, DC, counters the feminist line that taking medication for depression "will put the patient under the control and domination of the doctor." And recent issues of *Heartstrings* devote more space to reviewing the professional medical, psychiatric, and social science literature and list new professionals affiliated with the movement along with new volunteer telephone contacts than earlier issues did.

CONCLUSION

The origins of many contemporary women's self-help campaigns can be traced to the earlier feminist movement that thrived during the cycle of protest of the 1960s and '70s. This analysis agrees with the findings of others who view feminism as a "master protest frame" that provided both the ideological justification, or the "tool kit," and the initial networks that have spawned yet another round of mobilization by still more groups. Suzanne Staggenborg, for example, uncovers the feminist roots of the modern prochoice movement. In explaining the emergence of lesbian and gay antiviolence projects, Valerie Jenness finds that most groups succeeded by appropriating the feminist principles and tactics of the antirape movement. Beth Schneider and Nancy Stoller suggest that women's participation in the AIDS movement sprang from a feminist platform, and Nancy Matthews paints an identical picture of the antirape movement.

Examining the history of the postpartum support group movement allows us to recognize three ways in which feminism was a compelling force in its development. First, the women's movement of the 1960s and '70s promoted a *feminist world view* or mode of thinking that justified attention to a broad range of women's problems previously considered to be personal, and it linked these problems to women's disadvantaged social status. One of the major successes of the women's liberation movement was the massive change it brought in women's collective consciousness, specifically the widespread application of a feminist frame to problems such as violence against women, sexual harassment, and depression that had previously been understood as personal. Early editions of *Our Bodies, Ourselves*, still considered the feminist bible of women's health, emphasized the socially defined nature of postpartum emotional disturbances, placing some of the responsibility for women's problems on the male bias of the medical profession and some on the "societal pressures surrounding motherhood—the mystique of the maternal instinct, joys of child care, and fulfillment through others."

The feminist movement also supplied *preexisting networks of activists* who, by virtue of prior participation in feminist causes, had acquired some of the skills and organizational experience necessary to mobilize around the issues of postpartum depression and psychosis. In its heyday, the women's movement enlisted scores of women to feminism and gave rise to numerous organizations. Throughout the 1980s, the movement retrenched as it won some victories but lost others because the political tide ebbed as feminists encountered growing opposition. But this did not mean that seasoned veterans who had committed their lives to the fight for women's rights jumped ship. As Nancy Whittier demonstrated in her study of the biographies of radical feminists of the 1960s, most did not retreat into private life but moved the battle to other fronts. As the women who spearheaded the resurgent women's movement progressed through the life cycle, they felt the constraints of gender in their lives in new ways, turning their attention to problems that had not earlier seemed that pressing, such as postpartum depression, child rearing, menopause, and aging.

Not only did the emerging postpartum support group movement benefit from the prior connections and feminist world views of veterans of the women's movement, but feminism also supplied *a repertoire of tactics and strategies* of mobilization that activists could use both to pursue the movement's goals and to attract participants. The strategy was self-help. In an early article published in a perinatal nursing and women's health journal, D.A.D. founder Nancy Berchtold and office manager Melanie Burrough outlined "self-help support groups" as the principal tactic of the movement. But they envisaged self-help as more than simply a way to provide help to individual women. It was also a strategy for building a movement, because it nurtured the kind of grassroots commitment necessary to mount a challenge to the broad range of institutions and cultural practices activists hold responsible for the "tragedies"—by which they meant suicide and infanticide—that go along with postpartum illness.

As leadership in the movement has shifted to this younger generation of women, self-help has taken on a more therapeutic tone consistent with the medical and individual casework approaches that modern states embrace to deal with most problems that have social origins. But does this mean that the feminist agenda of self-help to change institutions has been subverted entirely, as critics have suggested? Or has this development expanded the reaches of feminism so that it remains a viable countervailing force in American society? In the next chapter we look at the transformation of the postpartum self-help movement and take up these questions.

GETTING AND GIVING SUPPORT

WOMEN'S SELF-HELP COMMUNITIES

Emotions

The phone rings.
I listen to a woman.
Baby,
three months.
This is when the emotions set in.

Women die.
Most are very sick.
Does anyone care?
Hello?
Is anyone out there?

Doesn't anyone realize,
What they are going through?

Help is on the way.
Please hang on.
Please try to understand.
The rollercoaster will end soon.
Just wait.
If needed, there is help.
But just wait.
Wait,
Wait...

—*Jeanette Honikman*

SIXTEEN-YEAR-OLD Jeanette Honikman, proudly described as an "ardent feminist" by her mother Jane Honikman, penned these lines for a high-school English class assignment. The volunteer-staffed "warm line" described in the last stanza of Jeanette's poem is one of the primary means by which the postpartum self-help movement provides support to women suffering postpartum illness.

For feminists such as Wendy Kaminer and Naomi Wolf, a major shortcoming of self-help is the fact that the support these groups provide is deeply personal, psychological, and emotional. According to such critics, self-help simply makes women feel better about themselves rather than mobilizing them to work to change the system of gender inequality that is the real source of women's suffering. On the basis of data from a 1991 national survey of support group participation among Americans, Robert Wuthnow presents evidence to the contrary. He finds that the kind of support people seek from self-help groups only has meaning within the larger context of the community building and collective redefinition of problems that takes place in such groups. And in fact when women and their families turn to self-help groups for assistance with postpartum depression, they are likely to be looking for more than simply individual help. Listen to the voices of some of the women who wrote hundreds of letters to Depression After Delivery in the years between 1989 and 1991, when self-help activists succeeded in attracting wide publicity on television talk shows and news programs and in stories featured in major newspapers and magazines:

Dear PPD Support Group,

I am in a mental health unit suffering with my second bout of postpartum depression after the birth of my second child, a daughter born October 7th. The midwife gave me an article from Working Woman Magazine *that discussed your group. I suffered panic attacks and thoughts or fears of harming myself and my baby with my first child, and they began again soon after the birth of my second child. I am wondering if you could* please *send me some literature on ppd. Is there any hope I will recover from this??! I have a wonderfully supportive husband, parents, and brother and sisters. I feel like a failure. Can you possibly put me in touch with another woman who has gone through this who I can telephone or meet or write to?*

> *—woman writing from the Mental Health Unit*
> *Glen Falls Hospital, Glen Falls, NY*

Dear Nancy,

The reason why I'm writing you is for help and for me to help you. Many people still don't realize the effect a child being born to a woman has. We need to make people familiar with it. I might have lost more than my son from postpartum psychosis. I could have lost my daughter or even my husband for that matter. I don't want to sit in prison for life and watch on television that other children have died because their mothers went through something that we both faced. We need to make this illness known! Let's get it into the eye of the public before more lives of the innocent are claimed.

> *—woman serving life sentence*
> *State Correctional Institution at Muncy, PA*

Dear Depression After Delivery,

My son was born on June 11, 1990. I suffered postpartum depression that lasted 5 months. It was hell. What should have been a really special time was not. I feel that our American society does not support new moms. Our society expects too much of new moms, especially when people brag, "she was up and around the very next day." I was not allowed the privilege of coming home to a safe and worry-free environment and didn't get much help or encouragement around the house. The resulting stress caused depression. I have gotten some help and advice from other moms, and I have offered my support to my new mom friends as they need it. Also I have been writing letters to newspapers to respond to articles about motherhood and careers, and also recently to Ann Landers. Thank you for establishing this organization.

—woman from Chelan, WA

Dear Supporters,

I entered the hospital three months after giving birth. The doctor in the emergency room told me that I might have a latent case of schizophrenia that the stress of childbirth brought out. My terror increased, and in retrospect I get very angry at the ignorance some professionals display in the face of postpartum illness. I had seen several talk shows dealing with postpartum depression and psychosis during my pregnancy, and I even saw one while hospitalized. It was during dinnertime and I had to beg the staff to allow the T.V. on. When I watched this program, the relief that I was not alone was enormous. I blamed myself thinking it was my character at fault. The reactions of others seem to promote self-blame. Imagine telling a heart patient to "wash your kitchen floor and that mean old ventricular fibrillation will disappear." Imagine telling a diabetic to "go out and buy a new dress and the diabetes will improve." I can only be thankful that because of your movement the future is brighter for ourselves and our daughters where ppd and ppp is concerned. Our generation must be the vocal one so no woman will ever again have to suffer in silence.

—woman from Coconut Creek, FL

As these letters suggest, it is impossible to understand the social significance of the self-help wave in American society if we fail to acknowledge that the emotional encouragement, self-validation, information, and tangible assistance that groups provide to individuals spring from a profoundly collective enterprise. The movement's growth increasingly depends upon the larger self-help industry for the spread of its message and upon medicine and mental health providers for the resources needed to help women. Given this context, to what extent has the movement been able to maintain the feminist goal of transforming the structures of gender inequality?

In this and the next chapter we shift our attention away from the leadership that gave birth to the postpartum support group movement, instead turning to the movement's grassroots support base. I draw from a survey of support group participants, intensive interviews with core activists, and my own observations of the movement to examine the way that self-help provides a space in which women express solidarity by mobilizing on the basis of lived experiences. I am interested here in the distinctive social movement culture, what Rick Fantasia might term the "culture of solidarity," that arises out of women's experience of coming together to define their commonalities as sufferers of postpartum illness.

All social movements, even those with fairly innocuous objectives, have a strong cultural focus. The production of new cultural patterns, displayed in language, symbols, and rituals, is central to mobilizing a group of collective actors. My interest in the type of women's culture created by the movement goes beyond the simple desire to describe the more expressive and symbolic dimensions of self-help. We need to know to what extent the cultural tools and resources of women's self-help are self-consciously brandished to challenge the structures that perpetuate women's disadvantaged status. Only by addressing this issue can we can begin to understand that when women come together to develop their own explanations and solutions to gender-linked problems such as postpartum illness, their actions can have implications for the reconstruction of gender.

In analyzing this dimension of the postpartum self-help movement, I ponder a question that has most often been debated by feminist scholars interested in whether contemporary women's self-help serves as an organizing tool for feminism in the 1990s. Does the postpartum depression self-help movement facilitate development of the type of women's communities that scholars of the women's movement find to be essential to feminist mobilization? Such intimate bonds between women have generally played an important role; as Estelle Freedman explains in her classic article "Separatism as Strategy," the decline of the U.S. women's movement in the 1920s can be attributed partly to the devaluation of women's culture and the decline of separate female institutions. Blanche Cook and Leila Rupp argue persuasively that female networks of love and support were vital to women's political activism in the early twentieth century. And Liz Kennedy and Madeline Davis consider the creation of a separate working-class lesbian community, formed in lesbian bars and house parties during the 1940s and '50s, as the key to the development of twentieth-century lesbian identity and consciousness. Although no monolithic women's culture has ever developed across lines of race, class, and ethnicity, women involved in a wide array of collective actions—from food riots in immigrant neighborhoods, to labor strikes, to protests against the lynching of African American men, to suffrage demonstrations, to neighborhood protests against the dumping of toxic wastes—have shaped oppositional cultures that sustained such struggles. If we are to understand the success of the self-help genre, then we must see it as linked to the caring and community it encourages among women.

Before we consider the forms of community within the postpartum support group movement, it is necessary to delve a little deeper into a more fundamental question raised in chapter 1: On what grounds is it possible to think of modern self-help movements—which make the construction of a collective identity their main task, sometimes by slighting other forms of change—as social movements?

PERSONALIZED POLITICS AS COLLECTIVE ACTION REPERTOIRE

Getting and giving support, which is the heart and soul of modern self-help, is not what most of us ordinarily think of as social movement activity. One of the features that distinguishes social movements from conventional groups such as political parties and professional associations is the use of noninstitutionalized means: marches and demonstrations, boycotts, sit-ins, speak-outs, strikes, and other direct-action strategies that are so much a part of American political culture that we automatically associate them with protest.

Social movement scholars Charles Tilly and Sid Tarrow use the term "repertoires of contention" to describe the distinctive forms and constellation of strategies that collective actors utilize to make claims on individuals and groups. Tilly and Tarrow attribute major changes in collective action repertoires throughout history to additions to the stock of knowledge available to collective actors who build on the repertoires of earlier groups and to shifts in the structural features of societies. What we tend to think of today as a social movement—dispersed and aggrieved individuals coming together to mount sustained national campaigns targeted at reforming institutions and winning rights and concessions from the state—is a repertoire that came into being with the rise of the modern capitalist state around the time of the European revolutions of 1848. The emergence of social movements was facilitated, in part, by the simultaneous expansion of government into the realm of social, economic, and political policies regulating the lives of individuals and the rise of mass-produced print media in the form of newspapers and books that made it possible for individuals to learn and act collectively on a national scale. While self-help movements share many of the fundamental features of the modern social movement—solidarity, the use of noninstitutionalized strategies, and the quest for societal change—I think of contemporary self-help movements in the United States as a fundamentally different kind of collective action repertoire that requires that we rethink some of the assumptions underlying general social movement theories.

Self-help groups are more likely to fall under the rubric of what John McCarthy and Mark Wolfson term "consensus" movements, whose forms of action and strategies of change are influenced by the fact that they tend to lack well-defined enemies and generally confront little organized opposition from the society at large. Nevertheless, former Canadian Minister of Health Monique Bégin insists: "Women's self-help groups are very threatening to the traditional medical health care system, since they question both the sacred status of experts and the authoritarianism of health professionals of all kinds." But even if the medical profession does not always embrace the world views and remedies advocated by self-help groups, it does generally find it advantageous to work with rather than against patient groups. In some hospitals, for example, physicians routinely refer women diagnosed with breast cancer to support groups, even though the advice and information imparted by grassroots self-help organizations can at times undermine standard medical protocols and physicians' professional authority. It is the easy cooptability of consensus movements by established institutions, along with their failure to generate controversy and resistance, that in part makes it so difficult for them to mobilize the mass membership and organizational strength necessary to serve as major vehicles for change. This dilemma is clearly illustrated by McCarthy and Wolfson's analysis of Mothers Against Drunk Driving (MADD), a self-help movement that was organized in 1980 to increase public awareness of the problems associated with drunk driving, to lobby for more stringent state laws applying to drunk drivers, and to provide support for victims. Because of overwhelming public endorsement of its goals, MADD was never able to recruit large numbers of supporters and, as a result, had difficulty maintaining local chapters. MADD has, nevertheless, accomplished many of its goals, winning stricter penalties for drunk driving nationwide, the establishment of victim assistance programs, and widespread public disapproval of driving under the influence of alcohol.

I use this example also to make the point that in modern self-help, a mass membership national organization is rarely the principal player. Most self-help movements do create umbrella organizations, like Depression After Delivery and Postpartum Support International, to coordinate communication and recruit participants. But it is the support group that is the site of most of the action. Like the modern social movement that came into being in the nineteenth century, the contemporary support group, I believe, represents a distinctive mode and strategy of collective action.

Some theorists of modernity view the number and diversity of small support groups that have arisen to address a wide range of matters once considered to be private and personal—such as illness, sexuality, major life transitions, family problems, and intimate relationships—as a response to the impoverished interactions that take place in late modern societies where large, rationalized, and impersonal organizations have replaced the more traditional associations of family, kinship, religion, and neighborhood. Few would disagree that in industrialized societies the social welfare and service delivery systems, both public and private, have become large, bureaucratic operations whose infrastructures reflect the inequalities of gender, race, and class in the society at large. In the typical health and human service agency, for example, the direct service providers, caretakers, and primary care workers are disproportionately women and minorities, whereas the decision-makers, executives, and power brokers are mostly male and white. Furthermore, the effects of gender categorization and hierarchy are so pervasive that, as feminist psychologists point out, they leave their imprint on women's inner and interpersonal lives. Feminist support groups develop, then, as a response to the male domination of medical and mental health institutions and provide a context in which participants can validate claims that their problems are a function not just of their own internal deficiencies but of social inequities that uniquely affect them as women.

Other writers hold a less pessimistic view. Although they see the life-political agenda that underlies today's support group movement as resulting, in part, from new grievances connected to the self-reflexivity of modern knowledge-based societies, they also view modernity as providing new opportunities for community building. The scientific premises of contemporary society open up more and more of our social practices and life experiences to examination and reconsideration in light of new discoveries. Research breakthroughs in medicine, mental health, and the social sciences increasingly command more time and space in the daily news. But, as Anthony Giddens emphasizes, these discoveries tend to be based in the internal logic and criteria of the highly professionalized and expert systems of knowledge of medicine, mental health, education, law, financial management, and the social sciences, not in the concrete life experiences and folk knowledge of individuals. These abstract systems

unwittingly propagate practices and identity categories that serve to reinforce inequalities of gender, class, race, ethnicity, and sexuality. For instance,
the concept of mental health implies a different standard for women than
for men by assuming that masculinity is organized around autonomy, self-
determination, and instrumental thinking and femininity around
connections with others, relational concerns, and emotional expressiveness. The fact that mental health definitions are tied to a gendered division
of labor that assumes that men's lives center on paid employment while
women's center on meeting the personal needs of their families is an
example of what Dorothy Smith has called "the gender subtext of the
rational and impersonal." As scientific discoveries make their way into the
media, they provide frameworks through which people filter their everyday experiences. To take an example, psychoanalytic theories that
dichotomize female and male identities and position women as the primary sources of nurturing provide a rationale for the contemporary
recovery movement that treats women's "codependency" as a compulsive
and pathological form of human connection. Even if psychological, medical, and legal categories are coming to replace class, gender, and race as a
basis for organizing, the point is that modern societies offer new reference points on which individuals can anchor identities.

New social movement theorists such as Alberto Melucci and Alaine
Touraine link the popularity of modern self-help movements to the tendency of people to create free spaces where they can come together to
monitor and respond to the ideas and information advocated by professionals and other specialists, and thus defend and expand their
individuality. It is in the context, then, of small groups or submerged networks that individuals apply the abstract discoveries of medicine and
mental health to their own lived experiences. Most analysts agree that in
postmodern information-based societies, the massive growth and influence of the mass media and communications industries, especially
television, provide unique capabilities and resources that make possible
new, artificially constructed, and more personalized forms of community
that would have been unthinkable in more traditional societies.

The expert systems of knowledge on which modern industrialized
societies are based provide the new therapeutic and scientific frameworks
that frequently supply what Dorothy Smith has termed the "discourses of
femininity," on which today's women's self-help movements are built. But
it is the communications technologies of modern societies—from radio
and television to telephone polls and computer networks—that make it
ever more possible for women with common concerns to organize, act
in unison with each other, and discover their own strength. An example

of a wide-ranging innovation of contemporary self-help groups is in the use of the Internet by individuals to access support groups for issues as diverse as panic disorders, sexual abuse, depression, divorce, adoption, infertility, cancer, obesity, and multiple sclerosis. While some computer mailing lists are private and moderated by individual facilitators, others are open to the public. There can be little doubt that the interactive devices used by television and radio talk shows that encourage audience response in the form of letter writing, telephone call-ins, and electronic mail, as well as the many computer bulletin boards that draw together people who share similar concerns, affect the speed with which individuals can develop a collective identity.

It is no accident that personalized political strategies, which were an important theme in certain sectors of the modern American civil rights movement, student new left activism, the anti-nuclear movement, the early feminist movement, and the early gay liberation movement, are becoming an important repertoire of collective action. And they have found especially fertile ground as they "spilled over" into the self-help movements that sprouted in the 1980s as offshoots of these earlier and more clearly political campaigns. Self-help groups take community building to the limit by practicing a type of togetherness that reflects the vocabulary and tradition of individualism peculiar to white middle-class Americans. This individualized form of community, as Paul Lichterman describes it, is a solidarity built on the empowerment, self-realization, and expression of individuals that makes room for the privacy and the cultural, social, political, and other types of diversity of its adherents. This means that self-help participants frequently enact their social and political commitments more as empowered individuals than as members of formal groups. Consequently, self-help communities reproduce in many ways the temporary, partial, and fragile relationships so characteristic of postmodern societies. Viewing self-help through a social movement lens leaves open the possibility that by bringing individuals together to define their commonalities in terms that connect their problems to larger social and political forces, self-help groups have the potential to pose significant challenges not only to conventional social roles and identities but also to the institutions to which they are moored. (Of course the leap from the individual to the collective may not always occur in every self-help campaign.)

Important to understanding the collective action repertoire of modern self-help movements, then, is the way that the distinctive nature of participants' grievances specifies the targets, goals, and strategies of collective action. Self-help movements frequently take matters of health, mental health, the body, problems of everyday life, and self-definition to be problematic, which makes the individual and the self the locus of change. But does this necessarily mean that self-help groups are either apolitical or antipolitical, as some social movement commentators have suggested? Scholars who write specifically about self-help movements say no, and the overwhelming majority of these writers contends that self-help groups are simply concerned with a different set of political processes, namely the politics of medical knowledge and treatment. As is evident from the struggle of AIDS activists to achieve greater public awareness of the dimensions of the epidemic, to redefine medical definitions of the disease, to win federal support for research on prevention and treatment of AIDS, and to obtain access to experimental medications, today's self-help movements are anything but apolitical. To the contrary, they frequently call on lawmakers and government agencies to arbitrate the conflict between patients and the medical and human service systems, as well as to answer needs that established medical providers refuse to meet. They furthermore reconceptualize the political by questioning and rejecting the power of dominant cultural codes, as in the case of AIDS activists who seek to overcome negative images of homosexuality.

Self-help communities start out as sites where participants can find personal support through sharing their problems, expressing their misgivings about the views of medical and scientific experts, and putting forward their own claims. So how do they make the leap from people's personal problems to the larger societal forces responsible for them? I focus on the women who are participants in the postpartum support group movement to show how the experience of being intensely immersed in a shared women's community offers participants the opportunity to reframe their individual biographies in socially and politically meaningful terms. In the next chapter, we turn our attention to exploring this process of redefinition, which social movement scholars think of as the construction of a collective identity. The insistence that the construction and expression of new identities is politics, which leads activists to contest traditional distinctions between the private and the public and between the personal and the political, is, to a large extent, what social movement scholars see as the core of what is "new" about the new social movements. Here we hone in on the communities within which women articulate and sustain a collective identity.

WOMEN'S COMMUNITIES OF SUPPORT

In the women's movement of the late 1960s and early 1970s, self-help was practiced mainly in direct-action or consciousness-raising groups, whose members embraced the view that women, as a powerless group, need spaces separate from men to express solidarity and create changes in their lives. Among early radical feminists, women-only groups, organized along egalitarian lines, held the belief that women can best empower themselves by taking direct charge of their own destinies and solving their own problems. The consciousness-raising and direct-action groups that scholars associate with the younger women's liberation branch of the modern women's movement planted the seeds for the myriad of small groups that exist exclusively to provide mutual aid and interpersonal support to women. As we have seen, support groups served as the springboard of the postpartum depression movement. To the extent that scholars of the women's movement have looked at women's support groups as mechanisms for recruiting women to feminism, it is sometimes easy to forget that their original purpose was to help women. Whether self-consciously or not, the construction of community that occurs through getting and giving support can be such a vibrant force that it functions as a form of what Wini Breines has termed "prefigurative politics."

Women's self-help communities, in other words, make a special claim to a better way of organizing society by constructing a distinctive women's culture of caring in which participants can find emotional support as well as receive practical help and information to understand and overcome their problems. To this end, the women's culture of the postpartum support group movement draws heavily from the emphasis on self-transformation, emotional expressiveness, collectivism, separatism, caring, and community advocated by feminist organizations in the late 1960s and '70s.

Despite the fact that the postpartum movement is overwhelmingly comprised of women, it differs in an important way from most earlier feminist self-help groups: it welcomes men. Husbands are invited to attend local support group meetings, even though they rarely do. In the San Diego and Philadelphia areas, fathers' support groups meet on occasion, and the national boards and officers of Depression After Delivery and Postpartum Support International include the husbands and fathers of women who have suffered postpartum illness. The movement's emphasis on men's role as caretakers is also evident in the fact that husbands of movement leaders frequently attend national conferences and are regularly featured in photographs and stories in the national newsletter. In almost every instance, the "Person of the Quarter" column in *Heartstrings*, which recognizes outstanding achievement on behalf of postpartum illness, pictures the recipient's husband and children. Now and then the award is even given to a male activist. Men in the movement not only advocate husbands taking responsibility for "restabilizing the home" during a woman's recovery, but they also urge other men to overcome the emotional detachment and inexpressiveness characteristic of conventional white middle-class masculinity in order to accept their wives' feelings and provide emotional support. In his June 1990 presentation to the annual conference of Postpartum Support International in Pittsburgh, psychologist Robert Hickman went so far as to challenge the traditional division of household labor between women and men by prodding husbands to "help out with the baby or clean up the house after work," suggesting that these types of support from a husband are important "components of an effective treatment plan" for a woman's illness.

Mobilization at the grassroots level swelled the ranks of the movement in the early years and laid the foundation for its growth. In response to calls and requests for information, activists who had recovered from postpartum illness mobilized to provide channels of support for other women by starting mutual aid and therapeutic support groups, volunteering to talk to other women on the telephone, speaking and writing about their experiences to public audiences, and participating in pen-pal networks.

As we saw in chapter 3, the face-to-face support group, patterned after the consciousness-raising groups that generated the women's liberation movement, was the protypical form of organization in the mid-1980s. But communications technologies, ranging from the telephone to the television, have made possible new avenues of support and spread the movement's message to women from more diverse racial, ethnic, and class backgrounds. As founders of the postpartum depression movement struggled to build a broad network of support for women, participation in women's self-help communities came to mean more than attending meetings of face-to-face self-help and mutual aid groups.

Telephone Support

In the 1990s, by far the most common way of giving and getting support in the postpartum self-help movement is through what members refer to as the "warm line." "We call it a warmline, as opposed to a hotline," Jane Honikman explains, "because we want parents to call any time they have questions, or when they are at wit's end, but before they are in crisis." Nearly half of the D.A.D. volunteers I surveyed indicated that they help new mothers primarily over the telephone lines. One volunteer explained: "New mothers barely have the time to manage everything at the same time they're learning to cope with their new roles as parents, so who has the time to attend counselling sessions?"

The national office of D.A.D. staffs a toll-free telephone line that provides support and information to roughly twenty-five women a day. However, the number of calls to the national office can climb to as many as several hundred a week after a nationally televised news program or talk show mentions D.A.D. To illustrate, during the last two weeks of October 1995, D.A.D. experienced a media blitz. Two major daytime television shows, Susan Powter's fitness program and the *Leeza Show*, featured the topic of postpartum depression. The *Bottom Line*, a news magazine aired in the Washington, DC—Baltimore, MD, market, followed with a focus on postpartum depression. Then on October 26th, Jane E. Brody titled her "Personal Health" column in the *New York Times* "Postpartum Depression: Shedding the Blues." In each case, the coverage featured self-help activists, including professionals and researchers connected with the postpartum support group movement, and concluded by giving the national D.A.D. address and 800 number. Over 1,100 calls, the usual average for a nine-month period, deluged the national office in less than one week. And, of course, there are no records of the hundreds of calls that local and regional telephone contacts answered.

D.A.D. maintains a list of 250 telephone contact people scattered throughout every region of the country that the office manager distributes to callers who request ongoing sources of support in their local communities. In the majority of cases, these telephone volunteers are women who have experienced postpartum anxiety, depression, or psychosis, although the list also includes a handful of husbands and professionals. To train these volunteers, D.A.D. issues a set of guidelines for telephone contacts and support group facilitators and a list of local referrals. D.A.D. telephone volunteers have a strict policy of following up with return telephone calls to women who seem particularly upset or suicidal, or who talk of hurting themselves or their children."

The average number of telephone contacts reported by local D.A.D. volunteers ranges from one or two a month to as many as ten to fifteen, but these numbers too can fluctuate sharply, especially when local and national media attention focuses on postpartum illness. Most telephone calls come from depressed women needing to talk to a caring and sympathetic listener, looking for validation of their experiences, seeking reassurance that their depression will end, searching for a support group, or requesting information and medical referrals; there are some calls from family members or professionals requesting information. One of the women I surveyed mentioned that it is not unusual for her to speak to the same woman several times a week, especially if the caller has no alternative sources of emotional support.

Judy, a nurse who operates a warm line out of her home in Madison, Wisconsin, emphasized the collective significance of telephone support. Recalling her own isolation during a severe postpartum depression that began seven months after her only daughter was born and led her to seek electroshock therapy, she sees the main benefit of telephone support as "helping other women realize they are not alone, that they will get through the depression and back to everyday life." Pat, a social worker from Tallahassee, Florida, receives so many calls that she has had a separate phone line installed in her home. She, too, emphasizes the collective validation women find through telephone support.

> One of our most recent calls was from a woman whose daughter in her twenties had committed suicide five days out of the hospital with a new baby. Today I see so clearly what happened to me when I went through my own depression. If I would have had information, I know I would have prepared much differently.

While early volunteers envisaged telephone support principally as a means of disseminating information, over the years it has functioned to create a sense of shared community, not only for nonemployed women isolated by the burdens of caring for a new infant but also for working women who have little time to participate on a regular basis in a face-to-face support group. Sharon, a woman from Louisville, Kentucky, who quit her job to raise three children describes her telephone contact as a "lifeline during the most difficult days." Like many women, she considers Nancy Berchtold, who offered information, understanding, and empathy through endless hours on the D.A.D. national warm line, as part of her "circle of friends." Betty, an optometric technician from Muncie, Indiana, who discovered that she carries major responsibility for parenting two children despite her husband's commitment to share equally in child rearing, characterizes D.A.D.'s warm line as "a light at the end of a very dark tunnel." But the single most important benefit of women's telephone contact with D.A.D. is, as one woman puts it, "finding out that I was part of something bigger than myself."

The Support Group

The second most frequently cited strategy for providing help is through small face-to-face support groups comprised mainly of women who have suffered postpartum anxiety, depression, or psychosis. Although a clear majority of the national network of telephone volunteers that I surveyed considered "support" to be the most important benefit of participating in the postpartum self-help movement, only about half of these women belonged to a small group of like-minded people who meet on a regular basis in a neighborhood setting such as someone's home, a coffee house, community center, church, or school to provide emotional support, information, and friendship around a common concern. Because of the spontaneity, informality, and lack of continuity of these types of small groups, it is virtually impossible to calculate the number and variety that exist. My survey of Depression After Delivery's telephone contacts turned up about seventy small groups linked in varying degrees to the national organization (see Appendix). These groups allow us to take a closer look at the distinctive kind of women's communities cultivated by therapeutic self-help movements.

More than two-thirds of the groups I located were of a mutual-aid nature and drew heavily from the ideas and practices of the feminist and other 1960s movements about informal group dynamics, egalitarian structure, expressiveness, and the cultivation of community. With the exception of two fathers' support groups, the groups I identified were all-female, although group leaders were quick to add that husbands are welcome but infrequent participants. For the most part, the participants were mainly white and middle class, but some groups, mainly on the West Coast, claimed a handful of Asian American and Latina participants; and others, in the Northeast and Southeast, drew small numbers of African American women. To the extent that therapeutic self-help groups tend to treat the expression of personal views both as an end in itself and a means of creating new knowledge about postpartum illness, the support groups I observed encouraged the open expression of emotion. Postpartum support groups are led by women who have themselves recovered from postpartum illness. A member of a Vancouver, Canada, group provides a feminist rationale: "We believe that the woman is expert and is capable of engineering her recovery." In most instances, groups get together weekly or monthly in women's homes and occasionally in other neighborhood and community settings.

Indicative of the increasing influence of medical and therapeutic models on women's self-help, one-third of the support groups I identified are professional therapy groups. Psychologists Susan and Bob Hickman, for instance, run separate therapy groups for mothers and fathers out of the Postpartum Mood Disorders clinic in San Diego, California. As the postpartum support group movement has become more inclined to mainstream obstetrical care and more closely aligned with orthodox birthing and psychiatric philosophies, it is not surprising to find that most professionally led therapy groups meet in hospitals. It is nevertheless significant that the vast majority of the hospital-based groups continue to be organized and facilitated by women professionals—usually nurses, social workers, or psychologists—who have firsthand experience with postpartum illness. "Having been there yourself" is seen as so vital, even in professional therapy groups, that Rita, a nurse facilitator of a longstanding group, reported that some group members distrusted her until she informed them that she had been treated for postpartum depression herself. It is not surprising, given the deeply personal, psychological, and emotional nature of the support provided by such groups that they tend, whether professional or peer led, to be highly democratic. Even semiannual business meetings of the national board of Depression After Delivery have a therapeutic quality. Not only are board meetings structured around collective decision making that allows participants to build their leadership and decision-making skills, but they serve as a kind of oasis where board members can share their doubts, fears, problems, and disappointments alongside their successes and accomplishments. At a statewide planning meeting I attended, Lucy, who suffered a serious bout of depression after the birth of her first child, admitted being terrified that she was pregnant again. Marsha crowed over her own personal victory in convincing her obstetrician to distribute D.A.D. brochures to his patients. Board meetings also give priority to the kinds of personal and family concerns that usually take a backseat in the modern impersonal workplace. At one annual D.A.D. meeting, a board member, along with organizational business, told a harrowing tale of a recurrence of psychosis, while another filled the group in on her mother's battle with cancer as she gave a subcommittee report.

The size of support groups ranges from two to twelve, although the majority have about four to five members. As might be expected, mutual-aid groups are more likely than therapy groups to be seen as a significant source of friendship and day-to-day support and to have been in existence for longer than five years. The emotional and concrete support that women get from long-term participation in a support group is emphasized by Sheila, a Pennsylvania woman who, despite having belonged to a postpartum support group for seven years, suffered a recurrence of psychosis outside the context of childbirth.

> *Someone from my group called everyday to see if I was okay and whether I just wanted to talk. . . . Almost every night for weeks after I got out of the hospital, they brought dinner for our family. Thank God I had my mother to help take care of my daughter, Ginger, and I knew a good psychiatrist this time because of D.A.D. But I really don't know how I would have managed without these caring friends, especially because I had a such a hard time adjusting to being on the lithium.*

The support and encouragement that even longstanding groups provide, as this woman suggests, is highly individualized. For this reason, membership and the life of a support group can be as transitory as the emotional crisis that leads women to turn to a support group for help. Furthermore, encouraging the forthright expression of emotion leaves members more vulnerable to personal criticism when individuals fail to cooperate with each other or use power in ways that are at odds with images of women as nurturing and supportive. When conflicts erupt in the movement, as they sometimes do between the leaders of D.A.D. and PSI, participants find them especially painful.

Robert Wuthnow concludes, from his survey of the variety of support groups in contemporary American society, that the small group movement is becoming one of the principal ways in which spirituality and a renewed commitment to faith is being fostered in modern society. Yet religion—in the sense of sharing one's faith, converting others, or using life experiences in defense of religious faith—plays a part in only a handful of the postpartum support groups. Likewise, only one of the seventy groups I surveyed reported using a twelve-step approach to recovery modeled on the Alcoholics Anonymous program, which explicitly incorporates spirituality into the solution of people's problems.

One of the main missions of the postpartum support movement has been to provide participants with a stronger sense of community, with a safety net for women and families during the transition to parenthood; it does this in part by constructing a special network of caring organized around what one telephone volunteer describes as the belief "that women do not share equal power in our culture and that they should." Participation in support groups provides women with the opportunity to forge solidarity with other women. This, as one woman explained, "gave me wings again by restoring my confidence and making me feel less alone."

It cannot be denied that when activists and mental health therapists alike began in the 1990s to recommend group participation for women who could not afford the expense of professional counselling or psychotherapy, the number of postpartum support groups began to grow more rapidly and took on an increasingly therapeutic flavor. Yet such groups encourage many women to think about their experiences not simply in individual and psychiatric but in more collective and social terms. Witness the solidarity that Becky, a woman from Manchester, New Hampshire, found in the movement. After the birth of her first and only child—like many women in the movement, she was afraid to have another—Becky endured a prolonged battle with depression that lasted nearly five years. Even though she saw a psychiatrist and several female therapists and took antidepressant medication for nearly four years, she "felt very shamed for having ppd." It was only when she "connected with other women who had experienced the same thing," and the postpartum support group opened her eyes to the fact that other women reacted to the burdens of motherhood in the same way, that Becky began to realize that perhaps she "wasn't so different after all."

Self-Help Reading and Talk Shows

Providing women with information about their problems may very well be the most consistent strategy of the postpartum support group movement. Indeed, most self-help movements produce a distinctive body of literature that focuses more on the personal experience of illness and offers lay explanations of and solutions to people's problems.

As might be expected, the perspectives advocated by self-help movements frequently conflict with professional notions of etiology and treatment. When I first began studying postpartum illness in the mid-1980s, around the same time that the self-help movement was getting off the ground, I located through the *Reader's Guide to Periodical Literature* a sample of one hundred popular writings on childbirth and mothering. I also read scientific and medical publications on postpartum illness, along with medical and nursing textbooks. As the analysis in chapter 2 reveals, medical professionals generally do not conceive of women's postpartum emotional problems as a disease but attribute them to social factors, namely the stresses of motherhood, the lack of social support for mothering, and the multiple demands of women's work and maternal roles. By contrast, activists in the postpartum support group movement, who are centrally concerned with women getting care and finding support, are pressing to have their problems treated as a bona fide illness, even if they admit to social as well as medical causes. It is significant that more than half of the women I interviewed who identified themselves as having suffered postpartum depression—none of whom was associated with the postpartum support group movement—considered the self-help discourse on postpartum illness found in popular books, magazines, and pamphlets on pregnancy, childbirth, and parenting as a major source of validation that what they were suffering was a medical problem.

Like most contemporary self-help groups, the postpartum support movement utilizes a variety of channels of communication to get across its message. Carol Dix's *The New Mother Syndrome*, which drew heavily from conversations with early self-help activists, was so important to the mass mobilization of the movement that nearly one-fourth of the telephone volunteers that I surveyed named it as their first source of information and support. National and regional newsletters geared to D.A.D. members generally contain first-hand accounts of women's personal experiences, member news, summaries of recent medical and social science research on postpartum illness, articles about new medications and treatments, information about activists' media appearances and recent publications, announcements of new support groups, telephone contacts, the names of professionals who have joined the support network, and lists of upcoming events. Nurses, childbirth educators, social workers, physicians, and other researchers active in the campaign author self-help books and articles in women's and parenting magazines or serve as consultants to professional writers. Both Nancy Berchtold and Jane Honikman have written numerous articles in scholarly and popular publications recounting their personal experiences with postpartum illness and describing the formation of their own support groups.

The trend of challenging the mainstream medical discourse stepped up as the movement spread. In 1992, psychiatrist James Alexander Hamilton and psychologist Patricia Neel Harberger edited a scholarly book, *Postpartum Psychiatric Illness*, a collection of writings by professionals in the movement who advocate the medicalization of postpartum illness. In *Mothering Twins*, published in 1993, D.A.D. member Debra Catlin from Eugene, Oregon, collaborated with Linda Albi and three other women to write about the severe depression she suffered for nearly three years as she confronted one barrier after another trying to cope with raising twins in addition to two other young children. D.A.D. members published three more popular self-help books in 1994, *The Postpartum Survival Guide: It Wasn't Supposed to Be Like This* by Ann Dunnewald and Diane G. Sanford; *This Isn't What I Expected* by Karen R. Kleiman and Valerie D. Raskin; and *Mothering the New Mother* by Sally Placksin. All draw heavily from the knowledge and perspective of the movement. Although not a member of D.A.D., psychiatrist Carl S. Burak, coauthor with Michele Remington of *The Cradle Will Fall*, credits much of his insight into postpartum illness to Nancy Berchtold and Depression After Delivery.

D.A.D. offers what the organization calls a "Mom pack," containing information about postpartum illness, a bibliography of research on postpartum disorders, referral information by region of the country, a list of support group contacts, the names of regional telephone volunteers, information about how to start a support group, and copies of back issues of *Heartstrings*. This information is the source of some women's self-assessments of postpartum illness, as is clear from the story told by Rose Marie, a thirty-four-year-old Puerto Rican woman from Miami, Florida, who

113

responded to my survey of D.A.D. telephone contacts. After the birth of her first baby, she found herself unable to sleep for nearly five days, suffered frequent anxiety attacks, and then sank into a depression that lasted for nearly six months. She relived the difficulty she had finding help and "returning to normal" until she managed to hook up with a postpartum support group. Rose Marie related how she telephoned Depression After Delivery after seeing the organization's name listed at the end of an Ann Landers column:

> D.A.D.'s "Mom pack" helped me so much because it described all of my symptoms. I was greatly relieved to find out just what I was experiencing and to understand how too many changes at once—loss of a job, staying at home with the baby, not enough knowledge about babies and parenting—contributed to the depression.

Esther, who was hospitalized for two weeks following the birth of her first baby and remained on antidepressant medication for nearly a year, emphasized that it was not merely the information contained in D.A.D.'s newsletters and articles that set her on the road to recovery, but also that the "pamphlets and information made me realize that I was not alone and that this was a temporary state and I could get over it."

When a request for information comes into the national office from a health or mental health professional, a library, hospital official, attorney, community group, or a childbirth or parent educator, D.A.D. responds by sending a special "pro pack" that contains material of a somewhat more technical nature. Each inquiry by a professional helps the national D.A.D. office to establish a list of referrals for women seeking professional help. The story of Celia, a thirty-five-year-old woman from New Haven, Connecticut, who had compulsive thoughts of harming her baby for several months, highlights the importance of the D.A.D. referral network. She saw "nearly twenty or so doctors, psychiatrists, and psychologists, all of whom dismissed the symptoms." It was not until she received D.A.D.'s pink brochure describing the signs of postpartum psychosis, depression, and anxiety, along with D.A.D.'s "mom pack" listing referrals in her region, that Celia found a psychiatrist willing to prescribe medication. She was "significantly better within a few months."

One of the strongest threads running through the tapestry of women's self-help is the belief that women's nature and modes of relating are different from men's. Some activists in the postpartum support group movement go so far as to assert the existence of a distinctive set of "female values" that include egalitarianism, collectivism, an ethic of care, respect for experiential knowledge, and cooperation, and they link these to women's biological capacity to reproduce. It is not uncommon for activists to use maternal metaphors to characterize the support provided by self-help, as in the case with *The Postpartum Survival Guide*, which begins by stating that "if it were possible to put a big motherly hug into words, this is what we'd do for every postpartum mom who picked up this book."

As important as books, articles, and newspaper stories have been, for many of the women I surveyed, television talk shows first alerted them to the collective nature of their problems. However sensational and shallow the treatment of women's issues, early talk shows such as the *Phil Donahue Show* and the *Oprah Winfrey Show* are credited by many feminist writers with raising women's consciousness and encouraging viewers to challenge the gender status quo. Of course, some talk shows encourage women to embrace the simplistic psychological explanations harped on in much of the commercial self-help literature. But the importance of talk shows to the mobilization of the postpartum self-help movement raises questions for analysts who have dismissed their potential to deliver feminism to wider audiences.

Between May 20, 1986, and 1990, the D.A.D. founders appeared on thirty-four media presentations. That talk shows serve to connect women in more isolated areas of the country, as well as those confined to the home caring for a young infant, emerges from the experience of Molly, a woman from rural South Dakota who found out about postpartum illness from D.A.D.'s members' appearance on the *Oprah Winfrey Show*. After the birth of her first baby she was hospitalized for anxiety and depression, and she frequently thought about hurting her child. Although several years later Molly was rehospitalized and treated for manic depression outside the context of childbearing, she continued to believe that postpartum illness is the basis of her problems. In effect, the validation D.A.D. provided through self-help reading, media presentations, and its pen–pal network allowed her to find a way to make sense of her feelings of inadequacy as a mother. She explained: "I got newsletters from D.A.D. and by watching them on talk shows I learned that I wasn't going crazy and the only one to have this."

The almost symbiotic relationship that has developed between television and radio talk shows and modern self-help movements provides clues about the kind of support people are seeking when they tune in. The centrality of talk shows to women's self-assessments of postpartum illness suggests that women watch these programs in pursuit of some understanding of their real or authentic selves, in hopes of finding themselves through others whose experiences are similar to their own. Even if reading, watching television, and listening to the radio are essentially solitary activities, they offer some of the same kinds of emotional support and personal validation that takes place in face-to-face encounters. Louise, who suffered manic depressive episodes for nearly a year, maintained that "as embarrassing as it is to admit, maybe it was in answer to her prayers" that she "learned about D.A.D. on *Geraldo*," but she emphasized that "what seeing the show provided was the validation" she needed to seek help.

The significance of self-help reading—or what Gloria Steinem terms "bibliotherapy"—to the personal reconstruction that takes place in contemporary women's self-help movements cannot be overestimated. Some feminist writers consider the advice books pitched to women that have flooded the market beginning in 1963 with the publication of Betty Friedan's *The Feminine Mystique* a distinct genre geared to those who shy away from the label "feminist" but may be willing to articulate their personal experiences in gender terms. Few would dispute the fact that self-help writings are oriented mainly toward individual rather than social change. Nevertheless, as self-help analyst Wendy Simonds points out, they validate a women's culture of caring and encourage the development of a sense of community among women. Reading self-help literature or tuning in to television and radio talk shows does more than provide concrete information about women's problems. Such activities open windows on new worlds and possible identities that rescue women from the drudgery and constraints of motherhood. The postpartum self-help movement offers individual women a therapeutic rather than a societal solution to the anger, guilt, depression, and anxiety associated with mothering. Yet like most women's self-help movements, it exhorts women to embrace broader understandings of their problems. For example, with only a few exceptions, the telephone volunteers I surveyed agreed that participating in the postpartum self-help movement has made them aware of the inferior ways women are treated in society.

Leaving aside the fact that self-help reading and media presentations frequently are the products of organized groups seeking to create wider audiences for their claims, the inherently social nature of self-help is to be found in the self-confirmation of seeing shared experience on the written page or watching it on the television screen. Julie, whose anxiety, depression, and suicidal thoughts following the birth of her baby made her resolve never to have another child, put her finger on the inherently social nature of self-help when she attributed her recovery to having received a list of other mothers who had experienced postpartum illness from the national office of D.A.D. "Just knowing I wasn't alone and that it was going to go away helped."

Pen-Pal Network

The files of Depression After Delivery and Postpartum Support International are filled to the brim with letters from women describing their personal ordeals and seeking help. The overwhelming majority of these writers acknowledge that they learned about the movement either from a story in a popular magazine or newspaper or a television program. An anonymous woman who signed her letter "Alone With My Shame" confessed to Jane Honikman that she killed her baby: "I watched the *Phil Donahue Show* today and now I know what happened to me nineteen years ago. I suffocated my eleven day old son. He was our first child." Although no one, not even her husband, suspected that this woman had murdered their child—physicians attributed his death to Sudden Infant Death Syndrome—the writer described her guilt and the consolation she felt once she discovered a psychiatric basis for her behavior. She nevertheless remained "terrified" that her act would be discovered. Another writer whose problems were not quite as severe described in a letter to Nancy Berchtold a desperate search for treatment that led her to three different doctors. The quest ended only after a friend called and told the writer to "watch Carol Dix on *Donahue*." A local bookstore ordered Dix's book, she read it, and it helped make sense of her "anxiety, crying spells, mood swings, nothing could make me happy, nervousness, dizzy headaches, and diarrhea."

When the postpartum support group movement was in its fledgling stage, both Jane Honikman and Nancy Berchtold took the time to answer personally nearly every individual letter and plea for help, most of which came from women who were themselves suffering emotional problems. In a few instances, these women's illnesses had been professionally diagnosed. More typically, however, women wrote because they wanted to understand what was happening to them, and something they had read or seen on television led to a self-diagnosis of postpartum illness. Occasionally a mother, sister, friend, or perhaps even a husband begged for help. Although a few of the letters made straightforward requests for information, most contained long and detailed personal descriptions of the writer's problems: suicidal feelings, fears of harming their children, anxiety attacks, depressions lasting for years, guilt over having failed to live up to an idealized image of motherhood, and isolation connected to a sense that they were "the only woman who has experienced this hell." Most women were eager to embrace biochemical and medical explanations of their problems that countered "the reactions of others that seem to promote self-blame." Even so, most set their difficulties squarely within the injustices in motherhood's present configuration, which assigns women the enormous responsibility of childrearing at the same time that it degrades women's labor as mothers. The following excerpt from a letter written to the national D.A.D. office by a woman from Portage, Indiana, illustrates:

> I saw the article on PPD in the Gary, Indiana Post-Tribune. I feel I may be suffering from this strange malaise. My husband works in a steel mill and I'm faced with "everything else." I quote that because he does cook dinner approximately 4–5 nights a week and does his own lunches. I do the bills, filing, laundry, groceries, cleaning, repairing home and cars, take care of 2 dogs, 5 fish, and our (thank goodness) wonderful 5 month old little girl. My daughter has been ill and my husband and I have been fighting. . . . I love my husband very much, but I want to leave him. He has a violent temper sometimes and I don't want my daughter to grow up with him. I know I'm not happy here but I have nowhere else to go. I feel that I'm not appreciated, that I do too much or not enough. I can't do anything right. My friends think I'm a wiz at mothering and wifery. I just don't feel adequate. I really feel that I need help. Please send information and the name of a contact person in state?

This letter is not unusual in its emphasis on women's traditional family roles and the oppressive aspects of motherhood as a source of women's emotional problems. At the same time that the letters provided an outlet for expressing dissatisfaction, they also conveyed optimism connected to the discovery that other women have experienced and lived through the same type of problems, as well as gratitude, as one writer puts it, to the women who have "brought this issue out of the closet."

As the movement expanded in size and requests for help skyrocketed, the personal letters Honikman and Berchtold composed in response to women's pleas for help gave way to other forms of support, such as D.A.D.'s and PSI's telephone contacts, face-to-face support groups, and bibliotherapy in the form of D.A.D.'s "Mom pack." However, letter writing continues to be a primary and unique form of support for one group of women who lack access to other avenues.

Since D.A.D.'s appearance on *Donahue*, women facing charges and serving prison sentences for murdering their children turned to the postpartum self-help movement for emotional support and legal assistance. At first the letters and telephone calls that arrived at the national headquarters of D.A.D. came mainly from the women themselves. Most had been convicted and were serving prison sentences, but it was also not unusual for women to write confessing to undetected murders that had taken place several years earlier, such as the woman discussed previously who admitted to having suffocated her child, and another woman from Pontiac, Michigan, who acknowledged that she had killed her son eight years earlier and covered it up by claiming that he was abducted.

As publicity about the link between infanticide and postpartum psychiatric illness stepped up in 1988 with a second *Phil Donahue Show* featuring Sharon and Glenn Comitz, Angela and Jeff Thompson, and Michele and Jeff Remington, requests for help picked up and took on a slightly different character. D.A.D. did continue to receive letters from women who wanted to get in touch with others in similar circumstances who might help them come to terms with their guilt and grief. For example, a woman wrote who is currently serving a ten-to-twenty year sentence for third degree murder in the State Correctional Institution at Muncy, Pennsylvania, even though physicians diagnosed her as suffering severe postpartum depression. She explained agonizingly how difficult women find it to live with themselves after killing a child:

> *In the beginning, I cried all the time, took psyche medicine to help me over the voices and delusions in my head and tranquilizers. For what? They either wanted me to remember in the beginning, as they said to confess to my violent crime. Now they want me to forget. I have low self-esteem but I know this much. I am not, nor ever was a violent person. My living daughter can testify to this. It hurts how people have convicted me and act like I don't feel a thing, if they were inside me they sure could see what I really feel. . . . It eats me alive inside, day after day. It gets easier but never better with time.*

But D.A.D. also started to receive requests for information from attorneys defending women facing criminal charges for infanticide. The D.A.D. national office responds to these requests by suggesting names of psychiatric and mental health professionals qualified to provide expert testimony in such cases and by sending the organization's "pro pack" that contains legal and medical information on postpartum illness. But providing ongoing support to incarcerated women presented a more difficult problem.

From her background in sociology, Jane Honikman had acquired a strong commitment to "emotional support as a natural component of society." While she believes that therapy and medication can be beneficial to women's recovery, she places the most value on the kind of support people can provide each other in more natural settings. In hopes of facilitating a supportive and caring community among women incarcerated for infanticide, she conceived of an informal pen-pal network to forge a connection from cell to cell. Honikman launched the network in 1990 by compiling the names and addresses of all the women who had written directly to her, to PSI, or to D.A.D. requesting information and support in connection with killing their children. She then sent each woman what she described as a "letter of friendship" inviting her to participate in a mutual support group and asking for permission to give her name and address to other women in the network so that they could all correspond with one another. About fifteen women wrote back expressing interest. At the end of each year, Honikman supplements women's letters to each other with a pen-pal newsletter that welcomes new members, reports member news, and tries to "link everyone into a single voice" that expresses connections above and beyond the relationships established by the personal one-to-one letters.

Between twelve and fifteen women generally participate in the network where there is frequent turnover. Women write each other about how to put together a legal defense based on postpartum illness, exchange ideas about how to get their sentences reduced or obtain early parole, and share information about home visitations, their health, and life in prison. But the network offers women much more than concrete information. It is here that women find the emotional and psychological support they need to voice their innermost fears and feelings. For instance, one woman wrote for advice to another network member who appeared on the *Phil Donahue Show* before stepping forward to share her own experiences with a newspaper reporter. Another sought suggestions about how to explain to her older child that she had murdered her baby. And another sought friendship and acceptance because even in prison she found herself ostracized by other inmates for the unspeakable crime she had committed. Women share their intense grief over what they typically describe as the "loss of a child to postpartum illness." Grateful not only for the written information provided by D.A.D. and PSI but also the mutual support provided by the movement, a woman from Texas described how participating in self-help can contribute to women's emotional well-being by helping women manage distressful feelings: "Your material has eased my confusion, guilt, and isolation and I thank you from the depth of my heart." Another woman whose outlook improved so much during the first year she participated in the network that she started college, was moved into an open ward of the prison, and began receiving day passes into the community, called the pen-pal network her "life support system." She went on to say that "all of the medication and therapy cannot compare with the understanding, support, and help she had been given by the other women in the network.

That these artificially constructed forms of community are built on close personal relationships between women and promote the kind of female bonding and emphasis on caring that scholars consider typical of communities of women activists is conveyed through participants' open expressions of love and affection for each other. One woman summarized the intensity of women's relationships and the impact of the group on her own life when she wrote to thank Jane Honikman for starting the network:

> *For me, this has been the best therapy. I feel so close to these women. I mean, we truly know and understand each other's pain and the craziness that accompanies PPP and other people's misconceptions. It is amazing what an understanding ear can do.*

Even if letter writing may not be an exact substitute for more immediate forms of community, the caring and support the pen-pal network provides is no less real. Certainly, prison authorities recognize the subversive potential of women's solidarity. On January 25, 1991, the Superintendent of the State Correctional Institution of Muncy, where three members of the pen-pal network are imprisoned, wrote to Jane Honikman informing her of an administrative policy forbidding inmates to correspond with those incarcerated in other institutions. Honikman successfully subverted this policy by having women channel future correspondence through friends and family. And so the pen-pal network lives on.

In order to manage the fact that they have failed to meet the test of ideal motherhood—and, for some, that they carry the added stigma of criminality and mental illness—women find solace in spaces that allow them to reconstruct their biographies in more positive therapeutic terms. Telephone support, face-to-face support groups, self-help reading and talk shows, and pen-pal networks promote the kind of solidarity necessary for women to take a stand on society's construction of the mother and on the ways their common experiences of motherhood depart from the cultural ideal. Although the letters and telephone calls from women who watch television talk shows suggest that the problems that lead women to turn to the postpartum support movement for help are widely shared, the women's communities that form the basis of the movement appeal mainly to the same group of white, middle-class women who historically have been drawn to feminism. Unlike the feminist self-help groups of the

1960s and '70s, however, these communities do not emphasize separation from men. Rather, they offer more palatable therapeutic rationales, expressed increasingly in the dominant medical discourse on childbearing, for expanding men's participation in the nurturing and caregiving roles generally performed by women. Because these self-help communities challenge as well as grow out of women's primary social identity as mothers, they can be seen as oppositional. Certainly, it is easy to consider women's violation of gender norms when they refuse to conform to a standard of the selfless mother as a part of the reconstruction of motherhood. But as Dorothy E. Roberts emphasizes in her 1995 essay on criminal mothers, for most of us it is much harder to accept the notion that women who engage in violence against their children by committing infanticide, for example, are also inadvertently helping to transform the institution of motherhood as it exists today.

THE GENDER LOGIC OF SELF-HELP COMMUNITIES

I have focused in this chapter on community rather than the individual because of my assumption that community is key to understanding the significance of women's self-help in American society. A variety of factors contributed to the emergence of the women's self-help communities that grew rapidly in the 1980s and show signs of continued vitality in the 1990s. There are several ways in which community building through support groups is consistent with the development of postmodern societies in which people turn increasingly to anonymous authorities for resolution of their emotional problems rather than to traditional spheres such as family or religion. First, in contrast to the more enduring kin, religious, and neighborhood groups—which exact a fairly high cost from participants in terms of reciprocity for the kinds of emotional, physical, and social support most of us need when we face major life crises—support groups promote the self-interest of each individual. Many critics consider this aspect of modern self-help to be detrimental to building effective and lasting communal ties. Yet for women struggling to find the time and energy for jobs, children, and relationships, the accessibility of magazines and advice books, television talk shows, telephone contacts, and weekly or bimonthly support group meetings are real benefits. I was not surprised to discover that, on average, women report participating in face-to-face postpartum support groups for less than a year. And, of course, the other more transitory forms of community support discussed here require even less time and commitment from individuals.

A second benefit of self-help is the significance it places on caring for others as a route to individual empowerment. In a society that values rationality and impersonality over emotionality and intimacy, self-help groups depart in a fundamental way from the general ethos of American society. Embedded in women's self-help communities is a logic that reflects the traditional pattern of gender differentiation found in American families. It is women who generally have primary responsibility for caring for families, neighbors, and friends. The structures and professions, and even the informal channels of support that have evolved to provide care, are essentially substitutes for or supplements to care that can no longer be provided within families. It is my view that self-help groups can be understood as what Joan Acker would term "gendered" organizations. That is, irrespective of their composition, they are structured on the basis of underlying assumptions associated with the traditional feminine responsibility for caring, what Sara Ruddick terms "maternal thinking" and Carol Gilligan associates with an "ethic of care." Modern self-help groups, furthermore, give caring moral significance in a society that otherwise devalues such labor and in which women, by virtue of their expanded participation in the work force, are increasingly less able to take care of others.

The task, however, of disentangling the feminine aspects of self-help from feminism is not so simple. The real question is, do the transient forms of community concocted by self-help support groups facilitate the formation of feminist consciousness and resistance to oppression? In evaluating the diverse forms of women's communities that appear in the historical record, Nancy Cott has identified three forms of consciousness that motivate women to engage in collective action: feminist consciousness, female consciousness, and communal consciousness. What distinguishes feminist consciousness from the other two forms of collective consciousness is its critique of male domination, the will to change it, and the belief that change is possible. Female consciousness, in contrast, is rooted in women's acceptance of the sexual division of labor. Although female consciousness has also been an important force propelling women to protest, as the contemporary antiabortion or "pro-life" movement illustrates, female consciousness is more likely to support the status quo. Yet female consciousness can sometimes be a force for change. Molly Ladd-Taylor demonstrates, for example, that middle-class women's welfare activism in the 1910s and 1920s was justified by a maternalist world view that sought to unite women across class, race, and national lines on the basis of the capacity for caring and nurturing that arises from women's common responsibilities of motherhood. Even if maternalist reform activity did not directly challenge the sexual division of labor, the concern that maternalists expressed for the welfare of women and children was a progressive force in the development of national child welfare policy in the period. Finally, women historically have mobilized around communal consciousness, or solidarity with men of the same group. African American women have created, for example, separate women's groups such as the National Association of Colored Women that struggled in concert with African American men to undermine racial apartheid. Similarly, working-class housewives have organized women's brigades to support labor strikes of predominantly male workers.

This typology points to the central concern I address in the next chapter. To what extent do the strategies and tactics of women's self-help, intended to provide emotional support and encourage personal reconstruction, contribute to feminism as a political project? To address the vexing question of whether feminism, despite the turn to thera-peutic explanations, nevertheless continues to point the way for women in contemporary women's self-help, I turn my attention to the creation of a collective identity in the postpartum support group movement.

THE METAMORPHOSIS OF FEMINISM IN WOMEN'S SELF-HELP

COLLECTIVE IDENTITY IN THE POSTPARTUM SUPPORT GROUP MOVEMENT

Two people can keep each other
sane, can give support, conviction,
love, massage, hope, sex.
Three people are a delegation,
a committee, a wedge. With four
you can play bridge and start
an organization. With six
you can rent a whole house,
eat pie for dinner with no
seconds, and hold a fund raising party.
A dozen make a demonstration.
A hundred fill a hall.
A thousand have solidarity

and your own newsletter;
ten thousand, power and
*   your own paper;*
a hundred thousand, your own media;
ten million, your own country.

It goes on one at a time,
it starts when you care
to act, it starts when you do
it again after they said no,
it starts when you say We
and know who you mean, and each
day you mean one more.

—From "Circles of Water" by Marge Piercy

SOME PEOPLE treat a crisis or traumatic illness as a private and individualistic experience. Others use such events as an opportunity to reflect on their lives and as a bridge to new and more public understandings of their biographies. The difference, according to C. Wright Mills, between seeing one's problems as having to do with one's own character and immediate relations with others rather than with matters pertaining to the institutional and cultural factors of the society as a whole is profound. For this difference determines not only whether we are able to relate our personal troubles to public issues and societal structures, but also whether we are willing to pursue collective solutions.

Probably the most fundamental of all the ways support groups help people solve their problems, as Robert Wuthnow observes, is by "providing occasions to do things and be things that the person cannot do or be alone." In American society, learning to be a mother is the kind of developmental task that can sometimes best be accomplished by watching and talking with other women. The loss of local community associated with the geographic mobility characteristic of modern industrial societies means, however, that new mothers often reside some distance from their own mothers or feel that they do not want to raise their children in the same way that they were raised. They may also be isolated from other women undergoing the same transition. Nearly two-thirds of the women active in the postpartum support group movement reported either that they lacked access to traditional mentors, such as mothers, sisters, aunts, or grandmothers, or did not want to turn to their relatives for advice. Another one-third emphasized their desire to interact with women whose conception of what it means to be a wife and mother had been influenced by the common experience of postpartum illness. What these findings suggest is the significance some women attach to self-help groups for the process of defining their social identities.

Thus, in order for people to pursue collective rather than individual solutions to their problems, they must come to some common understanding of their experiences. The concept of collective identity, as developed by scholars of the new social movements of the 1960s and '70s, addresses the question of how groups define and make sense of the question "who we are." Ultimately, the task of all social movements is to find some way to bridge the individual and societal levels by convincing people to interpret their problems in collective terms. Most collective actors do this by finding similarities in the biographies of a group of people and emphasizing them in such a way that the group's definition becomes a part of individual members' definitions of self. As suggested in chapter 3, David Snow and his collaborators, building on Erving Goffman's concept of "framing," argue that a group's ability to define itself collectively is linked to its capacity to inscribe people's grievances in some overall framework that identifies an injustice, attributes the responsibility for it to others, and proposes solutions. In a group's *collective action frames*, or the claims it makes about itself and its circumstances, one can often hear the echo of conventional cultural ideas. The resonance in the postpartum support group movement of the therapeutic world view that dominates American society thus comes as no surprise. But collective action frames also originate in the ideas of groups that challenge the status quo. David Snow and Rob Benford emphasize that longstanding and influential social movements such as feminism produce widely shared master *frames* that are likely to show up in the framing and identity construction processes of subsequent movements.

In this chapter, I elaborate the connections between feminism and the collective identity that is constructed and affirmed in the postpartum support group movement. In so doing I unveil the way that acting collectively in the context of a self-help movement provides an opportunity for women who have suffered from postpartum illness to create solidarity and to articulate new and more positive conceptions of themselves as mothers. I concentrate especially on the way that women use feminism to attempt to reconcile their individuality with involvement in the postpartum support group movement. Like most contemporary women's self-help movements, activists do this by borrowing feminist principles. But while it may be true that women's self-help extends the reaches of feminism by alerting new constituencies of women to their disadvantages, it also transforms the meaning of feminism in the process.

COLLECTIVE IDENTITY IN THE POSTPARTUM SUPPORT MOVEMENT

Collective identity is the shared definition of a group that derives from members' common interests, experiences, and solidarity. Groups articulate and sustain their collective identities within the context of social movement communities. These communities, according to some scholars, become a basis for distinct political cultures that are partly responsible for the increasingly fragmented and pluralistic nature of modern societies. As I have argued elsewhere, the formation of collective identity is the outcome of three interrelated processes. The first is the creation of *boundaries*, whether social psychological or physical, that establish differences between a group and the larger society. In contemporary self-help movements, the importance of accentuating differences between participants and nonparticipants is illustrated by the use of terms such as "recovering alcoholic," "breast-cancer survivor," "survivor of incest," "rape survivor," and "codependent," which identify persons primarily in terms of a common experience and locate them as members of a shared group. In describing the postpartum support movement, I am particularly interested in discovering whether the predominantly white and middle-class self-help groups serve as islands of resistance that affirm feminist values.

The second process is the development of *group consciousness*, which support groups advance by creating new collective self-understandings that specify participants' unique explanations of their problems and reframe individuals' biographies in more favorable collective and structural terms. This dimension focuses our attention on the way that feminism imparts larger social and political significance to the experience of postpartum illness. But critics continue to worry that the new identities self-help activists are embracing debase women by offering explanations that reaffirm traditional notions of women as neurotic, diseased, and biologically and socially inferior to men. Such concern directs our attention to the third process involved in constituting a collective identity, individual political expression.

In women's self-help, participants open the curtain on the intimate dramas of their personal lives not in the interests of voyeurism but as a political strategy. By connecting their personal experiences and everyday lives to the processes of gender subordination, they engage in personalized political resistance. This brings us to the final question that I take up in the conclusion of this chapter: To what extent do identity and self-expression, which are a major focus of therapeutic feminism, contribute to the eradication of institutional barriers to women's equality?

Boundaries of Gender, Race, Class, and Sexuality

To get a better idea of the composition of the movement at the grassroots level and to describe the beliefs and strategies of activists, I surveyed the telephone volunteers whose names are on file at the D.A.D. national office. The number of volunteers hovers between 230 and 250, of whom the 115 members I surveyed are broadly representative. Consistent with the emphasis on women's difference from men that underlies much of contemporary women's self-help, the movement continues to be comprised mainly of women, despite the participation of a few men; only one man responded to my survey.

Except for two women of Hispanic background and a woman who self-identified as an Indian from the Caribbean, all of the telephone volunteers are white European Americans. Most range in age from thirty-three to forty, although several are in their late twenties or mid- to late-forties. D.A.D. lists telephone contacts in every region of the United States as well as four in Vancouver, Canada. The largest concentration of volunteers (40 percent) can be found in the Northeast in Pennsylvania, New Jersey, New York, Washington, DC, and the Boston area, all of which lie in close proximity to the national D.A.D. headquarters. About equal numbers of D.A.D. contacts reside in the western United States (19 percent), in the Midwest (22 percent), and in the South (19 percent). Most of the volunteers live in small- or medium-sized cities (54 percent) and suburban areas (23 percent), rather than in large urban (17 percent) or rural communities (6 percent).

In terms of social class, educational background, and occupation, these women come from the educated upper-middle class thought to make up the demographic base of support of the new social movements. Slightly over half (52 percent) report annual family incomes between $40,000 and $69,000, which is well above the 1995 national family average of $35,000. As a further indication of the high economic standing of participants, nearly one-third (32 percent) have family incomes of over $70,000. The volunteers come to the movement with the kind of educational background, credentials, skills, and other resources that scholars have in mind when they speak of the "cultural capital" associated with participants in the new social movements. Not only have the vast majority (90 percent) of participants attended college, but more than one-third (38 percent) have received college degrees, and nearly the same number (37 percent) have earned postgraduate and professional degrees. Nearly three-fourths (72 percent) of the volunteers work outside the home, which is consistent with the national average for women between the ages of thirty-five and forty-four. It seems significant that more than half (54 percent) are employed in medical or mental health fields, although this is not to suggest that these women participate only because of professional interest, as only four of the 115 volunteers surveyed had not suffered postpartum illness themselves before getting involved in the movement.

But the characteristics of grassroots activists do more than confirm the writings of social movement theorists who trace the origins of contemporary movements to the grievances of a new middle class of educated professionals working in government, education, and human service occupations. This particular constituency calls attention to the structural origins of the movement in the problems faced by white middle-class women as their participation in paid employment has caught up with that of other groups of women. Throughout the 1970s the struggle to combine parenting with employment outside the home, which African American and poor white working-class women had endured since the turn of the century, began for the first time to plague large numbers of white middle-class families. It is little wonder that this is the group from which the postpartum support movement draws its greatest support.

The majority of the telephone volunteers are married (90 percent), although seven women are single parents, one lives with a male partner, and another resides with a lesbian partner. Only about 23 percent are full-time homemakers, which means that most volunteers come from two-income families that face the difficulties of raising children and maintaining a household at the same time that both parents are working. Two-thirds of the women share family financial responsibilities with their husbands, compared to less than a third (30 percent) who see their husband as the primary breadwinner. On the average, the women have two children, although it is almost as common for families to have one child as it is to have three or more. Given the composition of the movement, it is little wonder, then, that the traditional model of white middle-class motherhood that was seen as pivotal to women's subordination by feminists of the 1960s and '70s plays such an important role in women's definition of and solutions to their problems.

The public image that "only white middle-class women have postpartum depression" concerns some leaders who see the need to expand the base of the movement to include more minority women." Like other contemporary women's movement organizations, the postpartum support movement recognizes the dangers of assuming a universal and monolithic form of motherhood, even if it does not always put this belief into practice.

We turn now to look at the way that women's attempts to make sense of their negative experiences leads them to challenge, even while accepting tenets of, the prevailing white middle-class conception of motherhood. As we shall see, constructing women's commonalities in therapeutic terms makes it possible for the postpartum self-help movement to mobilize individuals who have stood apart from organized feminism.

Feminist Consciousness in Women's Self-Help: Linking Feminist and Therapeutic Frames

In 1977, when Jane Honikman laid the foundation for the movement by establishing the Santa Barbara-based Postpartum Education for Parents, feminist direct-action and self-help organizations were springing up around the country to address a wide range of women's problems. Even if most women's self-help groups founded in the late 1970s and early 1980s were feminist in the sense that they shared a fundamental commitment to ending male domination, the meaning of feminism was tied to the distinct politicizing experiences that shaped the collective identities of those who participated in the women's movement in this period. Because the women's movement overall placed a great deal of emphasis at that time on challenging the societal elevation of women's family roles over their paid work, Jane Honikman saw the burgeoning women's movement as exacerbating her problems by exerting additional pressure. "We were caught between our mothers who thought it was a noble cause to stay home with your children, and the next generation of feminists who asked, 'What do you mean, you're just a mom?'" Honikman found three soul mates in the Goleta Valley Branch of the American Association of University Women: "all new moms, college education, at home, and overwhelmed." These early activists connected their problems to the widely shared and broader feminist analysis and patched together a fledgling post-partum support movement in their local community. Looking back, Honikman acknowledges the insight of Margaret Mead, quoting her injunction to "never doubt that a small band of committed individuals can change the world, indeed, that is all that ever has."

The early founders of the movement did not set out to offer women a label—or psychiatric diagnosis—as much as they sought to connect women's problems to the burdens of motherhood and to male-domi-nated medicine. Laying out her group's agenda, Honikman outlined in a speech to community groups a "system for action" that would reach out to both the mother and father to offer ongoing resources and sup-port, and that would struggle to correct the medical profession's tendency to "brush aside the fact that postpartum is a period of stress compounded by fatigue" when "the mother feels neglected." Above all, Honikman linked women's problems to larger social processes expanding women's roles, specifically the "change from the traditional family unit, where the man went to work and the woman stayed home to raise the children." Although she advocated extending support to individual women and families, she did not consider individualized diagnosis and treatment a solution. Rather, she placed as much, if not more, emphasis on pressur-ing social service agencies and representatives from private industry to support "universal access to quality child care in all communities, urban, suburban, rural, and industrial, middle class and poor." That Honikman never pointed the finger at feminists is clear from her insistence in nearly every public speech she made and every article she wrote that women should not be expected to go back home "where, as some say, they belong and raise babies. That simply will not happen." Rather, Honikman clearly attributed women's postpartum difficulties to societal sources, going so far as to link the "economic future of our country" to its abil-ity to solve the growing problem of parenting and raising children. Obviously, psychiatric categories and treatments were not central to the self-definitions of early activists. As Honikman's approach shows, the postpartum support group movement from the start addressed women's problems from a feminist perspective.

As David Snow and his colleagues have argued, framing processes are not only central for mobilizing more broad-based support, but they also give collective significance to a set of actors. Collective action frames, that is, assert something about the commonalities shared by a group of people. The claims women's self-help movements make about what it is that participants share in common are integral to women's sense of self. The questions are, then, how did women's self-definitions get bound up with psychiatric nomenclature, and what are the implications for feminism?

As the mass feminist movement receded in the mid-1980s, women's self-help movements in general began to link feminist explanations of women's problems with a psychiatric and medical diagnosis and prescription for treatment. For the postpartum depression movement, an important turning point came in 1984 when Carol Dix introduced Jane Honikman to Dr. James Hamilton, who was teaching psychiatry at nearby Stanford University Medical School. Hamilton invited Honikman to attend the Marcé Society's 1984 annual meeting in Berkeley. In a speech delivered in 1990 at the Santa Barbara Birth Resource Center, Honikman described how this meeting set the stage for her conversion to a therapeutic understanding of her problem:

> Trial and error helped my husband and me through the tough road of postpartum adjustments, but years went by before I learned that I had experienced postpartum stress and depression/anxiety in 1972 and 1975. During that decade, I received emotional support from other mothers who have become lifelong friends. We were founders of Santa Barbara's own Postpartum Education for Parents (PEP). We have fulfilled our dream of establishing a support system for our community. Later, I was fortunate to be introduced to the scientific professionals who were conducting research into the causes and treatments of postpartum depression. It was from that education that I recognized the need to further refine the system.

That refinement meant resolving the dispute between self-help activists, who pointed to social and psychological explanations of postpartum illness, and those who looked to organic causes. To hold the movement together, Dr. Hamilton proposed using "ppd" as a "generic term to relate all of the groups to a common cause" and he gave the movement its name by suggesting that activists use the designation "support groups for ppd." Even though Hamilton clearly acknowledged the social factors in postpartum illness, the decision to emphasize the biological basis of women's problems in order to campaign for recognition as a bona fide psychiatric disorder was clearly strategic. In a letter written to Jane Honikman in June 1987, Hamilton elaborated:

> Let me explain my concern about technical words. After my bath of fire with criminal problems, I feel sure that we cannot get a fair hearing for infanticide cases unless we use the word "psychosis." We are reaching into the ancient common law concept of "not guilty by reason of insanity," and we cannot

*receive the benefits without flat-out use of the word "psychosis." That is why
my outline in the sheets I passed out had "postpartum" or "puerperal" psychosis for the early agitated cases and "postpartum psychotic depression"
for the late ones who pop up with an episode of violence after 6-9 months. It
is alright to just use the single word for depression, or postpartum depression
for less severe cases, but we cannot sell the courts to let a patient off easily and
call her some kind of a depression.*

To this end, Dr. Hamilton has dedicated much of his research and writing to the way childbearing affects the functioning of the thyroid gland,
producing biochemical abnormalities that make women vulnerable to
depression and anxiety. Even though Hamilton is generally credited for
his essentially hormonal explanation of postpartum illness, from the
beginning he recognized the need to widen the movement's appeal by
adopting as broad a definition of postpartum illness as possible:

> *If anybody tries to split the "organic etiology" people into one group, and the
> "psychological stress" people into another, and puts me in the former group, refer
> them to my chapter in Inwoods. Also, don't forget that the most important "psy-
> chological stress" attack is in the hands of the* Support Groups for PPD.
> *These problems represent an interaction between the two, and I choose to talk
> about the organic side because that has been the neglected side. Also, since you
> are far ahead on the psychological side, why should I tell you anything?*

There can be little doubt that a multifaceted approach to the problem
of postpartum illness has facilitated the growth and expansion of the movement. In the movement's own literature, one finds reference to a variety of
emotional problems that, according to one self-help source, are "much like
the spectrum of light in a rainbow; one color or category may blend into
the next one." Women are able to locate their feelings—and thus to define
themselves—along a continuum from postpartum blues to postpartum stress
syndrome to postpartum anxiety to postpartum depression to postpartum
panic disorder to postpartum obsessive-compulsive disorders to postpartum
psychosis. And while "ppd" remains the most often-used designation for
women's negative feelings, over the years Depression After Delivery and
Postpartum Support International have gradually adopted the shorthand
designation of "ppd/ppp" to call attention to the severity and organic origins of some women's illness. The following passage from a 1995 issue of
Mothering magazine, which relies heavily on the theories advanced by medical professionals associated with the movement, is typical of the
explanations found in the most recent advice literature:

The hormonal shifts that occur within 24 hours of giving birth are dramatic. Estrogen levels, for example, decrease by about 99 percent. In some new mothers, this tremendous hormonal drop alters the uptake of neurotransmitters in the nerve synapses of the brain. The minute changes in neurotransmitter concentrations are what bring on the not-so-minute changes in women's lives. For a portion of women with postpartum disorders, the altered brain chemistry is said to directly trigger the rapid onset of mental illness. For others, the altered brain chemistry, like a compromised "immune system of emotion," increases vulnerability to stress.

Despite increased attention to biological causes, it would be an oversimplification to suggest that the postpartum self-help movement subscribes to essentialist explanations of gender by attributing women's problems exclusively to hormonal processes: either to the routine hormonal changes that take place during pregnancy and childbirth, or to thyroid problems that bring on hormonal changes, or to hormonally induced alterations in brain chemistry. To the contrary, the self-help literature makes explicit the multiple causes of postpartum illness and in fact adopts such a long litany of social, cultural, and psychological explanations that one is left with no clear understanding of the causes. Everything from a difficult pregnancy, a complicated birth, medical problems with the baby, difficulties with nursing, or a recent change in work or family life can serve as "the straw that breaks the camel's biochemically weakened back." In effect, self-help writings call attention to the way that women's well-being is affected by the normal physical changes associated with pregnancy and childbirth—not only the increased production of estrogen and progesterone, but also the expansion of the uterus; the swelling of the breasts; the increase in the amount of blood circulating in a woman's body and the extra demands this makes on the heart, liver, and kidneys; the soreness associated with breastfeeding; and the pain and exhaustion women experience as their bodies return to a nonpregnant state. The movement aims, in other words, to bring the discussion of women's bodies and the bodily processes associated with human reproduction into the public domain.

Biological explanations do not undermine women's awareness of the significance of the social aspects of motherhood in delimiting women's place in society, as reflected in the stories activists tell about their own postpartum illnesses. Over half (53 percent) of the telephone volunteers I surveyed attributed their problems to multiple causes that included both the biochemical hormonal variations and the social responsibilities of motherhood. Only 19 percent of these women viewed their postpartum illness as exclusively "biochemical." Those who provided only biological accounts were likely to use these explanations as a way of clinging to nor-mality, as one woman did when she described herself as "normally a happy, well-adjusted woman in a stable relationship who loves mother-hood." This woman's comments make sense only when we recognize that many of these activists place mothering in a different light. Of those sur-veyed, 25 percent depicted motherhood as an oppressive role that saddles women with primary responsibility for caretaking, isolates them from oth-ers, and becomes a basis for women's devaluation and disadvantages in the workplace. Betsy, who suffered severe postpartum depression after the birth of her three children, was hospitalized once, treated with antide-pressants, and finally sought out a support group, illustrates the effects of defining motherhood as women's core identity:

> I had to look like a perfect mother, the motherhood myths. The work I did at
> home was unseen and unvalued. I was ill-prepared for motherhood, being led
> to believe that it was instinct. With the later children, I went through job
> changes, moves, "loss of dreams," independence, and even myself temporarily.

What holds together women with diverse angles of vision on post-partum illness is the common bond of having had a negative experience with motherhood, which appears to trouble the activists I surveyed far more than the stigma of having suffered mental illness. The fact that only six activists believed that a prior history of depression or other psychi-atric illness figured significantly into their problems suggests that most would agree with the title of a popular self-help book *This Isn't What I Expected*. For activists in the postpartum support group movement, men-tal illness is not the only frame on which their identities hinge. While medicine may offer explanations of and solutions for some of their prob-lems, it does not delineate who they are. Rather, women also interpret their past experiences and their present circumstances in terms of gen-der oppression and resistance.

As we have seen, the movement's shift to a more medical view of post-partum conditions is in line with the mainstream American tendency to conceptualize problems mainly in individual and therapeutic terms. This strategy has the potential to bring in a wider circle of women, but it does not mean that feminism is filtered out of the solution. In fact, almost all of the 115 D.A.D. telephone volunteers who responded to my survey fit some-where on the continuum of support for feminism devised by Melinda Goldner and Kim Dill. Reflecting both a commitment to equality for women and a response to the negative images of feminism conveyed in the public discourse, women positioned themselves differently with regard to their willingness to call themselves feminists. At one end of the spectrum were half of the telephone volunteers who *embrace the feminist label* when asked, "Do you consider yourself to be a feminist?" It is clear that the identities of a significantly larger proportion of women in the postpartum support group movement are bound up with feminism than is the case for women in general. For about half of the women who claimed the label feminist, their identity grew out of a history of prior participation in the women's movement, as Caroline an Oregon woman in her early forties made clear:

> *I was raised in the 1960s and was college age in the 1970s and had a lot of exposure, meaning that I am sensitive to gender issues and try to see the world in a balanced way. I had a lot of good role models as women who were both professionals and family oriented.*

Like Caroline, participants who came to feminism during the sixties' surge of activism had a broader and more theoretical conception of the societal basis of women's inequality. They tended to speak in terms of "women's disadvantages" and looked forward to a time when women will have "the same rights as men" and will no longer be "discriminated against because of their gender."

By contrast, the meaning of feminism for women whose feminist identities result from their participation in the postpartum self-help movement—or the other half of the women who claimed the label—is more bound up with either motherhood or a critique of the male-dominated medical establishment. Sara, who joined D.A.D. after twice suffering postpartum illness considered her experiences the turning point that raised her awareness of the extent to which motherhood contributes to what she calls the "victimization of women":

> *I had a mother who was battered and treated like a second-class citizen. I had a mother-in-law who was a single mom and got almost no encouragement just put downs. I see the way they both had to adapt to the ill-treatment they received. One with alcohol and temper. The other with passiveness and not being who she was meant to be. Neither of them appreciate my feminist philosophies and yet they're the biggest reasons I've been angry enough to ask why violence against women in any form is unacceptable. The women in my family were bright, strong, able women and never appreciated as such. They stood in the shadow of their partners.*

For Rita, a clerical worker and mother of two from Vancouver, Canada, feminism grew directly out of the treatment she received from "male know-it all psychiatrists." In the midst of a severe depression, she sought care from two psychiatrists who refused to "recognize pdd." When she finally found a "caring intuitive woman psychotherapist, oh what a difference it made." The therapist suggested she join a postpartum support group, and the group turned out to have a feminist orientation. Today, Rita considers herself a strong feminist who speaks out against "stereotypes and images that do not support this belief," and states rather emphatically: "I truly became a feminist by way of feminist psychotherapy and my association with the support group." In a similar vein, Alana, a full-time wife and mother of two from Massachusetts, attributed her feminist consciousness to "having had children" and learning that "our culture is male-dominated through dealing with the o.b. community."

Although the overwhelming majority (95 percent) of the activists I surveyed indicated that participation in the postpartum support group movement had raised their awareness of women's issues and of "the inferior ways women are treated in the society," about half of these women did not use the feminist label to describe themselves. Failure to identify as a feminist did not, however, mean that they rejected the principle of gender equality. Rather, it is more accurate to think of these women as falling into two camps. By far the largest proportion—88 percent—supported feminist beliefs about women's employment, pay equity, abortion, violence against women, and the empowerment of women, but they *disclaim feminism* because they believed that identifying with the women's movement would distance them from men, marriage, and maternity. That this position can be understood as a response to the growing backlash against organized feminism that began in the early 1980s is illustrated in the eagerness of a forty-five-year-old nurse from Akron, Ohio, who had a history of participation in the pro-choice movement, to describe herself as "not extreme." She qualified her feminism by stating, "I believe in equal rights but not to the point of negatively affecting the position of women. I don't really consider myself a true feminist because that word, for me, has militant connotations."

Many women who disclaimed feminism drew such an image of feminists as "extreme," "militant," and "antimale." Similarly, I found that most of the men who were actively involved in the movement took profeminist positions. But, like their disclaiming female colleagues, they accepted that "females have problems with males domination-wise" and "to a certain extent agree with women, more so than not," but would prefer that the postpartum movement "ignore the man-woman thing and get on with the other part [of the problem]."

One of the main differences between women who embrace the feminist label and those who do not is the importance those who disclaim feminism place on women's differences from men. In debating the kinds of health and social policies that best meet women's needs, feminists in the United States have tended to formulate their opinions on the basis of women's sameness or difference from men. The dilemma that has often divided feminists is whether treating women and men the same produces the fairest and most equitable results, or whether women's special concerns, especially as they relate to the unique burdens of motherhood, should be enshrined in maternity and family policies. Evoking the sameness position that dominated mainstream feminist groups in the 1970s and 1980s, several scholars accuse what remains of the organized women's movement of exalting women's victimization and retreating into a worship of female culture at the expense of pursuing societal change.

To the contrary, I found that women who shy away from the feminist label are most likely to advocate in the strongest terms a societal reversal of the cultural valuation of the male through the elevation of the female values of caring, cooperation, and connection thought to derive from women's maternal role. The definition of feminism offered by Roseann, whose local support group pays a great deal of attention to "gender issues," typifies this kind of thinking: "Even though I don't call myself a feminist, being a feminist means taking responsibility for myself and my actions, without using my sex, yet appreciating our differences and celebrating them." Since a significant number of women who disclaim feminism see their activism as a public expression of the domestic values of caring and nurturance traditionally associated with motherhood, it might be tempting to think of them as wedded to maternalist thinking that relies on the rhetoric of motherhood rather than of equal rights. But although activists who prefer to put some distance between themselves and the feminist label are more likely to use the discourse of motherhood to campaign for recognition of postpartum illness, the majority do not hold a sentimental biological view of motherhood that asserts women's special capacity for raising children. Rather, they consider the elevation of motherhood merely one step toward providing broader public support for families attempting to raise children.

At the other end of the continuum from those who identify as feminists is a handful of women who explicitly *reject feminism*. Only a very small number of the activists in the survey—around 6 percent—expressed antifeminist sentiments. These women not only rejected feminists as "anti-Christian, liberal, men-haters," but, as was found in a study of right-wing women, were turned off by what one respondent described as "the absoluteness of their seemingly collective beliefs." Like the antifeminist women described by Kristen Luker and Susan Marshall, they were more likely to be full-time homemakers, to have less education, and to think of themselves as highly religious than the rest of the women in the sample. And most reported a history of participation in pro-life activism. Although the majority admitted that women "get the short end of the stick" when it comes to medical and psychiatric care, they all quoted the Bible or made reference to religious beliefs to justify their opposition to feminism. Furthermore, most of these women subscribed to maternalist beliefs grounded in essentialist notions of motherhood. That even these women take contradictory stances about the social position of women is evident, however, in the way Marianne, a thirty-five-year-old woman from Louisville, Kentucky, who runs a Christian home school and is active in the pro-life movement, responded to the question, "Do you consider yourself to be a feminist?" She answered: "Not in the liberal sense. The Bible makes it clear that women are of infinite value and have equal share in salvation with men." At the same time, she acknowledged women's disadvantage when she went on to state: "Since my personal self-worth is rooted in God's love for me, I have not had to struggle in this area as many women seem to."

As this analysis suggests, an important element of self-help consciousness in the postpartum support group movement is the recognition and reevaluation of the negative side of motherhood. In attempting to understand why so many women find themselves unable to live up to society's image of what constitutes a good mother, the founders of the postpartum support group movement sought to remove women's experiences and self-definitions from the deviant clinical realm and to place them in the somewhat more acceptable feminist arena. But over the years, as feminists became the targets of virulent criticism and the movement formed closer alliances with medical and mental health professionals, activists in the postpartum support movement grew more receptive to identity accounts that play up women's biological uniqueness. Unlike strict maternalists, such as the La Leche League described by Linda Blum and Lynn Weiner, activists in the postpartum support movement do not believe that the only way women can reclaim control over motherhood is by turning away from the advances of medicine by, for example, resorting to natural childbirth and extended breastfeeding. Rather, they are willing to embrace the new technologies of scientific medicine and to use them to provide maternal support.

As we have seen, implicating the body in the processes of gender is not the same as biological determinism. Scholars of contemporary feminist organizations note a tendency beginning in the 1980s for many of the direct-action self-help groups founded at the height of the modern feminist movement to adopt mental health models that rely on psychological interpretations and remedies, or medical explanations that have the potential to expand further medical control over women's bodies through hospitalization and drug therapy. While the postpartum support group movement has followed this same path, it also demonstrates that psychiatrization does not automatically translate into the obliteration of feminism. Feminism continues to serve as a collective political vision for activists. Furthermore, the combination of feminist and therapeutic frames has been a particularly potent means of recruiting both feminist and nonfeminist women to the cause. This, I will argue, has not only opened up women's bodies as a site of protest, but women's emotional lives as well.

Personalized Political Strategies in the Reconstruction of Motherhood

The slogan "the personal is political," coined by radical feminists in the early 1970s, continues into the present to express the essence of contemporary women's self-help. To make identity, or personal experience, the focus of political work stems from the recognition that gender inequality is embedded and reproduced in images and codes of femininity that link women to the private realms of home, motherhood, and sexuality. Sociologist R. W. Connell refers to this dominant construction of women's roles and identities as "emphasized femininity" to highlight that, in our society, femininities are in reality far more diverse. Gender is embedded in the most routine interactions of everyday life, whether medical or therapeutic encounters or the way people divide up the daily tasks of parenting and doing household chores in marriages and domestic partnerships. Because women's self-help movements direct attention to the specific ways that gender is played out in the lives of participants, they rely upon tactics and strategies of change that emphasize the political expression of individuals as much as of organizations. The postpartum support group movement utilizes two tactics that are central to the "repertoire of collective action" of contemporary women's self-help: *survivor narratives* and *empowerment*. I focus on the way that activists use these personalized political strategies to challenge dominant representations of motherhood that valorize women's nurturing and caring roles, to contest medical practice organized around the idea of the male body as the universal body, and to reconstruct the patriarchal model of parenting in which child care falls exclusively in women's laps.

It is a good guess that all self-help groups make use of personal testimony as a means of transforming what were once private experiences into public events and to normalize experiences once thought of as deviant. Turning illness into narratives of self-change is certainly not new. Steven Epstein credits the AIDS movement with being the first social movement in the United States to use lay and experiential knowledge to "accomplish the mass conversion of disease 'victims' into activist-experts." While he is undoubtedly correct that the AIDS movement takes self-expression and redefinition as an important political project, Epstein overlooks the fact that survivor narratives have long been one of the most striking features on the landscape of feminist politics. In the early pro-choice movement, women routinely held "speak outs" where they described in moving terms the agonizing consequences of illegal abor-tions. Battered women, anti-rape activists, and survivors of incest rely upon survivor narratives to raise awareness of the pervasiveness of sexual vio-lence. And in another contemporary support group movement, patients tell their stories to demedicalize the experience of breast cancer.

As we have seen, survivor narratives are one of the principal means by which the postpartum support group movement has been able to garner media attention. Women who have suffered severe postpartum illness bare their souls on television, at conferences attended by health and mental health professionals, at the office, and to countless others they encounter in the course of their daily lives. They make their stories public by writing about them in popular books and magazines, newspapers, and even profes-sional and scholarly publications. But beyond their flash, survivor narratives are also a strategy for exposing internalized oppression. Speaking out is such a critical event in the reconstruction of self that takes place in the postpar-tum movement that one woman serving a prison term for infanticide would not agree to talk to the media without first seeking the advice of other women who had given testimony to public audiences. It is no coin-cidence that the movement, in describing the willingness of more women and their families to share their postpartum illness publicly, refers to the act as "coming out of the closet." The reference to "coming out," borrowed from the gay and lesbian movement, is particularly appropriate. For when women come out as having suffered postpartum illness, they make a clear and visible break with the conventional view of motherhood. The guilt, anxiety, depression, and anger women associate with postpartum illness are not feelings women ordinarily connect with the joys of becoming a mother. Like much of the movement's literature, a recent popular book on post-partum survival begins by contesting the dominant construction:

> Society is quite clear about what your emotions are supposed to be once
> your baby is born. Television, movies, magazines, newspapers all give you the

*message that happiness, calm satisfaction, joy and pride are the norm when
a new baby arrives. Family friends, and medical professionals tell you to "relax
and enjoy your baby," as if relaxation played even the smallest role in the
drama of life with a brand-new child.*

When women express their negative feelings, they experience themselves as different from traditional—and ideal—mothers. Solidarity with
other women and the group consciousness that grows out of participation in self-help makes it possible, however, for women to use cherished
ideals about motherhood for their own purposes. Activists openly discuss
the "need, as women, to replace the myth of maternal bliss with a more
inclusive view of motherhood" that is "more realistic and accurate" and
places more emphasis on "the challenges and difficulties that are part of
the territory." It is not by coincidence that the emotions depicted in typical survivor narratives bring to light entirely different dimensions. For
instance, the book *The Cradle Will Fall*, which tells the story of D.A.D.
member Michele Remington who shot and killed her baby and then
attempted to end her own life, attributes Remington's severe postpartum
depression to her failure to bond with her son Joshua. Separated from
Joshua for over a week because he suffered oxygen deprivation that
resulted in brain damage at birth, Remington recalls how she felt the first
time she held him in her arms in the hospital:

> *I felt almost paralyzed. Mechanically like a robot, I held out my arms. I was
> holding Joshua just as I had held many other infants, but there was no joy. I
> tried to act the part of the happy mother, but I was terrified. . . . All I could
> think of was bonding. Bonding, bonding, bonding.*

The overriding message of *The Cradle Will Fall* is that women who fail
to enact the maternal script, even if they commit an act of murder,
should not be led down the prison corridor but instead offered compassion, understanding, and medical and psychiatric care. If it is possible
to speak openly about the almost unthinkable act of murdering one's
child, it is much easier for activists to air some of the other "less socially
acceptable feelings of new motherhood," such as guilt, anxiety, panic,
anger, and depression.

Activists frequently use the expression of emotions as a deliberate tool
for change. They do this, on the one hand, by providing "authentic" representations of their maternal feelings, which are intended to call into question
the unifying view of clinical medicine that erases postpartum conditions.
Regional and national D.A.D. and PSI conferences on postpartum illness

typically are sponsored by medical schools under the auspices of continuing education programs and are usually attended not only by self-help activists but also by physicians, nurses, and other medical practitioners. A standard feature at these conferences is a panel of women and, in keeping with the movement's goal of holding men accountable for caretaking, almost always at least one husband and wife pair who provide vivid first-hand accounts of postpartum illness. Frequently, the failure to find satisfactory medical and psychiatric care emerges as the moral of these survivor narratives. But participants are not left without hope. Researchers allied with the movement swoop in to confirm the view of activists that postpartum illness should be treated as a bona fide illness. Even if featured research presentations tend to advocate biochemical explanations of postpartum illness as hormonally induced, they invariably connect the denial of postpartum illness to gender bias and discrimination directed against women and women's health concerns by the medical establishment.

At times, confrontations erupt between lay activists and medical professionals, as was the case at a national conference of PSI held in Pittsburgh in 1991, when Dagmar Celeste gave a controversial keynote address. Celeste not only lashed out at the "culturally defined emotional imperatives directed toward new mothers" but pointed the finger at male-dominated medicine as contributing to the "emotional costs of mothering" by denying women's actual feelings, "both good and bad." Referring to her own institutionalization, Celeste charged that when women's "real experiences become too severe to ignore, we are referred to psychiatrists who treat us with magic potions (drugs) and other treatment modalities, even though there is no official diagnosis (DSM-III) for our ailment. This so-called treatment," she concluded, "is the socially imposed sanction for our failure to obey the rules." I interviewed a male psychiatrist shortly after the speech. Although supportive of the movement, he described the talk as "very emasculating," not just to him as a professional but "because a lot of husbands were there." Another man who is part of the inner circle of D.A.D. considered Celeste's comments "strong and offensive" but conceded that "they were probably true, but not put across the right way and, if they were rephrased would have been fine." He went on to validate her claims by saying, however, "it's the truth, what she's talking."

The importance of survivor narratives goes along with the insistence, which is fundamental to women's self-help, that collective self-expression is politics. In her concluding speech at a 1990 conference held at Children's Hospital in Columbus, Ohio, Nancy Berchtold emphasized the political significance of women using their personal experiences to become a part of the medical discourse on postpartum illness:

I think today we've been able to see the relationship between the personal and the political. This is more than a women's problem, a parent problem, or a sibling problem. It is the community's, the state's, the nation's.

As activists' narratives imply, the self-change that women undergo by virtue of their participation in the self-help movement often results in a fundamental redefinition of their feelings. Eileen, a woman from Eugene, Oregon, who suffered depression after the birth of her twins, credited participation in a support group with helping her to overcome her shame and guilt by focusing her anger "where it belongs, with our cultural practices." Another woman from Manchester, New Hampshire, Carolyn, attributed her activism to anger, saying there "are some serious problems with the way women are forced to raise children in our culture." She saw her commitment to the cause of postpartum illness as a way to "help change this." To the extent that it is much less acceptable for women than for men to exhibit anger, the fact that the postpartum movement encourages women to trade their shame and depression for anger and, furthermore, to express it can be seen as a kind of personalized political strategy in it own right.

Women's survivor narratives intend not only to contest dominant discourses of motherhood and postpartum illness but to proclaim the way that participation in self-help contributes to women's empowerment, which in many respects can be considered the *sine qua non* of all self-help movements. Although some feminist scholars have tended to think of empowerment primarily in individual terms as an outcome of participating in feminist organizations, I am interested here in the consequences for transforming institutions. Thinking of empowerment in this way makes the individual the site of political activity. In women's self-help, it is often more accurate to conceive of the empowered individual, rather than the social movement organization, as the primary instrument of change. In the postpartum self-help movement, as in many contemporary women's self-help movements, empowerment is expressed in strategies that challenge the subordinated position of femininity in the gender order.

Much of the work that self-help participants are engaged in is a reinterpretation of their own lives in relation to organized medicine and the world around them. Activists emphasize the way that participation in self-help encourages women to reflect on their interactions with physicians and to question medical knowledge, authority, and decision making in ways they otherwise might never have dared. The feelings aired by Celia, a woman who suffered a year-long depression following the birth of her seventh and last child are fairly typical. This woman "still feels angry" when she thinks about the way that the professionals she saw for help "let her down." But how specifically did they fail her and why was this failure political rather than individual?

To the extent that health and mental health care are delivered in a larger social context, the structural features and inequities of gender, race, ethnicity, class, and sexuality that are woven into the fabric of daily life inevitably impinge on the doctor–patient relationship. Many of the women who are actively involved in the postpartum support movement complain of the unwillingness of obstetrician-gynecologists and psychiatrists to acknowledge a connection between their problems and the biochemical changes and other physical and emotional stresses associated with childbirth and motherhood. For these women, empowerment translates into confronting the gender bias and power dynamics of medical knowledge and practice. Some women criticize physicians for failing to diagnose and treat their problems, as in the case of Marilyn, who suffered such severe anxiety that she cleaned the bathroom until she "literally pulled material off the walls" and had frequent panic attacks, coupled with such prolonged bouts of depression that she would lock herself in the closet and rock to get away from the baby. In attempting to find help, Marilyn lashed out at medical providers when she discovered that both her "ob-gyn and psychiatrist didn't have a clue" about what was wrong or how to help her.

Other women report just the opposite problem, complaining instead of overzealous treatment. Barb, whose incision from a cesarean section got infected, ended up spending five days in the psychiatric unit of a local hospital. Diagnosed psychotic, she was prescribed low dosages of lithium followed by other antidepressants and sleep medication for a subsequent depression that lasted nearly six months. Looking back at her unfortunate experience, Barb explained the role that self-help played in empowering her to stand up to physicians:

> I was actually better when I got off all meds. Joining D.A.D. and going to conferences and being in on the early days of the ppd movement gave me a feeling of greater power. I was asked to speak about my ppp at an event. That was something I never thought could happen to me.

Today this woman considers herself an "ardent feminist" who continues to "speak out about the abuse of women by the medical, legal, and political systems whenever possible."

For the overwhelming majority of activists in the postpartum movement (78 percent of the telephone volunteers surveyed), empowerment finds expression, then, in deliberate attempts to challenge physician authority. Showing what it means to consider routine medical encounters a site of political activity, most woman emphasize that they know their own bodies better than what one activist describes as the "so-called professionals." Another avows: "I feel that I am the expert on my own life, and I have the right to choose which treatment is right for me."

It is nonetheless true that many women are eager to obtain antidepressants and other pharmacological interventions to help them get back on their feet until the worst is over. Marla, a D.A.D. support group leader, who suffered a prolonged depression after the birth of her first child and then chose to take antidepressants almost immediately following the birth of her second in order to prevent a recurrence, rationalized her use of medication in political terms:

> It may take decades for us to tear down the motherhood myths and convince the powers that be to take postpartum depression seriously. In the meantime, if taking antidepressants makes me better able to manage my own life, why not take them? After all, when I have a cold, I take medicine to be able to go to work, don't I? Still, I wonder what this says about our society, that so many women are having to take pills just to be able to function as mothers.

Given the emphasis the postpartum support movement places on medical access and recognition, it may seem paradoxical that women who have experienced postpartum illness are likely to use their own lives as vehicles to question, rather than to corroborate, the legitimacy of organized medicine. But whether women reject or accept medication, the issue is the same: control. In contrast to the woman quoted above, Melinda, a telephone volunteer from Vancouver, Canada, refused to seek professional care during a six-month depression because "having the power to say 'no' to treatments that I don't believe in or feel might not be right for me" was the foundation of self-help.

Empowerment in the postpartum support movement means more, however, than staking out some claims on medicine's terrain and resisting the gender bias of organized medicine and mental health. Some activists go so far as to restructure their marriages and partnerships in ways that undermine the dominant ideology that women are uniquely suited for nurturing and domestic work. And in so doing, they are contesting in yet another way the prevailing notions of femininity and women's place. Indeed, I found a great deal of variety in the way that women structure their lives to accommodate both work and family roles. In studying how modern families combine raising children with employment, Arlie

Hochschild found that women use three different gender strategies in marital roles, what she calls "traditional," "transitional," and "egalitarian," depending upon whether women identify to a greater extent with home or work and how much power they have in the relationship. I found this categorization useful for differentiating among activists who are consciously struggling in their own lives to dislodge the ideology of the monolithic nuclear family in which child care, housework, and kin work is strictly a woman's responsibility and other activists who embrace—and sometimes even idealize—a traditional form of family.

From my survey of telephone volunteers, I found that a third (34 percent) of the participants considered their families to be *traditional*, meaning that the woman bases her identity mainly on the roles of wife and mother even if she works outside the home, while her husband is tied to his work, giving the woman less power in the relationship Although it might be tempting to dismiss these women's lives as supporting the gender status quo, many of them interpreted their marriages in the context of a larger conservative movement attempting to turn back the clock and reinstate the traditional family. Alice, a full-time homemaker from San Jose, California, who had given up a nursing position until her children get older but who facilitates postpartum support groups in her church, demonstrated the way traditional women draw upon religious doctrines and beliefs to justify strong marital bonds:

> *Jesus gave women more status and recognition than the culture of the day. I encourage the husbands of the women to love their wives in the same way Jesus commanded. . . . Basically women with ppd need husbands to love them sacrificially, unconditionally, and with understanding. My husband did this for me, and his love, proven to me by his actions, boosted my self-esteem and made me feel like I came back to life again.*

As Alice illustrates, some women, however traditional they might seem in terms of the gender division of labor, see their marriages as a site for addressing the devaluation of women and motherhood and go so far as to term their relationships, as one woman did, "part of the ministry of God." Although not all traditional women couch their experiences in terms of religion, some postpartum activists do.

On the other end of the scale, 49 percent described their relationships as *egalitarian*, which means that both partners identify with both career and home and that each has a relatively equal amount of power in the relationship. Perhaps not surprisingly, all of the women in nontraditional families, including seven single mothers, an unmarried heterosexual partnership, and a lesbian couple, described their relationships in this way. Several women considered their marriages or partnerships egalitarian prior to their bout of postpartum illness. It was not unusual for these women to attribute their recovery to what many described as a "supportive" husband or partner. But in many instances, the negotiation of egalitarian family arrangements is inextricably linked to a woman's postpartum illness, because the husband or partner is forced to step in and assume the lion's share of the household work. Bob, whose wife suffered severe depression and anxiety followed by an obsessive-compulsive disorder that still persists several years later, sold two businesses that "were going down the tubes" because of the time he was spending on his wife's illness. Reducing his commitment to work allowed Bob to spend more time with his wife and daughter and to assume greater responsibilities in the home. He described how the "untraditional" division of labor in their household evolved as a result of his wife's depression:

> Prior to the depression I would do the laundry. She'd do the cleaning. But during the depression, I did everything. It was just everything. And I picked up from there. And I still do the laundry, and I still do the bathrooms every Saturday morning. And I do the sheets and the beds and clean the kitchen and straighten up when the baby's down at night. Amy's a handful, but in the evening and weekends I spend just about as much time with her as my wife does. I was raised in a traditional family, you know, my father expected dinner on the table at six. . . . But marriage changed me because I realized that marriage takes two, and for one person to do it alone, it's not fair. If my parents heard me now, I wonder what they'd think. For my mother to do everything, that was a shame. She accepted it, but that's something she should never have done.

Bob goes on to explain that the thing that kept their marriage together through his wife's hospitalization, long-term treatment, and the strain of having to pay psychiatric bills totaling over $10,000, was their friendship. "Without our friendship, we really wouldn't have made it through this together." This couple is not unique. Many egalitarian couples consider the way that they structure their relationships and divide up household and child-care responsibilities as far more than a source of individual support paving the way to women's recovery. One woman realized that by making her husband more aware of her own emotional needs and insisting he get more involved in raising their children, she is "responsible for her own cure." She considered her own marriage a reflection of the movement's aims, because it was contributing "in a personal way to crushing the fantasy of the perfect mother image."

It is surprising that only a small proportion of activists (17 percent) considered their relationships *transitional*, meaning they are still plowing the road to egalitarian partnerships. It is surprising because most couples fall into this category. I found that most women who claimed transitional gender strategies considered career and family to be of equal importance in their own lives but nevertheless expected their husbands or partners to "assume major responsibility for family finances." It is not surprising, however, that women in these types of marriages are more likely to describe their emotional problems as putting a strain on already troubled relationships. The problem is that transitional men, although they acknowledge women's right to work outside the home, still tend to place most of the responsibilities for child care and housework on their wives. Such is the case with Gwen, a thirty-four-year-old woman from Providence, Rhode Island, whose marriage ended in divorce after a severe case of postpartum depression that led to acute anxiety attacks. Gwen now resides with a male partner and is using what she has learned from serving as a volunteer on the movement's "warm line" to try to build a more "coequal relationship" this time around.

A final way in which women weave their commitment to postpartum issues into their lives is by using their activism as a pattern for starting new careers. For a significant number of women, participating in support groups led them to pursue professions connected to helping women and families suffering from postpartum illness. In fact, of the 115 telephone volunteers I surveyed, 12 percent worked in jobs that allowed them to merge their personal and professional lives. Shana, an activist from Vancouver, Canada, who had never worked outside the home, went back to college to complete a degree in counseling psychology after her depression. She considers the work she does as a postpartum support group facilitator an expression of her commitment to "the family of women." Several women have earned master's and doctoral degrees in nursing, social work, and counseling with a focus on pre- and postnatal education or mental health, and today they work in hospitals or women's health centers facilitating postpartum support groups.

As the postpartum support group movement brings personalized strategies of change to the forefront, women become aware through shared narratives of the systemic nature of gender inequality, and they become empowered to make changes in their everyday lives. But individual transformation can also have larger collective implications. Mary Katzenstein, in her research on Women-Church, a feminist self-help movement in the Catholic Church, introduced the term "discursive politics" to underscore the nature of the work women activists often do when they come together. That is, they rewrite through talk, text, and symbolic acts their own understanding of themselves and the relationship of women's lives to the world around them.

Women in the postpartum self-help movement, as we have seen, are engaged not only in providing help to individual women but also in the construction of a new kind of mother. This new mother is not wholly fulfilled by her motherhood experience, but is ambivalent about her children and the loss of freedom that motherhood entails. She is no longer the sole caretaker of children, but is shifting some of the responsibility to fathers and partners. She is not deferential to medical professionals who have both idealized and insulted motherhood. She is unwilling to accept the views of experts who treat women's bodies as a site of social control in the reproduction of femininity. And she is no longer willing to accept family structures that require the sacrifice of her own goals and dreams. While in reality contemporary mothers are far more diverse than the portrait painted by the postpartum support group movement, these activists are engaged in a struggle to reverse the public definition of the dominant white middle-class institution of motherhood.

THE TRANSFORMATIVE POTENTIAL OF WOMEN'S SELF-HELP

Thus far, I have focused primarily on the postpartum support group movement's use of collective self-definition—by constructing women's failure to meet the test of ideal motherhood as postpartum illness—as a strategy to resist the ideological and structural constraints of motherhood. Critics of women's self-help contend, however, that organizing around identity reveals an unrealistic view of how social change takes place and has led to the depoliticization of feminism. Taking aim at the radical feminist self-help groups of the 1970s, Alice Echols charges that tracing change to the empowerment of individuals rather than to institutional transformation demonstrates "a stunning disregard for the material barriers to women's liberation. The struggle for liberation became a question of individual will and determination, rather than collective struggle." Debates about the merits of identity politics also find fault with the narrowness of a politics based on a specific identity. Holding feminism responsible, in part, for the fragmentation of other social movements such as civil rights, peace, and socialism, L.A. Kauffman goes so far as to accuse some strands of contemporary feminism of a kind of "anti-politics of identity." Such groups embrace self-transformation to such an extent that it "encourages the view that politics need not necessarily involve engagement with external structures of power."

Not all writers have been so unabashed in their criticism of the recent trend toward organizing around personal experience. Some social movement scholars consider women's self-help as one of the primary bases of feminist politics. After observing women's music festivals and interviewing participants, Suzanne Staggenborg, Donna Eder and Lori Sudderth concluded that it would be a mistake to interpret even the most conspicuous cultural strands of feminism as escapist, individualistic, and apolitical. As we have seen, taking part in postpartum self-help groups not only provides emotional support, but it encourages women to attribute their experiences at least in part to the gender bias of the medical system and the social constraints of motherhood. This change in world view comes about because participants form a collective identity, or what Bert Klandermans has termed, an "interpersonal life circle" that offers solidarity with other women and conveys that it is possible to alter their situation through collective action. In this sense, the construction of a collective identity is a necessary stage in the mobilization of all social movements. Writers such as Alberto Melucci take the argument much further. They believe that in postmodern societies the definition and expression of new collective identities is a significant form of change in its own right. For example, much like women who have been the victims of rape, of childhood sexual abuse, and of battering, postpartum depression activists have sought to carve out a public identity based on their experiences. But, in this instance, as for most groups, organizing around a shared identity is only a prelude to changing the institutions and challenging the societal inequalities responsible for an undesirable situation.

To demonstrate how constructing a collective identity can encourage women to engage in various other strategies of change, it seems fitting to conclude this chapter by looking at how women's self-help deploys tactics and strategies targeted at both individual and at social and institutional change. It is interesting that scholars have so rarely scrutinized women's self-help on its own terms. What are the biographical consequences of self-help? Does participating in self-help groups have a positive effect on women's emotional well-being? No matter what critics might have to say about the pitfalls of therapeutic feminism as a political project, after all is said and done, most women get involved with self-help groups to improve the quality of their own lives. Nevertheless, as we have seen, the process of getting and giving support in women's self-help almost inevitably gives way to the creation of women's communities that generate the solidarity and collective consciousness necessary to propose solutions to postpartum illness that go beyond merely providing help to individuals. But to what extent do the strategies of self-help actually undermine the institutional supports for the dominant white and middle-class construction of motherhood? I turn to these questions in order to address the larger debate about the consequences of identity politics as practiced in contemporary women's self-help.

Activism and Women's Psychological Well-Being

If there is a single sin of which contemporary women's self-help is most guilty, according to the chorus of feminist writers who have raised their voices in a lament about therapeutic feminism, it is the preoccupation with women's victimization. Although the data I have presented in this chapter suggests that getting involved in self-help does make women more aware of the roadblocks to women's equality, we can also see how activism can open the way to women's psychological well-being. I use the term "well-being" here as situated at one end of a continuum that locates psychological distress at the other. Psychological distress encompasses the feelings of depression, anxiety, and anger that we typically associate with mental illness. As we saw in chapter 2, these are the emotions women describe when they speak of having experienced postpartum illness. In addition to suffering a variety of unpleasant physical and psychological symptoms, distressed people usually feel demoralized, sad, lonely, and hopeless, whereas people who enjoy physical and psychological well-being are happy, able to enjoy life, and hopeful about the future. The activists that I surveyed from the postpartum support group movement almost unanimously sang the praises of self-help's enhancement of their psychological well-being. To be precise, 96 percent of the women stated that being a part of a self-help movement had improved their mental health. Typical was Emma, one woman who suffered such a severe depression after the birth of her only child that she, in a familiar refrain, resolved never to have another child. Even though Depression After Delivery referred her to a psychiatrist whom she found helpful, "the support groups proved to be most vital" to her recovery.

Social scientists increasingly find that people who believe they have personal control over their bodies and their destinies, because they are likely to work actively to solve problems and take actions to prevent anticipated difficulties, enjoy better physical and psychological health than those with a sense of powerlessness. From their preliminary studies of the breast-cancer self-help movement, for example, Catherine Ross and Marieke Van Willigen have proposed a model to explain how becoming actively involved in a social movement organized around an issue affecting one's own health or mental health can enhance physical and psychological well-being. Van Willigen and Ross start from the premise that the positive collective identities constructed by self-help groups provide activists with a greater sense of control over their lives. Self-help encourages women to develop solidarity with other women and to redefine seemingly personal experiences in more favorable collective terms. This process enmeshes women in networks that provide the kind of caring and social support researchers have found to be linked to improved physical and mental health. Self-help also gives women access to others who have experiential and professional knowledge of their problem, its treatment, and available resources. Nearly two-thirds of those I surveyed placed the greatest weight on the empowerment that resulted from self-help; a common sentiment was, "I feel I now have more control over my own life."

Considering the positive consequences of self-help activism for women's well-being brings the discussion back full circle to an important debate raised by the labeling theories of women's mental health, discussed in chapter 2. What are the implications of labeling women's problems in psychiatric and therapeutic terms, even if the defining of emotional deviance that takes place is, by and large, self-labeling? Labeling theory has, for the most part, emphasized the negative consequences, suggesting that stamping people's problems as psychiatric disorders results in punishment and stigmatization when individuals attempt to return to normal roles. Feminist labeling theories take this scenario one step further by suggesting that psychiatric labeling denigrates the feminine and contributes to women's subordination by defining the normal female as diseased. Yet by looking at the myriad of changes women are able to make in their lives by virtue of participating in self-help, we must wonder if labeling theorists have overstated their case.

Certainly this study suggests that in the context of the collective transformation of self that takes place in women's self-help, labeling can have positive as well as negative effects. And at the top of the list of the benefits is the way that participation in contemporary self-help promotes women's psychological well-being. As long as women are unable to identify their problems in a way that connects their experiences to both the lay resources and professional treatments available to help them, they remain powerless to overcome their problems. Even though women's self-help, as we have seen, often raises women's awareness of the structural impediments to gender equality, this change in consciousness does not appear to leave women feeling powerless. Rather, participation in the postpartum support group movement provides women with an opportunity to strike a blow at what one group leader terms the "conspiracy of silence surrounding the existence of postpartum depression" and its relationship to the hard emotional work of motherhood, and to advance their own claims to expertise about their emotions. In the aftermath of her own illness, Eva, a full-time home-maker whose severe depression after the birth of her first child motivated her to reach out to other women by becoming a telephone volunteer, admits: "If anyone ever told me ppd would have positive effects on my life, I never would have believed them. But it is true."

Self-Help Strategies and Institutional Change

To what extent, however, does the kind of collective self-transformation that takes place in women's self-help translate into other more conventional strategies of social and political change? Marieke Van Willigen traces the three main tactics used by contemporary women's self-help movements—consciousness-raising, direct service, and lobbying—to the early women's health movement of the 1970s. In the postpartum support group movement, these first two strategies not only provide emotional support and a sense of community but also, as we have seen, can contest the everyday practices and symbolic representations of the "good mother." As is the case with other identity-based movements, even if these strategies are fundamentally directed at individual women, they serve to politicize experiences that previously had been categorized as merely personal. It seems significant that the postpartum movement is not the only national women's self-help organization that has burst onto the scene brandishing a challenge to society's construction of the mother. The La Leche League, which promotes breastfeeding and maternal nurturance, and Momazons, which provides support to lesbian women who become mothers without out a male partner, are merely two examples of this trend. Such women's self-help groups do not stop, however, at the reconstruction of women's individual identity. They also use more conventional strategies to lobby for changes in the medical and mental health systems, the law, family policy, and society at large.

The postpartum self-help movement grew from the idea of organizing women into a movement to force the medical establishment to recognize postpartum illness. Formulating this as a goal proved to be easier, however, than agreeing upon strategies and tactics. The postpartum self-help movement has followed the same trail toward medicalization blazed by most contemporary women's self-help groups, and the movement's strategies also reflect an ambivalence toward medicine that is likewise characteristic. Some of the movement's tactics derive from what Steven Epstein terms a politics of distrust, or extreme skepticism about the credibility of male-dominated medical and scientific authorities whose knowledge is thought to be fueled by gendered assumptions. Giving more weight to personal experience as a basis for understanding postpartum illness is seen, therefore, as a way of holding medical experts accountable for their failure to acknowledge women's problems. In the Summer 1993 issue of *Heartstrings*, a review of Karen Kleiman and Valerie Raskin's book on postpartum depression, *This Isn't What I Expected*, exemplified the way self-help activists use personal experience to chip away some of the power of established medical authorities. The reviewer set this book apart from purely professional accounts of postpartum depression when she wrote:

> Refreshingly, in the prologue, Kleiman and Raskin indicate that their discussion of PPD is framed by the realities of their own experience with motherhood, which followed their professional training. And the authors are clear about their intent "to help you understand postpartum depression and to engage you in an active effort to recover."

At the same time, by identifying the authors as professionals, the reviewer made it clear that she did not reject outright the medical and scientific way of knowing and even praised the book for its strong contributions to medication therapy. That the coauthors of this self-help book, which has been heavily endorsed by the movement, are a social worker and a psychiatrist illustrates the extent to which female medical and mental health professionals are using self-help to stake out some territory on which to advance their own claims to expertise, both from an experiential and a scientific standpoint.

As the postpartum movement has become more closely aligned with medical and mental health professionals, it has increasingly seized upon tactics that target the knowledge systems of medicine and mental health by asserting the expertise of self-help-based experts. For the most part, activists have struggled to obtain control over the content of medical knowledge rather than the process by which it is produced. By that I mean that, instead of rejecting science as a way of knowing as some "New Age" self-help movements, the postpartum self-help movement has tended to embrace scientific medicine by encouraging professionals and researchers affiliated with the movement to produce an alternative body of research that confirms activists' positions. Several dozen medical and social science researchers are members of D.A.D. and PSI. They draw from their research and experience working with women who have suffered postpartum illness to validate the movement's claim that postpartum illness should be treated as an independent syndrome.

For example, Dr. Katherine L. Wisner and Dr. Deborah Sichel appeared on the June 1, 1993 *CBS Evening News* segment on postpartum illness.

Dr. Sichel has experimented with alternative pharmacological approaches to treatments not sanctioned by the medical establishment, and Dr. Wisner is principal investigator of a major research study on repeat episodes of post-partum depression funded in 1994 by the National Institute of Mental Health. Because of her medical credentials and the credibility she gives to women's experiential knowledge, Dr. Wisner has become virtually the "dar-ling of the movement," frequently appearing in the media and at professional conferences with activists. The story of how she hooked up with the post-partum self-help movement demonstrates not only the close ties between women physicians and women's self-help groups, but also the central role played by women doctors struggling to reform medicine from the inside. As Dr. Wisner tells it, "When I first started the research, a group of women from D.A.D. knocked on my office door and said 'you say we're at risk for having postpartum depression again. So do something!'" And she has.

Along with Marcia Greco, a member of the D.A.D. board of directors, Dr. Wisner appeared before the Gore Task Force on April 15, 1993, in Washington, DC, to present recommendations to the Presidential Commission on Health Reform about providing appropriate care to those suffering from postpartum illness. Wisner and Greco urged the task force to recommend seed money for a model mother/baby hospital unit for women suffering from postpartum illness; insurance coverage for unlim-ited outpatient psychiatric visits, home health care aids, and inpatient treatment; educational materials on postpartum illness in the National Institute of Mental Health-sponsored DART (Depression Awareness Recognition and Treatment) public education project; depression training for obstetricians, gynecologists, pediatricians, and psychiatrists; funding for research on treatments and prevention; and funds for the development of a standard of care for postpartum illness.

As one of these policy recommendations reveals, activists are eager to win insurance reimbursement for medical and hospital expenses incurred by women treated for postpartum illness. At national and regional con-ferences, women and their husbands testify to the dire consequences of insurers' denial of coverage by recounting the enormous expenses asso-ciated with hospitalization and outpatient treatment. To some extent, this problem stems from the fact that most health insurance policies either provide no coverage or sharply limit payment for mental illness. But even if insurance coverage includes mental health treatment, physicians treat-ing patients with postpartum illness are limited by the *Diagnostic and Statistical Manual of Mental Disorders*, which does not contain what activists point to as "an accurate, descriptive portrayal of what medical science now knows about postpartum psychiatric illness." To get around this problem, self–help advocates have developed their own tactics. At the annual conference of Postpartum Support International, activists regularly organize workshops on "how to construct a strategy to qualify postpartum psychiatric illness as a complication of pregnancy" rather than as a mental disorder. Such sessions point out that when it can be shown that the claim results from childbirth, it can be paid in full or at least is subject to the same rate of coverage as any physical illness.

Conducting and presenting research that confirms the movements's own position on postpartum illness at meetings of physicians, mental health professionals, public health officials, and childbirth educators is an ongoing strategy for challenging the failure of the medical establishment to recognize postpartum illness. Professionals affiliated with the postpartum self-help movement frequently present both research findings and experiential accounts of postpartum illness at in-service medical education seminars and at "grand rounds," as they are called, in medical centers. Winning an invitation to make a grand rounds presentation qualifies as such an important victory that when D.A.D. professional affiliate Dr. Zachary Stowe presented the results of working with postpartum depression patients, he made headlines in the D.A.D. newsletter. Dr. Stowe has since established a postpartum support program at Emory University Hospital Department of Psychiatry in Atlanta, Georgia, similar to one at Duke University. That Dr. Stowe in his presentations emphasizes the need for "ppd sufferers to speak to one another on a regular basis" is undoubtedly one of the reasons that activists praise him as "easy to speak to, enthusiastic, has good humor, and is truly dedicated to helping mothers recover from PPD."

In attempting to challenge and undermine the dominant medical line on postpartum illness, the postpartum support group movement has adopted a strategy pioneered by the AIDS movement that has received fairly wide documentation in the media. AIDS activists have demanded scientific studies of potentially useful treatments not sanctioned by the medical establishment. Similarly, some researchers allied with the postpartum self-help movement have advocated "investigative approaches that fall short of ideal experimental conditions" in hopes of discovering new pharmacological approaches to treatment and prevention. A good deal of this experimental work has focused on treatment regimens that derive from the view that postpartum illness is related to hormonal deficits, regimens that include administering estrogen or progesterone injections immediately after birth. Such experimental treatments, intended to prevent rather than treat postpartum illness, are predicated on the view, which remains largely untested by medical researchers, that high levels of gonadal hormones (estrogen and progesterone) during pregnancy and their abrupt withdrawal after birth can trigger postpartum mood disorders. These approaches differ from the standard treatment regimen, tested and reported in the medical literature, which rely mainly upon psychotropic medications such as lithium, antidepressants, and antipsychotic drugs.

Almost from the beginning, activists have worked at the grassroots level to wrest the definition of postpartum illness from the medical establishment in order to define women's problems as a bona fide medical condition. Nearly half of the telephone volunteers I surveyed participate in lobbying efforts in their local communities targeted at making individual physicians, the staff of hospital obstetric and gynecology units, and local medical societies and mental health associations aware of postpartum illness. Volunteers distribute informational brochures to physicians, hospitals, and other health providers, urge physicians to place them in the waiting rooms of their offices, and suggest hospital personnel hand them to women following childbirth. For example, D.A.D. Ohio's "Feelings After Birth" brochure, funded by the Ohio Departments of Health and Mental Health in connection with the state's annual Women's Health Month, is widely available in Ohio. In other regions of the country, activists rely on various sources of funding, including contributions from individuals, hospitals, pharmaceutical companies, and community agencies, to distribute similar pamphlets and other kinds of information about postpartum illness.

As a result of such means of pressuring medical and mental health professionals to take postpartum illness seriously, some change is evident. In Columbus, Ohio, where the movement has considerable visibility, the Departments of Obstetrics and Gynecology and Psychiatry of the Ohio State University Hospitals have jointly established a clinic on postpartum illness in response to lobbying by self-help activists. Similar clinics exist in other areas of the country, and they usually have their origins in pressure from self-help groups. In St. Louis, Missouri, D.A.D. board member and psychiatrist Dr. Christa L. Hines initiated a mother/baby unit at St. Mary's Health Center to provide inpatient treatment that allows the baby to remain with the mother whenever possible. Dr. Hines has also worked to inform physicians and other health professionals about postpartum psychiatric disorders through lectures, interviews, and publications.

Even though the postpartum self-help movement is sometimes willing to join force with other groups, most activists attach a great deal of importance to distinguishing postpartum disorders from depression that is not associated with childbirth and motherhood. For example, activists waged a campaign to win a category in the *Diagnostic and Statistical Manual of Mental Disorders, Fourth Edition* but were unsuccessful. But activists lost this battle. At Postpartum International's 1991 Annual Conference in Pittsburgh, the program organizers invited Dr. Ellen Frank, psychiatrist from the University of Pittsburgh School of Medicine and member of the task force revising DSM-IV, to explain the decision not to include separate diagnostic categories for either nonpsychotic or psychotic postpartum mental disorders. In response to a series of very pointed questions, Dr. Frank reported that the dearth of evidence for "symptom specificity" stemmed from the lack of a sufficient number of studies based on a minimum of fifty subjects and using a standardized set of criteria to diagnose postpartum disorders. It is little wonder that D.A.D. founder and then-director Nancy Berchtold soon afterward stepped up her letter-writing campaign to the National Institute of Mental Health and the National Institute of Health demanding greater support for funding of research on maternal mental health. Meanwhile, professionals affiliated with D.A.D. such as Dr. Miriam Rosenthal, psychiatrist and professor of reproductive biology at MacDonald Hospital for Women in Cleveland, Ohio, worked from the inside by serving on an NIMH research review panel. It was no accident, then, that in 1992, research guidelines published by both federal agencies targeted proposals focusing on the risk factors for postpartum illness. The campaign for recognition of postpartum illness continues, as self-help activists work to win hearts and minds by sending delegations to the American Psychiatric Associations' Annual Meetings.

The rejection of postpartum illness as an independent syndrome related to childbirth means that some women are serving prolonged prison sentences for infanticide because psychiatric testimony, critically important to an insanity defense, has been discredited on the grounds that their supposed illness presumably does not exist. Activists point to the fact that in England the law is more lenient in its treatment of infanticide related to childbearing. Two sets of British legislation, one specifically intended for psychotic mothers (the Infanticide Act of 1938) and the other aimed at enshrining the concept of diminished responsibility, or the insanity defense (the 1957 Homocide Act), are used fairly successfully by British lawyers and doctors to avoid murder convictions for women who kill their babies. The Infanticide Act, which tacitly acknowledges the existence of postpartum psychosis, states that in the first twelve months after a woman gives birth, she cannot be charged with the murder of her infant, only the lesser offense of manslaughter.

In the absence of similar legislation in the United States, self-help advocates have carved out several strategies to challenge the criminalization of maternal infanticide linked to postpartum illness. First, because the insanity defense is the only legal strategy available to defend women who kill their children against a murder charge, D.A.D. and PSI maintain a file of psychiatrists familiar with recent research on postpartum illness, as well as with the applicable legal standards and interpretations necessary to relate their clinical findings about a particular case to the insanity defense. When a woman or her attorney writes to the national director of either organization, she is referred to a list of psychiatrists who have experience testifying in cases where women have been charged with murdering their children. The insanity defense depends not only on the expert testimony of psychiatrists, but also on the ability of police, prosecutors, and judges to recognize and acknowledge the clinical manifestations of postpartum depression and psychosis in order to distinguish this type of child killing from killings not resulting from psychotic motives.

Self-help activists have, therefore, used a second strategy, which is to educate police officers to become aware of postpartum disorders. In 1990, the movement played a leading role in the passage of legislation in California mandating a basic training course for law enforcement officers focused on detecting and referring for treatment, women who might be suffering from postpartum psychosis. The law mandates that a mother suspected of infanticide receive a psychiatric evaluation within 24 hours of her incarceration from mental health professionals who have expertise on postpartum illness. It also mandates training for police officers to enable them to recognize symptoms of postpartum illness. This legislation is largely the result of lobbying by self-help activists Angela and Jeff Thompson. Jeff Thompson is a lobbyist for the California Correctional Peace Officers Association, and Angela, who was acquitted of the murder of their nine-month-old son Michael, served on a state-wide task force set up to implement the legislation. A similar campaign to provide police training in the state of Pennsylvania has been launched by Rick Baker, Chief of Police of Sugarcreek Borough near Erie, Pennsylvania, who had investigated an alleged abduction of a six-week-old infant. Two days later, the mother admitted fabricating the story and suffocating her child before placing his body in a dumpster.

Self-help activists have also sought to sensitize prosecutors, judges, public defenders, and correctional officials to postpartum illness through state-wide and regional conferences. In Columbus, Ohio, First Lady Dagmar Celeste served as the force behind a conference held at the Governor's residence in 1990 aimed at making legal, judicial, and correctional officials aware of postpartum psychosis and depression as a defense against criminal liability. As a result of the movement's strong presence in Ohio, public defenders in the state have been proactive in applying the insanity defense to cases in which women have been suspected of suffering postpartum illness. When Columbus, Ohio, resident Kim Chandler shot and killed her three children—a seven-month-old daughter, four-year-old son, and another six-year-old daughter—on September 25, 1991, the movement's lobbying efforts paid off. Chandler, a single mother overwhelmed by the care of her children and financially strapped, had told relatives many times that she did not want to have the third child and had even threatened to kill the children several times. She had been in touch with Children's Services staff, who assessed her as a competent if stressed caregiver just weeks before the killing. This report lent credence to activists' campaign to have Chandler evaluated at Timothy B. Moritz Forensic Center, a maximum security psychiatric hospital, where she was treated for more than a year before standing trial. Because psychiatric reports did not confirm that Chandler suffered postpartum illness at the time of the killings, her attorneys did not use postpartum psychosis as a defense. As it turned out, Chandler was convicted of 3 counts of murder.

But self-help advocates do not always find themselves with as much access to the criminal justice system as they have in Ohio. Sometimes they are forced to rely on more grassroots strategies to win support for individual women charged with killing their children. Kate Carpenter, who has been an active member of a postpartum support group in Harrisburg, Pennsylvania, for nearly nine years and who served as a member of the first D.A.D. national board, coordinated one of the first such campaigns. Carpenter worked closely with Glenn Comitz on behalf of his wife Sharon, who was serving an eight-to-twenty-year sentence at the State Correctional Institute in Muncie, Pennsylvania for the death of their son. The phenomenal growth of D.A.D. resulted, in part, from activists' strategy of using Sharon's case to call attention to the existence of postpartum illness. The movement has had less success in winning either a pardon or early parole for Sharon Comitz.

When activists organize on behalf of women accused of murdering their children, they have in mind multiple goals. One aim is to help individuals by raising funds for the defense and by mobilizing public support for a pardon or a reduction in sentence. But organizers view these campaigns as collective strategies for opposing the criminalization of maternal conduct and advocating more therapeutic approaches. That the tragedy of infanticide can serve as an impetus for questioning the institution of motherhood is illustrated by a recent grassroots campaign in the predominantly working-class and African American neighborhood of Linden in Columbus, Ohio. After a resident killed her two children and then committed suicide, a group of mothers organized a series of meetings to make the community aware of the problems facing single mothers and to mobilize support for helping these women care for their families.

The combination of personal change and institutional transformation embraced by women's self-help movements signals that the distinction in writings on the contemporary women's movement and on social movements in general between strategic and identity-oriented movements has been too rigidly drawn. As the postpartum support group movement illustrates, women's self-help uses collective identities that draw upon the discourse of feminism as a critical resource for calling institutions to account for sustaining, reproducing, and legitimating the centrality of women's position as mothers. Once we begin to recognize the broader implications of the various strategies of resistance and change employed by women's self-help, then we must ask what are the implications of this modern repertoire of activism for the reconstruction of gender relations in American society. In the next and final chapter, I look out from the postpartum self-help movement to examine the connections between gender and contemporary women's self-help movements.

THE REVOLUTION FROM WITHIN

GENDERING SOCIAL MOVEMENT THEORY

P ERHAPS THE first recorded case of a woman afflicted with post-partum depression who made something positive of her condition can be found in *The Book of Margery Kempe*, the earliest known autobiography of an English person. Margery Kempe, born around 1373 to a prosperous family in King's Lynn, married at the age of twenty and, after the birth of her first child, fell into madness. Although herself illiterate, she dictated to two clerics the story of her difficult pregnancy and labor, her fear of death and damnation, and her experience of going "out of her mind . . . amazingly disturbed and tormented with spirits for half a year, eight weeks and odd days." Although she regained her sanity through a vision of Christ, she was a changed woman. She developed a strong aversion to sexual relations with her husband and eventually, after the birth of fourteen children, persuaded him to live chastely with her. She also began to weep and wail loudly and profusely (a trait that priests found most annoying), to engage in conversations with Christ, and to dedicate her life to pilgrimages. Her behavior won her both admirers and enemies, some of them quite powerful figures in the Church.

Whether or not Margery Kempe's story can be likened to a modern American woman's experience of postpartum depression, what is striking is her transformation of illness into a source of strength, even if she attributed it all to divine providence. What is different is the solitary nature of her quest, although she did engage in one instance of what might be described as self-help. One day she met a man, much distressed, who explained that his wife had just had a baby and gone out of her mind, roaring and crying and striking out. Kempe went to see her, talked with her and prayed for her, and reported with evident satisfaction that the woman then regained her sanity.

Like Margery Kempe, who turned her tears to the service of heaven, offering solace along the way to at least this one woman, a group of mostly white, middle-class, American women are in the process of transforming their deviant emotions following the birth of a child into a collective challenge to the meaning of motherhood. We have seen how the guilt, anxiety, depression, and anger that some women experience come as a bolt out of the blue, given the societal emphasis on the "joys of motherhood" and the profound silence of the medical and mental health professions, at least until recently, about the "possibility" of postpartum depression. Coming together to support one another, women in the postpartum self-help movement have forged an alternative discourse that both undermines the traditional expectations and at the same time confirms them.

In the face of demanding responsibilities for family and work and cutbacks in medical and social services, women have insisted both on greater male participation in childrearing and on more attentiveness from medicine and mental health, in this way combining feminist and therapeutic solutions. What started as small networks among already committed feminists who found their realities of motherhood almost diametrically opposed to what they had anticipated has grown into two social movement organizations with wide appeal. In the course of giving and getting support over the telephone, in face-to-face groups, by reading self-help books and watching talk shows, and by participating in pen-pal networks, women have built communities in which feminism reaches a whole new constituency. In the process of constructing a collective identity, women in the postpartum support group movement have given larger social significance to experiences that otherwise might be seen exclusively as individual problems. Not only do self-help participants empower themselves, but they also challenge the gender code embedded in medical, legal, and mental health institutions.

Yet the metamorphosis of feminism as it has combined with the therapeutic frame of contemporary women's self-help, although not deserving of the scorn heaped upon it by feminist critics, has limitations as well as possibilities. For treating women's negative response to motherhood as an illness can, ironically, reaffirm the model of the self-sacrificing and blissful mother by insinuating that therapy and medication are the keys to normal motherhood. But I have argued that the turn toward therapy is less a sign of the decline of feminism as a political strategy than of the resilience of the sexual division of labor and the devaluation of the female role, and of American medicine's tendency to expand its domain to address women's problems.

I began this book by taking issue with those who have failed to acknowledge the connection between the varied manifestations of gender inequality and the characteristics and strategies peculiar to contemporary women's self-help movements. This study, I hope, will help debunk the myth that the therapeutic feminism that thrives in women's self-help is excessively concerned with women's weaknesses rather than with gender disadvantages, and with women's personal development rather than with political and social transformation. Certainly identity politics, which has been widely criticized by scholars and activists, comes naturally to modern feminism, which holds that male domination is accomplished through structural, cultural, interpersonal, and psychological means. That the kind of activism flourishing in today's self-help has been overlooked by the mainstream writings on social movements can be attributed, I think, to the fact that it is largely a female enterprise. Even if therapeutic feminism is beginning to diffuse into mixed-sex movements (such as the peace movement; the lesbian, gay, and bisexual movements; and the men's movement) and men are increasingly being drawn to the self-help genre to tackle problems (such as job loss, divorce, and parenting), the distinctiveness of women's self-help requires that we come to terms with the gendered nature of social movements.

Gender, or the process of differentiating the sexes and giving males advantage over females, is an organizing principle of all groups and a pervasive feature of social life. Inequality processes connected to gender, race, and class have as much effect on groups seeking to change society as on mainstream institutions. In an influential article published in 1985, Judith Stacey and Barrie Thorne summoned readers to launch what they deplored as the "missing feminist revolution" in sociology. In this last chapter, I take up their charge by using the postpartum support group movement as a starting point to ask a more general question that has only recently begun to capture sociologists' attention: What does a focus on gender add to our understanding of social movements? In considering this question, I also rely upon recent research by other scholars who are beginning to use the lens of gender to examine social protest. But it is not only the scholarship on social movements that comes up short when we scrutinize it for insights pertaining to women's self-help. Gender theory recently has been preoccupied with the ways women resist and promote changes in the gender order, most of the major theorists have yet to discover the rich body of scholarship on social movements. So we can see as well how the literature on social movements contributes a useful set of conceptual tools for those interested in understanding gender resistance, challenge, and change.

GENDERED SOCIAL MOVEMENTS

To consider social movements as gendered is to recognize that the concept of a two-gender system that constructs women to be the subordinates of men is central to the emergence, nature, and outcomes of social movements. Treating gender as an analytic category opens our eyes to the ways that all social movements—regardless of whether they are focused on issues pertaining specifically to women and irrespective of their sex composition—are engaged in the social construction of gender. Of course, the significance of gender is more obvious for some groups than for others. The redefinition of gender in contemporary lesbian feminist communities that separate masculinity and femininity from sexuality is fairly apparent. But gender is also affirmed in movements that do not evoke the language of femininity and masculinity or of gender conflict. In her autobiographical account of the Black Panther party, former member and Party head Elaine Brown recounts the way that the organizational practices and strategies of the party reproduced male domination. In her view, the party's male power rituals—its military structure, use of violence and aggression, and promotion of sexual rivalries—could be blamed not only for women's virtual absence from the black power struggle but also could be seen as serving as the seeds of the Panthers' destruction. So attention to gender will increase our understanding of processes influencing the nature and course of all forms of collective action. To develop this argument, I offer a framework that demonstrates how gender relates to social movement formation, mobilizing frames and identities, organization and strategies, and outcomes.

Gender as an Organizing Principle of Social Structures

One of the major premises of social movement scholars is that changes in the larger political and cultural environment can stimulate or discourage people from participating in collective action. The assumption that gender inequality is embedded in political, economic, legal, medical, human service, and other institutions suggests that shifts in gender policies and in the larger cultural climate with respect to women's sameness or difference from men are critical for understanding the changing contours of women's collective action. Nancy Whittier attributes feminists' preference for strategies that address internalized oppression in part to the conservative and antifeminist backlash of the 1980s that closed off the political domain. The election of an obviously antifeminist president, Ronald Reagan, fueled the growth of a grassroots religious right that mobilized to defeat the Equal Rights Amendment (ERA); campaigned against the Family and Medical Leave Act, which addressed women's need for maternity benefits; launched an attack on abortion rights; and accused the women's movement, as Pat Robertson flamboyantly charged, of encouraging "women to leave their husbands, kill their children, practice witchcraft, destroy capitalism, and become lesbians." Underlying the conservative political turn was a spirited debate over the meaning of gender, with feminists for the most part emphasizing the commonalities between women and men and antifeminists insisting on women's distinct nature and responsibilities.

In her study of the evolution of public policy with respect to pregnancy and motherhood, Lisa Vogel demonstrates that policies and strategies for addressing women's needs have historically been formulated either by treating women and men as the same and developing gender-neutral solutions, or by recognizing women's special needs as childbearers and mothers and providing female-specific benefits. Nineteenth- and early twentieth-century reformers tended for the most part to support special female labor legislation consistent with women's primary identity as mothers and nurturers. Beginning in the 1960s, however, the feminist campaign to formulate public policy directed to the needs of mothers and families switched to the sameness side of the sameness/difference divide. As Jane Mansbridge pointed out in her book *Why We Lost the ERA*, the Equal Rights Amendment—in many ways the quintessential expression of this sameness strategy—went down to defeat in 1982 largely because it denied women's special qualities and raised fears that women would be treated the same as men. Yet by the 1990s, policy concerning pregnancy and motherhood embodied in legislation, court opinions, government regulations, and employer practices was framed almost exclusively in terms of sameness rather than difference. For example, the Family and Medical Leave Act finally signed into law in 1993 after Democratic President Bill Clinton took office provides unpaid time off for both female and male employees for a variety of reasons, including pregnancy, childbirth, and care of a newborn or ill family member. It disregards, in other words, the gender specialness of pregnancy and motherhood.

The medical field is uniquely positioned to recognize the vocabulary of female difference spoken among American mothers who historically have gotten remarkably little support from the state. The way that childbirth and child care places women at a disadvantage in the United States is especially evident when we compare their circumstances to those of European working women, who enjoy comprehensive and for the most part government-funded maternity benefits and rights. As we have seen, in contrast to federal, state, and local political bodies, which turned away from women's problems in the 1980s, American medicine was willing to acknowledge women's burdens and to recognize the connection between women's social roles and their physical and mental health. The gender-neutral approach to women's health endorsed by mainstream feminists in the 1980s nevertheless blinded medicine to many health problems that are unique to women, such as postpartum illness. The historical tendency for medical professionals to use women's health issues to expand the boundaries of medicine, increase profits, and consolidate medical influence has in this instance worked to women's advantage. The entry of large numbers of women into the medical profession over the past decade has made medicine more receptive to women's claims. As a result, the demand for equal medical care has not automatically translated into the medical field denying women's differences by endorsing the mind-set "that a woman can either react physiologically like an honorary man, or she can lump it." The conservative political tide of the 1980s that began the erosion of the broad-based community mental health services put into place in the 1960s and '70s ironically made medicine a fertile ground for the growth of therapeutic feminism. For feminists, this choice of venues makes self-help a logical strategy for curbing the power of male-dominated medical knowledge and institutions. We would be hard pressed to find anyone who would deny, for example, that the breast-cancer movement is not actively involved in changing medical definitions of the disease when it estimates the scope of breast cancer to be of epidemic proportions or lobbies for increased federal funding for research and services.

Paul Burstein argues that politics proceeds in numerous relatively self-contained policy domains, with each site of struggle operating more or less autonomously with its own issues, actors, and processes. Understanding what R. W. Connell has termed the "gender regime"—or the pattern of power relations between men and women in the sociopolitical and cultural institutions concerned with a particular issue—provides insight into the broad range of external social and political factors that affect the mobilization, claims, tactics, and, ultimately, the success of social protest.

Division of Preexisting Networks along Gender Lines

As we have seen, the various support groups that lie at the heart of women's self-help are potential centers of feminist activism. Whether women cement their ties through face-to-face interaction, as did the two women who formed the first postpartum support groups, or through indirect channels of communication such as the telephone, the Internet, or the mass media, support groups represent the kinds of networks out of which social movements arise. Today's self-help movements might appear, at first glance, to be drastically different from those of the nineteenth and early twentieth centuries, and even of the 1960s and early '70s, but they all mobilize through the same fundamental social processes. As several recent studies have established, we cannot fully understand a movement's patterns of mobilization without attending to the power dynamics of gender, race, and class. These inequalities are embedded in the preexisting networks that provide incentives to get people to take the risks associated with participating in collective action, and they operate in insidious ways. Bernice McNair Barnett and Belinda Robnett, for example, attribute women's absence in formal leadership roles in the early civil rights movement to the gender exclusion of the black church. Doug McAdam traces women's lower rates of involvement in the 1964 Mississippi Freedom Summer campaigns to gender-bias among the recruiters and organizers. But gender does not always serve as a barrier to women's participation.

Gender divisions can actually facilitate mobilization, as has often been the case in sex-segregated women's colleges, clubs, and associations, which have been fertile grounds for the growth of feminism. And gender differentiation almost everywhere tends to precipitate, at least among certain groups of women, the creation of informal interpersonal networks that make it possible for women to fulfill their responsibilities for the care and nurturing of children and family members and for household survival. Women's relational orientation, according to Phil Brown and Faith Ferguson, explains why women predominate in the toxic waste movement; they generally become activists after a child becomes ill and they begin to suspect the illness is caused by exposure to hazardous substances. Kevin Neuhouser describes gendered patterns of mobilization in mixed-sex social movements in Brazil, where women recruit participants in the female-dominated urban squatter settlement campaign through informal survival networks developed to exchange food, money, and the unpaid labor of children. The importance of the social role of motherhood for women's activism also helps us to understand why the low-income African American and Puerto Rican women studied by Nancy Naples consider their community advocacy work as "not political in the classical sense."

Work by sociologists of emotions calls attention to the ways that emotional experience and expression are differentiated on the basis of gender and reinforce the gendered division of labor. Even if ideas about a correct maternal role are giving way as the practice of motherhood is shifting and becoming more diverse, my research suggests that the affections and dispositions of motherhood have not succumbed so readily to change. Women essentially remain responsible for much of the "emotional work" of family and community life. It is astounding that so many mothers are able to provide the prescribed kind of continual love, caring, and responsibility for a child. It is little wonder that, for those women who cannot, postpartum illness has been such a recurring theme throughout history.

Women's high rates of depression, in particular, and the division of emotional labor, in general, have been the backdrop against which a booming women's therapeutic self-help industry has appeared. Focusing on experiences within the traditionally female domain that modern self-help scrutinizes so intensely opens the door for social movement scholars to recognize how emotions figure into feminist resistance. Attending to the gender processes at work in both the informal interpersonal and the formal institutional networks that are the building blocks of collective action furthers our understanding, then, of the ways individuals come to participate in social movements.

Gender as a Mobilizing Frame

The postpartum support group movement provides a window through which we can glimpse the way feminism is being amplified to address the "caring work" that is so disproportionately allocated to women. Even the most vehement of critics would have to acknowledge that the language of gender difference and power is pervasive in women's self-help, serving as a framework for understanding the problems that trouble women. And that is precisely the point: gender holds a preeminent place in modern therapeutic discourse. Herein lies the paradox of women's self-help, if I might borrow Judith Lorber's term in her recent book *Paradoxes of Gender*.

Connecting people's problems to individual essences—and it is common for the continuous stream of advice and self-help books to link women's problems to gender—can reinforce the idea that masculinity and femininity are oppositional dichotomies. The very concept of a two-gender system distorts the realities of individual women's and men's lives, namely the varied expressions of femininity and masculinity and the fluidity of gender in everyday life. And it conceals the fact that, in many ways, women and men are far more alike than different. The paradox is that, in using gender as a mobilizing framework, women's self-help movements reinforce the very gender categories and hierarchy that figure into women's subordination. But gender distinctions, once in force, can also have the opposite effect by serving as a basis for resisting social control. For example, breast-cancer activists have politicized the assumption that women should hide the physical effects of breast cancer under clothes and with breast prostheses and reconstruction, and have openly refused to engage in these practices since, to them, hiding a missing breast shores up dominant conceptions of femininity as expressed through the female body.

To treat gender as an institution that gives meaning to our experiences and patterns our interactions requires that we acknowledge the centrality of gender processes in the collective identities, group consciousness, and solidarities on which social movements are built. This holds true even for groups that, on the surface, might appear to be unconcerned with gender issues but where gender stratification is, nevertheless, implicit. Only recently, for example, have scholars come to recognize how profoundly gendered the Nazi movement in Germany was. Not only was masculinity glorified and male bonding considered the foundation of the Nazi state, but gender oppositions served as the metaphor for the polarization of Jews as weak and emotional and "Aryans" as strong and rational. In her work on striking steelworkers, Mary Margaret Fonow notes that gender can frame men's and women's participation in the same struggle in different ways. For working-class men, the strike actions conveyed cultural standards of masculinity. But working-class women saw themselves as protesting the conditions of work in jobs that are stereotypically male, "jobs that in effect signified that they were 'not women.'" In this way, women's resistance to cultural standards of femininity was a factor in women's strike participation.

Myra Marx Ferree and William Gamson use the term "gendering" to characterize campaigns in which gender distinctions are explicit and central to the discourse and mobilizing strategies of activists. They contrast the movement for abortion rights in the United States—where abortion is linked to a larger culture war that includes gay and lesbian rights, "family values," welfare reform, school prayer, and gender relations—to the movement in Germany. In Germany, where abortion is a part of the state's family policy, the gendering of public discussion about abortion has been much less prominent, and women's movements play a less significant role in the national political debate. To take another example, gender differences were major components of women's organizing in the Buffalo lesbian community of the 1940s and '50s. By creating butch and fem identities that paralleled (although they did not precisely reproduce) the male-female roles in heterosexuality, lesbians managed to overcome their invisibility and create a public presence. In the mixed-sex peace movement in the United States, which historically has established close ties with feminism, gender has figured heavily into the movement's form and strategies. The importance of community-building, the nonhierarchical leadership structure, the value that activists placed on emotional expression, and the personalized politics found in the direct-action wing of the movement all stem from its emphasis on gender difference, in particular women's unique concerns as the nurturers of life.

One of the primary contributions of social movements is to take up the process of naming in ways that resonate with widely shared experiences. Activists develop collective action frames that get encoded in the discourse, symbols, and rituals of activists. A collective action frame, according to William Gamson, defines an injustice, empowers participants by suggesting they can do something about the injustice, and defines the "we," or the collective identity, whose interests will be realized through banding together around a common cause. We have seen how the acronym "D.A.D.," chosen at a moment's notice, evokes both a nonseparatist community in which women find validation and the reevaluation of men's parenting roles. To the extent that gender differences and hierarchy are ingrained in society, it is not surprising that images of masculinity and femininity are reproduced in the language and ideas that activists use to frame their messages, define themselves and their shared interests, and build solidarity. Only by connecting our analysis of activists' frames of meaning to the larger structure of gender relations, then, can we understand fully why social movements mobilize around particular sets of ideas and not others.

Gendered Organizations and Strategies

Formal organizations with clearly defined leadership are the kinds of groups social movement scholars have found to be the most effective for mounting challenges to political institutions. Women's self-help movements do not follow such a pattern. To be sure, the postpartum self-help movement gains direction from Depression After Delivery and Postpartum Support International, which serve as centers of strategic activity in the battle to bring attention and funds to the problem. But the crux of modern self-help is to be found in the social movement communities that coalesce loosely around the informal leadership and personal relationships stitched out of participants' giving and getting emotional and other very individualized kinds of support. These "communities of discourse" are structured around women's work of caring for people, and they make use of the language and practices of femininity both to build solidarity and to develop strategies of resistance to women's oppression. The postpartum support group movement employs community-building, discursive politics, and personalized political strategies to bring to light the realities of mothering where there is little social support or respect for childrearing and to challenge the cultural view of motherhood as intrinsically satisfying and fulfilling.

This type of organizing is typical of the way many feminist groups use politics in order to address the issues of gender inequality within society. In the Catholic Church, which has been so resistant to women's demands for change, activists participate primarily as members of local liturgical communities. These communities, known as "Women-Church," engage in practices such as storytelling, potluck meals, and leadership roundtables that articulate participants' commonalities as women and embody feminist values of collective structure to redefine women's relationships to the power of the Church. Of course, gendered social movement strategies are not always based in feminism. Kathleen Blee's research on women in the 1920's Ku Klux Klan highlights the way women drew on familial ties, traditions of church suppers and family reunions, and on women's gossip in the form of "poison squads" to spread a message of racial and religious hatred. That women's gendered experiences also figure into the organizational forms of political movements where women's participation is more indirect, is illustrated by Karen Beckwith's research on the Lancashire Women Against Pit Closures (WAPC). WAPC organized to support predominantly male miners' protests against the British government's 1992 announcement that it would close more than half of the remaining deep coal mines in Britain. To support miners and the threatened pits, women pitched camps that provided all the comforts of "home"—food, company, shelter, nurturing, a place to sleep, and warmth—and asserted their roles as working-class women in banners, songs, speeches, press releases, interviews, and other protest symbols.

In women's self-help, belief in fundamental differences between female and male values, whether they are seen as socially or biologically determined, is the basis for a prefigurative politics that asserts a distinctive women's community organized around female values and the primacy of women's relationships. This paves the way for the development of "emotion cultures" that cultivate a unique set of feeling rules and expression rules that both draw upon and challenge the dominant ideal of women as nurturers. Self-help organizations make explicit claims to an "ethic of caring," even if in reality the conflicts endemic to all social movements frequently erupt. The feminist emphasis on caring even provides a political rationale for female bonding. Activists justify references to each other as sisters, open expressions of love and affection, and caring and nurturant relationships on the grounds that they pose a challenge to societal pressures for women to orient themselves almost exclusively to the needs of men and children. To take an historical example, the white upper-middle-class members of the National Woman's Party who carried the torch of women's rights from the end of the suffrage campaign until the resurgence of the women's movement in the mid-1960s expressed strong bonds of friendship and joy over participating in the ERA campaign, leading one woman to exclaim that "It is as thrilling as a love affair, and lasts longer!!!"

The emotion cultures of women's self-help grow out of a conscious awareness of the significance of emotional control for upholding gender differences. Activists struggle to resist this imperative by encouraging women to express and to transform the emotions that arise from subordination, to redefine feeling and expression rules to reflect more desirable self-conceptions, and to declare solidarity with other women. We cannot fully understand the vitality of women's therapeutic self-help movements without recognizing the wide range of feelings generated by male domination and the way they figure into the self-conceptions, strategies, and forms displayed by these repertoires of collective action.

As we have seen, the emotion work that women do in caring for others and the kind of self-sacrificial love expected of mothers not only give meaning to women's deviant emotions but also organize women's resistance to oppression as well. Expressing anger, for example, is less acceptable for women than for men. When a mother feels and expresses anger toward the very persons she is expected to love and cherish, she is resisting strong gender norms. When she admits depression rather than basks in maternal satisfaction and pride, or guilt when the bonding she anticipates does not come automatically, or anxiety in connection with the enormous responsibilities of caring for her family, she abandons the script of American motherhood.

Modern women's self-help encourages women to express these feelings in a collective context. In most contemporary women's self-help movements, gender is central to the emotional vocabularies activists use to present new and more acceptable identities. But explicitly feminist self-help groups take the challenge to conventional gender definitions one step further by channeling the emotions tied to women's subordination into feelings more conducive to protest. Feminist organizations such as Sisters of the Yam, an African American women's recovery network described by bell hooks, encourage women to trade the fear and shame that follow from experiences linked to gender and racial oppression— such as sexual violence, forced sterilization, poverty, unemployment, and inadequate access to health care—for anger and pride. The antirape movement relies heavily upon strategies such as all-female "Take Back the Night" marches and survivor narratives to downplay the fear, guilt, and depression women suffer in the wake of victimization, emphasizing instead emotions that empower women. In effect, women's self-help plays a major role in challenging the emotion norms surrounding love and anger and is contributing to an historical shift in American society toward free expression, individualism, and self-development.

Caring and nurturant personal relationships are, in a way, the essence of all self-help groups, whether or not the group is explicitly feminist. But their significance, however important to the individuals involved, is as social as it is personal. In self-help groups, "the good of self is not separate from the network of care for others." For such relationships provide a point of connection and identification with others that is not only therapeutic but empowering, permitting participants to cultivate new understandings of their problems that run counter to orthodox and purely individual medical and mental health solutions. The collective redefinition of self is possible because the forms and strategies of the self-help genre are in many ways diametrically opposed to the organizations and structures that perpetuate gender inequality. In *Men and Women of the Corporation*, Rosabeth Kanter shows that gender differences in women's and men's behavior in large corporations is the result not of their characteristics as individuals but of features connected to the organizational structures themselves. Gender, she argues, is built into organizational roles that "carry characteristic images of the kinds of people that should occupy them."

If a masculine ethic of rationality and reason that necessitates setting emotions and personal considerations aside governs the workplace and the bureaucratic organizations that are the engines of modern societies, then feminist discourses rooted in women's historical experiences of nurturing and caring pose a fundamental challenge to the gendered logic of modern organizations. This logic is built upon what R. W. Connell describes as "hegemonic masculinity," or the image of the strong, authoritative, sexually potent leader with a family who keeps his emotions in check and his personal life under control. The emotion cultures of self-help, I think, express a rather different kind of logic, one that is essentially feminine. Self-help groups reproduce the discourses and practices of femininity, bringing to the forefront questions of emotionality, sexuality, procreation, and bodies, aspects of human life that generally are suppressed in the organizations of modern industrialized societies. Whether mixed-sex and predominantly male self-help groups gain much of their current popularity from being femininized is a question that springs to mind. From his research on the AIDS movement, Barry Adam suggests that this may just be the case. Adam uncovers a culture of coping among AIDS self-help communities that has broken through the strong cultural taboos that suppress intimate caring relationships between men.

By recognizing the pervasiveness of gender categorization and the way it interacts with race, class, sexuality, and ethnicity to serve as an organizing principle both for social identities and for social structures, we gain, then, considerable insight into a set of processes that shapes the structures, cultures, strategies, and identities of social movements. In the case of many United States social movements, the influence of multiple statuses is apparent. Ignoring gender dynamics has led to a failure to understand a major potential for internal divisions as well. To treat gender as an institution whose manifestations are cultural, structural, and interactional forces us also to recognize, as Nancy Whittier has argued, that social movements are as much about culture, community, and identity as about formal organizations and strategic action. Bringing gender squarely into the analysis of social protest perhaps even leads us to ask whether collective action repertoires might themselves be gendered.

Gender Change as an Outcome of Collective Action

I began this study of the postpartum self-help movement with a fundamental question that has troubled me for nearly two decades, ever since one of my oldest and dearest friends—who was also the most radical feminist I knew at the time—announced she was an alcoholic. I couldn't have been more surprised. Since then I have watched her come to terms with being an incest survivor and, after bottoming out, putting her life back together. Through all of these years, I have never doubted the role feminism has played in her journey. But on more than one occasion I have asked her whether she considers her personal political project to have had an impact on changing the system of gender inequality that she holds responsible for her problems. In this last section I address this question head on. To what extent do the ideas and strategies of women's self-help, tied as they are to notions of gender difference and hierarchy, bring about any real changes in the broader gender order? Is women's self-help an effective strategy for challenging women's subordination? Or does the tendency of women's self-help to mobilize around the language of femininity, to construct organizations that affirm women's caring roles, and to use personalized and expressive political strategies end up reinscribing gender?

Before taking up these questions, I should note that scholars of social movements have had a great deal less to say about what social movements accomplish than about how they mobilize. Reviewing the main writings on the effects of social movements, Suzanne Staggenborg discovers three main types of outcomes: political and policy, mobilization, and cultural outcomes. Conventional social movement wisdom would probably lump gender changes in with the shifts in norms, roles, identities, behaviors, and consciousness generally thought of as cultural change. While Staggenborg's scheme is an improvement over writings that adopt a strict political interpretation of success, it needs further refinement if we are interested in scrutinizing the effects social movements are having on gender relations. Gender is an institution that serves its own particular purpose—just like other core institutions such as the family, religion, the economy, and politics. The purpose of gender as an institution is "to construct women as a group to be the subordinates of men as a group." The question I am interested in here is to what extent women's self-help challenges and transforms gender as a social institution.

In the process of completing this research, I have been convinced that the postpartum support movement, like many contemporary self-help campaigns, is deeply engaged in the social reconstruction of gender and the female role. To the extent that motherhood is so closely intertwined with femininity in American society, appropriating the label of postpartum illness is subversive of the gender status quo. For, like women's hysteria of the nineteenth century, postpartum illness announces women's lack of conformity to a maternal script so fundamental to the social construction of gender that to violate it is to go against the very grain of what it means to be a woman. But the difference between modern self-help activists and nineteenth-century hysterics (or Margery Kempe) is significant. By making their claims within the context of a collective struggle, self-help activists are questioning the ideology and institutions that reinforce the view that "all women need to be mothers, all mothers need their children, and all children need their mothers." Further, bringing the discussion of deviant motherhood into public discourse breaks down the boundary between "good" and "bad" mothers, a division that has historically been used to set apart the celebrated white, middle-class ideal from presumably less exemplary single, African American, Latina, Jewish, lesbian, working-class, and other marginalized mothers. In addition to calling attention to the diversity of motherhood, the postpartum support group movement poses a clear challenge to gender oppositions by opening its arms to fathers and husbands and by urging fathers to become more involved in raising their children.

As Joshua Gamson argues, social movement scholars have overemphasized the role modern movements play in fashioning new collective identities that accentuate the commonalities among a group of people. In their attempt to renegotiate the meaning of femininity, women's self-help movements, like many contemporary social movements, must first struggle to break down the rigid gender categories that are the basis of women's subordination. If women's self-help finds its strength in the impulse to take apart the social categories of femininity and masculinity by highlighting the diversity of femininities and masculinities, what most critics object to is the weight some groups give to biological differences between women and men. But does attentiveness to biologically based questions—particularly as they relate to women's health and mental health issues—necessarily mean that self-help activists have abandoned the pursuit of gender equality begun by feminists in the 1960s and '70s?

Even if the postpartum support group movement sometimes stresses gender distinctions, the belief in female difference serves, as we have seen, as a rationale for support group structures and other forms of organizing that do not perpetuate gender hierarchy. For instance, in a society that hails selfless altruism as the chief maternal virtue, self-help provides a place where mothers themselves can turn for nurturance. When examining the results of women's self-help, it is essential that we recognize, then, the way that this collective action repertoire disrupts gender differentiation and inequality processes embedded in organizations and everyday interactions.

But modern women's self-help contributes to the reconstruction of gender in another very profound way. Feminist theories have long treated the ideological and structural division between the "public" sphere of states and markets and the "private" sphere of family and kinship as basic to the organization of gender and the devaluation and subordination of women. In the 1980s, when the feminist organizations that had emerged in the late 1960s receded into the background, women's "truth-telling" gained nationwide visibility. On television talk shows, in an explosion of self-help writings, in reading groups, in professional networks that support women in the workplace, on the Internet, and in twelve-step and other therapeutic support groups, women began to tell their own stories of sexual abuse, violence from men in their households, sexual harassment, lifelong struggles with depression, and much more. The postpartum self-help movement emerged as part of the nationwide diffusion of small groups interested in connecting women's private and public worlds. By moving the discussion of deviant motherhood—especially of the private and painful experiences of white, middle-class mothers—into the public domain, women who have organized around postpartum illness have brought to light the heavy demands on modern mothers and are calling attention to the way that maternal self-sacrifice undermines women's identities and well-being. In telling their stories, women disrupt the divisions between "private" and "public" that have been central to the subordination of women. And by so doing, they alert scholars of gender to a new wave of collective action aimed at the cultural and political liberation of women.

Thus, to paraphrase Marge Piercy, two women talk on the telephone, three or four form a support group, a dozen start an organization, a hundred flock to a national conference, thousands read Ann Landers or watch Oprah Winfrey. Or, in Gloria Steinem's words:

> It doesn't matter whether we call them testifying or soul sessions as in the civil rights movement; consciousness-raising or rap groups as in early feminism; covens, quilting bees, or women's circles as in women's history; or councils of grandmothers, "speaking bitterness" groups, or revolutionary cells as in diverse cultures. The crucial thing is that they are free, no bigger than an extended family, personal/political—and everywhere.

Those of us interested in understanding the way that gender change is taking place in the contemporary American landscape ignore at our own peril these fundamentally collective forms of resistance going on all around us, every day, all across the country.

APPENDIX

POSTPARTUM SUPPORT GROUPS

Name & Location	Leadership	Meeting Site & Frequency	Group Size	Group Age in 1996
Postpartum Depression/ Psychosis Support Phoenix, AZ	peer	home 1/month	12	2 yrs.
Postpartum Assistance for Mothers Castro Valley, CA	professional	unspecified 2/month	5–7	7.5 yrs.
Beyond Baby Blues & Postpartum Health Alliance Folsom, CA	professional	unspecified 2/month	6–12	1 mo.
Postpartum Support Group Fresno, CA	peer	home 2/month	8	2 yrs.
Postpartum Assistance for Mothers Lafayette, CA	professional	clinic 4/month	5–7	7.5 yrs.
Postpartum Mood Disorders Clinic San Diego, CA	professional	clinic 4/month	8–15	10 yrs.
Christian Assistance for Postpartum Depression San Jose, CA	peer	home 1/month	16	4 yrs.
Postpartum Assistance for Mothers San Jose, CA	peer	phone contact mainly	100	6 yrs.
Circle of Stone Santa Rosa, CA	peer	home 2/month	5–6	2 mos.
M.O.M.S. (Mothers Offering Mothers Support) Lodi, CA	peer	home 1/month	2–4	1.5 yrs.
Postpartum Support Group Toronto, Canada	peer	home 2/month	1–6	7 yrs.
Pacific Postpartum Support Society Vancouver, Canada	peer	varies 4/month	8	10 yrs.
M.O.M.S. New Haven, CT	peer	home varies	varies	unknown
Postpartum Disorders Therapy Group Chicago, IL	professional	hospital 4/month	6	3 yrs.
D.A.D. Central MA	peer	hospital 1/month	up to 17	unknown
D.A.D. Marshfield, MA	peer	unspecified 1/month	varies	3.5 yrs.

Name & Location	Leadership	Meeting Site & Frequency	Group Size	Group Age in 1996
Postpartum Support Group Middlesex, MA	peer	unspecified dormant	varies	2 yrs.
D.A.D. Springfield, MA	professional	hospital 1/month	0–16	2.5 yrs.
D.A.D. Grand Rapids, MI	professional	hospital 2/month	6–10	3 yrs.
Mothers with Postpartum Depression Royal Oak, MI	professional	hospital 2/month	6–10	3 yrs.
Postpartum Adjustment Support Group St. Louis, MO	professional	hospital 4/month	2–8	2 yrs.
Postpartum Support Group Hackensack, NJ	peer	hospital 1/month	varies	1 yr.
D.A.D. Montclair, NJ	peer	hospital 1/month	2–6	2 yrs.
D.A.D. Newark, NJ	peer	unspecified 1/month	15	6 yrs.
D.A.D. South NJ	peer & professional	hospital 2/month	3–5	4 yrs.
P.M.S. Support Group New Jersey	professional	hospital 1/month	4–10	unknown
Capital District PPD Support Group Albany, NY	peer	unspecified 2/month	8–10	4 yrs.
D.A.D. Erie County, NY	peer	home 1/month	25	2.5 yrs.
Postpartum Adjustment Support Group Long Island, NY	professional	unspecified 2-4/month	3–5	1 yr.
Welcome Baby Greensboro, NC	professional	unspecified varies	10	2 yrs.
Duke Postpartum Support Program Raleigh, NC	professional	hospital	2–8	3 yrs.
Northeast Ohio D.A.D. Akron, OH	peer & professional	home 1/month	6–7	5 yrs.

POSTPARTUM SUPPORT GROUPS

Name & Location	Leadership	Meeting Site & Frequency	Group Size	Group Age in 1996
D.A.D. Cincinnati, OH	peer	YWCA 1/month	4	7 yrs.
Postpartum Depression Support Group Salem, OR	peer	home 1/month	4	2 yrs.
D.A.D. Doylestown, PA	peer	hospital 2/month	4	11 mos.
Depression & Anxiety After Delivery Harrisburg, PA	peer	Woman Care East 1/month	5	6 yrs.
Parents' Network Philadelphia, PA	professional	unspecified 4/month	6–12	9 yrs.
Postpartum Support Group Philadelphia, PA	peer	hospital 2/month	3–6	4 yrs.
D.A.D. Southeastern, PA	peer	unspecified 2/month	5–6	8.5 yrs.
Weeding Out the Blues State College, PA	professional	church 1/month	5–10	6 mos.
Postpartum Support Providence, RI	peer	home 1/2/month	varies	unknown
D.A.D. Fort Worth, TX	peer	parent education center 1/month	10	10 mos.
D.A.D. Salt Lake City, UT	professional	hospital 4/month	6–12	7 yrs.
PPD Support Group Burlington, VT	peer	coffeehouse 1/month	3–10	2 yrs.
Postpartum Support Group Hampton Roads, VA	peer	unspecified varies	2	5 yrs.
Postpartum Support Group Woodbridge, VA	peer	home 4/month	5	8 wks.
D.A.D. Tacoma, WA	peer	home 1/month	varies	5 yrs.

NOTE: Source of data is mailed survey of Depression After Delivery telephone volunteers, 1994. Information about local support groups is available from the National Office of Depression After Delivery, P.O. Box 1282, Morrisville, PA 19067. Or call D.A.D. at 1-800-944-4PPD.

NOTES

NOTES TO CHAPTER 1

page number

1 "Rock-a-by, Baby" is as found in Commins 1941. The authorship of "Rock-a-by, Baby" is generally credited to Effie Canning Carlton, who in 1874 put to music the words of the Mother Goose rhyme. Then a young girl of fifteen, she was caring for a neighbor's restless child in an outdoor hammock. The melody is believed to have originated in 1854 in Nebraska with an American Indian woman.

2 For discussions on "puerperal insanity," see Theriot 1990 and 1993.

3 The quote on "there is disagreement . . ." is from Hamilton 1992a, 18.

3 The most often cited early studies on postpartum illness are Dalton 1980; Welburn 1980; Atkinson and Rickel 1984a; 1984b; Saks, et al. 1985.

3 For the full transcript of Princess Diana's interview, see "Diana: The Interview," *London Daily Mirror*, November 22, 1995.

3 Reskin and Padavic (1994) report the incidence of mothers combining raising children and working outside the home; see pages 144–46.

4 For more on the controversies surrounding work and motherhood, see Luker 1984; Rothman 1989; Moen 1992; Berry 1993; Vogel 1993.

4 Thurer 1994 discusses the chasm opening up between conservative and liberal factions over "the family".

4 The variety of women's self-help groups is covered in McCormick 1992; Blum and Vandewater 1993; and Weiner 1994.

4 The quote "mothering must now be defined and controlled by women" is from Trebilcot 1984, 17.

5 Ryan 1992 and Ferree and Hess 1994 track this retrenchment of feminism in the 1980s.

5 Analyses of the political and abortion policy struggles in the 1980s appear in Gelb and Palley 1982; Mansbridge 1986; Staggenborg 1991.

5 For more information on the feminism backlash, see Faludi 1991; Ferree and Martin 1995; Whittier 1995

6 The evolution of the contemporary women's movement is reviewed in Taylor and Rupp 1993; Taylor and Whittier, 1993; Mansbridge 1995; Whittier 1995.

6 The quote of "rewriting through language texts . . ." is from Katzenstein 1995, 40.

7 Criticisms of the self-help culture can be found in Kaminer 1992, 1993; Haaken 1993; Tavris 1993; and Wolf 1994.

8 To illustrate how the recovery movement treats women's victimization as caretakers as a therapeutic rather than a social issue, see Beattie 1987.

8 On support groups, see Katz 1993; Sered 1994; Wuthnow 1994.

9 Throughout this book, I use the terms "modern," "late modern," "postindustrial," and "postmodern." Strictly speaking, I think of modernization as the processes of social change initiated by industrialization. Postmodernity, on the other hand, signals the rise of the information age and the social developments associated with a postindustrial society. In my mind the question as to whether postmodernity has brought about fundamental changes in social patterns remains to be answered.

9 On the self-help industry in the 1990s and its function, see Katz 1993; Hochschild 1994; and Wuthnow 1994.

9 The function of anonymous authorities in contemporary society and their place in helping people deal with emotional problems are discussed in Giddens 1991; Hochschild 1994. The role of the medical establishment in this burgeoning industry is looked at in Conrad and Schneider 1980; Starr 1982. The impact of feminism in social services is covered in Skocpol 1992; Gordon 1994; Ferree and Hess 1994; Matthews 1994; Gagne 1995.

10 Giddens 1991 analyses the interconnections between social institutions and personal life in the modern world of organizations and bureaucrati-

zation. He shows how sociology and the social sciences contribute to the institutional reflexivity of modern social life by providing new opportunities for self-development.

10 In participatory projects, the researcher seeks to blur the boundaries between the researcher and those who are the subjects of the research. See Stanley and Wise 1983; Cancian 1992.

11 On feminist research, see Fonow and Cook 1991; Mies 1991; Cancian 1992; Reinharz 1992.

11 To approximate the quasi-experimental design that the sponsoring agent wanted, I originally compared the experiences of the women who self-identified as having experienced postpartum illness in the year following the birth or adoption of a child to a "normal" sample of fifty women who had given birth or adopted within the past year. Perhaps the most interesting finding from this comparison is how little difference there was between the groups in terms of women's actual emotional responses to motherhood. The main difference was in the labels women used to make sense of their feelings. See Taylor 1987.

12 The interview philosophy and methodology are discussed in Smith 1979; Oakley 1981; Collins 1989; Krieger 1991; Mies 1991; Reinharz 1992; Taylor and Rupp 1991.

13 For material about women's self-help literature, see Simonds 1992; Hochschild 1994.

13 The quote "fixation on gender war" is from Heaton 1995, 47.

14 Gender and its role are discussed in Kessler and McKenna 1978; Connell 1987; Smith 1987; Reskin 1988; Acker 1990; Thorne 1993; Lorber 1994; Reskin and Padavic 1994.

14 I rely upon Judith Lorber's conceptualization of gender as an institution, which emphasizes the structural, symbolic, interactional, and institutional basis of gender behavior and meanings.

14 The "doing of gender" quote is from West and Zimmerman 1987, 126.

14 The quote "signifying power relations" comes from Scott 1988, 42.

14 Connell 1992 uses the concept of "hegemonic masculinity" to emphasize the privileged position of white, economically successful, and heterosexual men relative to other less powerful groups of men.

14 See Collins 1990 for discussion of "matrix of domination."

14 On motherhood and its connection to gender inequality, see Firestone 1970; Rich 1976; Chodorow 1978; Huber and Spitze 1983; Chafetz 1990; Jones 1984; Rossi 1984; Adams 1994; Glenn, Chang, and Forcey 1994; Jores and Laslet 1995; Ross 1995; Ruddick 1989; Rothman 1989; Collins 1990.

15 Discussions of the fluidity of gender roles can be found in West and Zimmerman 1987; Butler 1990; Stacey 1991; West and Fenstermaker 1995; and Chodorow 1995.

15 The description of "sissies" and "tomboys" is in Thorne 1993, 121–25.

15 On black mothers, see Jones 1985; Stack and Burton 1994.

15 On infanticide, see Hine and Wittenstein 1981; Roberts 1995. On the use of depression, psychoses, and physical illness as oppositional acts, see Ehrenreich and English 1973; Smith-Rosenberg and Rosenberg 1973.

15 The quote, "Resisting is a very different process . . ." is from W. Gamson 1995, 6.

16 For analyses of the significance of social movements for gender change, see Huber 1976; Chafetz 1990; Taylor and Whittier 1992; Melucci 1994).

16 The gendered structure of social movements is examined in West and Blumberg 1990; McAdam 1991; Naples 1991; Barnett 1993; Brown and Ferguson 1995; Neuhouser 1995; Robnett forthcoming.

16–17 For classical definitions of social movements, see Lofland 1985; Turner and Killian 1987; Gusfield 1989.

17 On the distinction between expressive and instrumental movements, see Blumer 1969.

17–18 The term new social movement theory is often used to refer to the perspective of several mainly European writers, including Foucault 1980, 1986; Habermas 1984, 1987; Giddens 1991; Touraine 1981, 1985, 1992; Melucci 1989, 1994. For an overview of the new social movement approach, see Klandermans and Tarrow 1988.

18 For more on the resource mobilization model, see Oberschall 1973; W. Gamson 1975; McCarthy and Zald 1977; Tilly 1978; McAdam 1982; Jenkins 1983; Zald and McCarthy 1987; McAdam, McCarthy, and Zald 1988; Tarrow 1989; Jenkins and Klandermans 1995; Traugott 1995.

18 For works that conjoin various social movement models, see Morris and Mueller 1992; Laraña, Johnston, and Gusfield 1994; Tarrow 1994; Johnston and Klandermans 1995; Kriesi, Koopmans, Duyvendak, and Giugni 1995.

19 On the high level of knowledge in some self-help groups, see P. Brown 1992; S. Epstein 1996.

20 For more on what constitutes a self-help movement, see Gusfield 1994; Whittier 1995; Chesler and Chesney 1995. For benefits to participants, see Chesney and Chesler 1993.

20 On consensus movements, see Schwartz and Paul 1992 and Michaelson 1994.

20 Criticism of the self-help movement as a form of identity politics can be found in Boggs 1986; Kaufmann 1990; Plotke 1990.

NOTES TO CHAPTER 2

24 "Eat for Two" recorded by 10,000 Maniacs on *Blind Man's Zoo*, Elektra/Asylum Records, 1989.

28 The quote "a primal agony" is from Rich 1976, 161.

29 See McGrath, et al. 1990; Mirowsky and Ross 1995 for the incidence of depression in women and men. For studies on biological causes of depression in women, see Hamilton 1962, 1984; Dalton 1980; Hamilton, Parry, and Blumenthal 1988.

30 Sociological explanations of women's mental health are discussed in Miles 1988.

30 On the social causation approach, see Pearlin and Lieberman 1979; Mirowsky and Ross 1989; Hankin 1990; Menaghan 1990. On links between gender inequality and women's depression, see Gove and Tudor 1973; Gove and Geerken 1977; Tudor, Tudor, and Gove 1977; Thoits 1983; Ross, Mirowsky, and Huber 1983; Menaghan 1989; Mirowsky and Ross 1989.

30 Stack and Burton 1994 discuss the social support networks in place for African American mothers.

31 On labeling theory, see Scheff 1966; Broverman, et al. 1970; Chesler 1972; Gove 1975; Kaplan 1983; Schur 1984; Allen 1986; Lunbeck 1994; Dixon, Gordon, and Khomusi 1995.

32 For other writers who discuss the lack of attention to postpartum illness, see Nixon 1985; Hamilton 1992b.

32 On the medicalization perspective, see Zola 1972; Smith-Rosenberg and Rosenberg 1973; Ehrenreich and English 1979; Oakley 1979a; Conrad and Schneider 1980; Scully 1980; Oakley 1986; Fisher 1986; Ransdell 1990.

32 Strong 1979 questions the sociological bias underlying the medicalization perspective.

32 On the transformation of the mental health industry, see P. Brown 1985; Kirk and Kutchins 1992.

33 On women's own role in the construction of medicine and mental health care as gendered practices, see Leavitt 1986; Martin 1987; Rothman 1989; Theriot 1990; Broom 1991; Haaken 1993.

33 Poststructural analysis of mental health and gender issues can be found in Foucault 1973, 1980; Smith 1990. On feminist poststructural writings about the effects of psychiatric discourse on women, see Weedon 1987; Smith 1988; Leahy 1994.

33 For studies that demonstrate the self-initiated basis of most mental health treatment, see Gove and Geerken 1977; Gove 1980; Thoits 1985.

35 The term "emphasized femininity" is from Connell 1987, 186. As it is linked to the private areas of home and sexuality and reinforced in popular and expert discourses, see Smith 1990.

36 In an effort to find some meaningful criteria for selecting among the dozens of self-help books on pregnancy and childbirth, I have relied most heavily (though not exclusively) on a list of the "top ten" books listed in MacPherson 1990.

37 In recent years, self-help organizations have called attention to a variety of postpartum conditions—including depression, panic disorder, obsessive compulsive disorder, and psychosis—suffered by new mothers. As a result, postpartum self-help groups increasingly use the term "postpartum mood disorders" to describe the range of problems with which they are concerned.

37 Competing constructions of motherhood are discussed in Nock 1987; Ireland 1993; Seguara and Pierce 1993; Collins 1992; Glenn 1994.

37–38 Jane Israel Honikman, "Cries for Help from Postpartum Women," speech in personal papers of Jane Israel Honikman, Santa Barbara, CA.

38 For a discussion of the importance of submerged activist networks for the reconstruction of identity in modern societies, see Melucci 1989; Taylor and Whittier 1992.

38 The quotation is from "Postpartum Illness Feels Like a Thief," *Depression After Delivery Newsletter* (Fall 1989), p. 3.

40 The quote "to bathe in the glow of maternal love" is from DeLyser 1989, 282.

40 For an analysis of the history and functions of bonding theory, see Eyer 1992.

40 On feminist biological determinist views of motherhood, see Snitow 1990; Vogel 1993.

40 On biology and women's subordination, see Firestone 1970. On biology and women's empowerment, see Rich 1976; Chodorow 1978; Rossi 1984; Ruddick 1989.

40 The quote from *A Good Birth, A Safe Birth* (Korte and Scaer 1984) is on page 185.

40 The quote on "falling in love with your child" is from Arney 1980, 547.

40–41 Quote on "Not only weren't my feelings . . ." is from Eisenberg, Murkhoff, and Hathaway 1989, xxiii.

41 Quotes "not to feel guilty . . ." and "when the PPD begins to lift . . ." are from "Telephone Contact Guidelines," *Volunteer Update, Depression After Delivery Newsletter* (January 1991), p. 6.

41 The Hotchner quotes can be found on page 538.

41 Quote "not be judged harshly. . . ." is from Harberger, Berchtold, and Honikman 1992, 48.

41 On the functions of shame and guilt, see Scheff 1990.

41 Quote on "overwhelming rush of love . . ." is from O'Meara 1992, 2. Quote of "steals away their sense of motherhood" is from "Postpartum Illness Feels Like a Thief" in *Heartstrings* (Fall 1989).

41 The quote from Kleiman and Raskin's *This Isn't What I Expected* is on pages 47–48.

42 The quotes on offloading guilt are in Dix 1985, 185 and 196.

42 Resnick 1969 looks at the connection between maternal psychosis and child murders.

43 Barbara Katz Rothman defines patriarchal motherhood in her 1989 book *Recreating Motherhood*.

43 On the social and technological foundations of mothering, see Huber and Spitze 1983. On the patterns of mothering in society, see Birns and Hay 1988; Solinger 1992; Berry 1993; Glenn, Chang, and Forcey 1994.

43 The quote urging "a certain amount of 'special' help . . ." is from Romito 1989, 1433.

43–44 For more on how the medical establishment continues the supermom myth, see Ball 1987; Romito 1989; Beck 1992, 1993. For popular literature's contribution, see Bing and Colman 1980; DeLyser 1989; Eisenberg, Murkhoff, and Hathaway 1988.

44 For an example of the way medicine urges women to accommodate the female role, see Danforth 1982, 524.

44 See Berry 1993 for more on "father-care" and "other-care" as alternatives to "mother-care."

44 The quote advising husbands to "adapt to the changes they see . . ." is from Hickman 1991, 1.

44 "There is rarely an apprenticeship for parenthood" is from McMahon 1993, D1.

44–45 The quotes from *Mothering the New Mother* are on page 76.

45 For research documenting the relationship between sense of control and psychological distress, see Mirowsky and Ross 1986.

45 Self-help activists' discussion of the anxiety and fear associated with postpartum illness is found in Harberger, Berchtold and Honikman 1992.

45 Barbara R. Lewin, "The Moon and the Mythbegotten: Distortions About PPD," *Heartstrings* 3 (Winter to Spring 1993), p. 2.

45 The connection between loss and depression appears in most accounts of nonpostpartum depression, as evidenced by William Styron's observation that "loss in all of its manifestations is the touchstone of depression—in the progress of the disease and, most likely, in its origin." Analyzing the themes in depressed women's narratives, Dana Crowley Jack (1991) concludes that women's conformity to traditional notions of femininity—i.e., those that dictate that a woman submerge her own feelings and desires in order to cultivate, maintain, and preserve relationships with others—is a major factor in women's higher rates of depression.

46 For a discussion of the way black women's community activism contributes to "race uplift," see Gilkes 1983. For an explanation of the role of "other-mothers" in the extended network of parenting in black families, see Collins 1990, 65.

47 Kemper's (1978, 1987) structural theory of emotions centers on the significance of power and status inequalities in the production of emotions. Depression, according to this view, is produced by status deprivation, in this case by women's recognition that motherhood is not the esteemed role women expect it to be.

47–48 The passage from the obstetrics textbook is in Friederich 1982, 975.

48 On the working mother in medical literature, see Blum and Vandewater 1993.

48 Examples of research literature on maternal depression are Ross, Mirowsky, and Huber 1983; Hock and DeMeis 1990; McGrath, et al. 1990.

48 *Williams Obstetrics*, 19th ed., is edited by Cunningham et al. 1993.

48 How the medical and psychiatric world labels symptoms of postpartum depression is discussed in, for example, Gabbe, Niebyl, and Simpson 1991.

48 The passages quoted here are from Gitlin and Pasnau 1989, 1413 and 1420. These authors provide an overview of the medical perspective on postpartum illness, premenstrual syndrome, and post-hysterectomy depression.

48 See Romito 1990 for other recent summaries of medical research on postpartum disorders.

49 In 1995, women comprised 70 percent of the health care work force and nearly 40 percent of all medical students. Yet they continued to be in the minority as practicing physicians, held few positions of power, and exerted little influence on how research funds were allocated. For more, see Lorber 1984; Lawrence and Weinhouse 1994; Healy 1995.

49 Quote on the "possible adverse effects . . ." is from Romito 1989, 1443–46.

49 For more on hormonal/biological connections to postpartum illness, see Dalton 1980; Hamilton 1992b.

50 The quote on women being "miserable during one of the happiest times of their lives" is from Eisenberg, Murkoff, and Hathaway 1991, 398.

50 "The myth of blissful parenthood . . ." quote is from Harberger, Berchtold, and Honikman 1992, 46.

50 The quotes about postpartum emotions being "the little sister" of "severe illnesses" are from Harberger, Berchtold, and Honikman 1992, 45.

51 The passage on the joy of Mother's Day is from *Heartstrings* Spring 1991, 3.

51 For a sociological explanation of depression as social distress, see Mirowsky and Ross 1989. See Jack 1991 for a psychological theory and Kemper for a social psychological theory that links women's depression to conformity to the traditional feminine role.

51 For more on anger and depression and mental illness, see Weissman and Paykel 1974; Kemper 1978; Ehrenreich and English 1979; Frye 1983; Cancian and Gordon 1988; Mirowsky and Ross 1989, 1995.

53 Studies of lesbian mothers can be found in McCormick 1992; Lewin 1994. For more on the racially charged rhetoric and policies that affect black mothers, see Solinger 1992.

54 Medical text references to women's postpartum anger can be found in Tauber 1984; Cherry, Burkowitz, and Kase 1985; Gleicher 1985; Sciarra 1989.

54 The quote from *Pregnancy and Childbirth* is on page 536.

54–55 The quotes from *Jane Fonda* are on page 259.

55 For an example of a movement article critical of the male-dominated medical establishment, see Anonymous, "Depression During Pregnancy . . . One Woman's Story," 1988.

55 The excerpt from Honikman's untitled speech is from circa 1984 and is part of her collection of personal papers in Santa Barbara, CA.

55 The remarks of Dagmar Celeste come from a speech given at the National Women's Studies Association conference, June 21, 1990, Akron, OH.

55 For a discussion of the critical stance many self-help groups take toward medicine, see Simonds and Rothman's 1992 study of self-help for grieving mothers.

55–56 To illustrate how the postpartum support group movement encourages women to cast off the sick role in favor of the survivor identity, see Berchtold 1991, 3.

56 On symptoms of psychological distress, see Kemper 1978; Pearlin and Lieberman 1979; Mirowsky and Ross 1989.

57 On the common occurrence of "baby blues," see Oakley 1979b; Stern and Kruckman 1983. Saks, et al. 1985. Atkinson and Rickel 1984 look at more severe depression associated with the postpartum period.

57 The Freud quote is cited in Lunbeck 1994, 306.

57 In *Discipline and Punishment,* Foucault 1979 argues that women's bodies have become a focal point for the exercise of power. Through their discourses and practices, institutions such as medicine, science, and the law have, according to Foucault, pathologized women's biological and reproductive processes.

NOTES TO CHAPTER 3

59ff Quotes and synopses from the *Donahue* show are taken from *Donahue* Transcript #05206 of the show aired May 20, 1986. Available from Multimedia Entertainment, Inc., Cincinnati, OH.

60 A written evaluation of psychotic dissociation is contained in a letter from Joseph B. Silverman, M.D., a psychiatrist who evaluated Sharon Comitz, to Lianne C. Scherr, A.C.S.W. This information was part of a report prepared for Sharon Comitz's sentencing in August 1985. These data are from the organizational files of D.A.D., Morrisville, PA.

61 For further discussion of the way that the larger political, social, and cultural climate figure into the development of social movements, see McAdam 1982; Tilly 1978; McAdam, McCarthy, and Zald 1988; Ferree 1994; Jenkins and Klandermans 1995; Tarrow 1994; Gamson and Meyer forthcoming.

61 The importance of group organization and other internal resources for the coalescence of a social movement is documented in Gamson 1975; McCarthy and Zald 1977; and Staggenborg 1991.

61 The construction of collective identity in social movements is treated in Melucci 1989; Hunt, Benford, and Snow 1994; Taylor and Whittier 1992; Rupp 1994; Whittier 1995.

61 On the significance of collective actions frames for the mobilization of protest, see Snow, Rochford, Worden, and Benford, 1986; Snow and Benford 1988; and Snow and Benford 1992.

62 For more on the continuities linking social movements, see Rupp and Taylor 1987; Meyer and Whittier 1994.

62 "Movement families" is from McAdam 1995, 218.

62 On the role of women's associations in American history, see Epstein 1981; Yee 1992; Scott 1992.

62 On the antifeminist backlash in the 1980s, see Marshall 1989; Faludi 1991; Ferree and Hess 1994; Whittier 1995.

63 For more on the early women's health movement, see Ruzek 1978; Zimmerman 1987; Davis 1991.

63 Carol Downer's words are found in Zimmerman 1987, 459.

63 For more information on the variety and topics covered in the women's health movement, see Davis 1991.

63–64 For more on the Boston Women's Health Collective, see Beckwith 1985. The quote is from Beckwith 1985 and is found in Zimmerman 1987, 457.

64 On the role of women's culture in feminist self-help, see Taylor and Rupp 1993.

65 On separatist women's communities, see Taylor and Whittier 1992; Staggenborg, Eder, and Sudderth 1993/94.

65 Zimmerman 1987 covers feminist health centers as alternatives to traditional medical care.

65 On the evolution to therapy in the 1970s, see Morgen 1986, 1995.

65 Ironically, it was engaging in political work to target the social institutions and policies that promote male violence that led some feminist self-help groups to stray so far from their earlier dreams of changing the institutions thought to be the root of women's problems (Schechter 1982; Martin 1990; Matthews 1994). During the 1970s, conservative forces mounted a strong antifeminist attack to defeat the ERA and overturn the legalization of abortion. Even if the growing conservatism of the state in the 1980s can be seen as partially responsible for coopting many early feminist self-help groups into more conventional individualistic psychological explanations and therapeutic solutions, as Nancy Matthews notes in her study of the feminist antirape movement, "the roots of a more therapeutically oriented movement were there all along" (1994, 8).

65 Cassell 1977 describes the consciousness-raising groups that fueled modern feminism.

65 For more on feminist psychotherapy, see Allen 1986; Mirkin 1994.

65 "The revolution from within" is from Steinem 1992a.

66 Simonds 1992 examines what self-help reading reveals about gender relations in contemporary American culture.

66–67 On the feminization of psychiatry, see Philipson 1993.

67 A strong social movement orientation continues in the 1990s in self-help groups such as antirape and battered women's collectives that had their origins in the modern women's movement; see Ferree and Martin 1995.

67 On the variety of self-help campaigns, see Zimmerman 1987; Van Willigen 1993; Gagne 1995; Ferree and Hess 1994; Levi 1995.

67 I conducted the interview with Jane Mansbridge on March 26, 1992, in New York City.

68 On the significance of *Our Bodies, Ourselves*, see Zola 1991.

68 Meyer and Whittier, 1994. Students of social movements with different orientations have recently begun to recognize what Joseph Gusfield (1981) has termed the "carry-ons and carry-overs" from one movement to another. Many studies trace the historical roots of modern social movements in established organizations such as churches and colleges (Morris 1984), nationalist groups that harbor strong oppositional cultures (Johnston 1991), longstanding activist subcultures (McAdam 1982; Laraña 1994), and earlier cycles of protest by the same constituency (Rupp and Taylor 1987; Shin 1994; Taylor 1989; Weigand 1995). Only recently, however, have schol-

ars begun to highlight the way that one social movement influences an entirely different one through its "spillover effects" (McAdam 1988; Staggenborg 1991; Whittier 1995). By this Meyer and Whittier mean that the ideas, tactics, style, participants, and in some cases even the organizations of one movement extend beyond its boundaries to affect the nature and course of subsequent movements.

68 Research on how small groups are the building blocks of social movements appears in McAdam 1988; Kriesi 1989; Melucci 1989; Snow and Oliver 1995. For more on how groups establish ties among people, see Mueller 1992; Emirbayer and Godowin 1994.

68 A description of the networks that gave rise to the National Organization for Women can be found in Freeman 1975 and Rupp and Taylor 1987.

68 According to Doug McAdam (1988), it is not a coincidence that the predominantly white students who risked their lives in 1964 to register black voters and start "freedom schools" in Mississippi were already acquainted with one another before joining the Freedom Summer campaign.

68 On collective action frames, see Snow, et al. 1986; Snow and Benford 1992; Hunt, Benford, and Snow 1994.

69 "Cultural toolkit" is from Swidler 1986.

69 The background information on Jane Honikman was gleaned in an interview I conducted with her on June 28, 1991, in Pittsburgh, PA.

69 The quote is from an undated speech, "Cries for Help," from Honikman's personal papers.

70 David Snow and Rob Benford (1992) describe the way activists draw upon widely shared "master frames" to convince others of the legitimacy of their cause.

70 "Frame bridging" is discussed in Snow 1987.

70 Honikman, who refers in her speeches to the link between the "position of women in any civilization" and "the care given her" at the birth of her child, has outlined a broad "system for action" that includes not only the need for medical attention to maternal mental health problems but also broader societal solutions such as affordable quality child care for working parents and expanding fathers' responsibilities for parenting. From "A System for Action," an August 1984 speech, from Honikman's personal papers.

70 The information on *Our Bodies, Ourselves* and the formation of Postpartum Support International comes from an interview I conducted with Jane Honikman on April 7, 1992, in Santa Barbara, CA.

70 Quote on how the Marcé Society opened Honikman's "eyes . . . to the world of psychiatry . . ." is from "Cries for Help," undated speech from Honikman's personal papers.

71 These quotes are from an interview I conducted with Nancy Lee, April 7, 1992 in Santa Barbara, CA.

71–72 For further discission of political generations in women's movements, see Schneider 1988; Whittier 1995.

72 Information and quotes on the organization of D.A.D. are from an interview I conducted with Nancy Berchtold, July 30, 1991, in Yardley, PA.

73 The quote "I had the baby of my dreams" appears in Bebb 1995, 20.

74 As a result of the increased recognition of self-help and self-care from federal agencies such as the National Institutes of Health and the Center for Disease Control, a number of state-financed self-help clearinghouses formed in the mid-1970s to provide activists with an organizational model and the other necessary resources to begin self-help ventures (Katz 1993). The earliest and best financed of these were in New Jersey, California, New York, Illinois, and Minnesota.

74 On the antipsychiatry movement, see Hoffman 1989; P. Brown 1992.

74–75 The quotes and information on Ricardo J. Fernandez are derived from an interview I held with him on July 26, 1991, in Lambertville, NJ.

75 See Resnick 1969 on postpartum psychosis–induced infanticide.

76 Angela Thompson's story is as I transcribed it from the broadcast of "Baby Killers: The Oprah Winfrey Show," January 22, 1991 and from the organizational files of PSI.

77 Having previously testified in child abuse cases, Susan Hickman knew the public defender well enough to request and gain access to the accused woman's court records.

77 Quote from S. Hickman from an interview I conducted with Susan and Robert Hickman on June 29, 1991, in Pittsburgh, PA.

77 Scholars interested in the impact of the media on movements document that media publicity often triggers the rapid spread of collective action (Aguirre, Quarantelli, and Mendoza 1988) and facilitates public acceptance of the movement's claims (Gamson and Modigliani 1987).

78 The quotes on "teaching health care providers . . ." to "be knowledgeable . . ." are from a personal transcription of a speech delivered by Angela Thompson at the Annual PSI Conference, June 26, 1992, San Diego, CA.

79 This material is from an interview I conducted with Melanie Burrough on July 30, 1991 in Morrisville, PA.

79 "D.A.D. President Elected," *Heartstrings* 5:2.

79 Nancy Berchtold's personal story and the founding of D.A.D. are featured in Bebb 1995.

79 For more on "professionalized" social movements, see McCarthy and Zald 1973.

80 In her study of the history of the prochoice movement, Susan Staggenborg reveals that the crusade to legalize abortion in the United States in the 1960s illustrates the tendency of many contemporary self-help movements to rely upon a combination of both established groups and outside challengers. According to recent studies of social movements (Tarrow 1989; Staggenborg 1991), it is the combination of elite support and grassroots protest that produces the mass mobilization and institutionalized groups necessary to build and sustain a social movement. To generalize in this way, of course, glosses over the enormous inroads feminism has made in the world at large.

80 The term "femocrat" is from Eisenstein 1991.

80 Mumford also suffered a depression in 1981 after the birth of her first child.

81 Information and quote on women "with a common experience . . ." are from my interview with Karen Mumford on May 20, 1991 in Columbus, OH.

81 Mumford quotes on postpartum depression being a "community problem" are from "Report on the Ohio Effort," dated August 22, 1989, in Mumford's personal papers.

81 The term "cultural capital" is from Bourdieu 1986.

82 Dagmar Celeste's recollection of her psychotic episode appeared in the Columbus *Dispatch* of July 20, 1984.

82 The Celeste administration is documented in Gagné 1993; 1996.

82–83 It seems unlikely that there is any other state in which feminism penetrated as deeply into the reaches of state government as it did in Ohio from 1982 to 1990 during Celeste's two terms in office. As first lady, Dagmar launched an Interagency Council on Women's Issues to examine state policies and programs and their effects on women and to make policy recommendations to the governor regarding administrative and programmatic recommendations. This group was influential in the establishment of a broad set of initiatives including the creation of on-site child care centers for state employees, the initiation of an Executive Order in 1984 forbidding discrimination on the basis of sexual orientation in state government, the foundation of a State Employee Assistance Program in 1984 to fund a network of recovery services, the establishment of a Women's Health Program in the Ohio Department of Health to fund services geared specifically toward the health and mental health problems of diverse populations of women, and the creation of an annual "Women's Health Month." Indicative of the Celestes' continuing commitment to progressive causes, the Governor's office established the Ohio Peacemaking Education Network to pull together 150 organizations, comprised mainly of grass-roots and professional social movement organizations, under whose umbrella the governor and the first lady undertook a sweeping set of reforms that included the development of a curriculum on Holocaust education for grades K-12, a statewide parenting program implemented through Maternal and Child Health Centers, a set of programs to combat racism in departments throughout state government, and a campaign to abolish capital punishment. The latter eventually resulted in the governor's widely publicized and controversial decision to grant clemency during his final weeks in office to twenty-six women incarcerated for killing or assaulting abusive husbands, lovers, or fathers. It seems almost fitting that the governor would end his term by returning to the feminist cause that propelled him when he took office as Lieutenant Governor over fifteen years earlier, for the governor cited "the battered woman syndrome" as grounds for the pardons (Gagné 1993). Included among the women was one serving time for killing her children.

83 For more on the women's movement in central Ohio in the 1970s, see Whittier 1995.

83 The quote "the normal state of motherhood" comes from an interview I conducted with Dagmar Celeste on March 15, 1985, Columbus, OH.

83 The quotes on "miracle drugs," "playing God with the mind," and "support of family and friends" are from Laurie Loscocco, "Depression Cures Disputed: Celeste, a Victim Herself, Says Drugs Alone Aren't Answer," Columbus *Dispatch*, November 4, 1987.

83 The quotes "raise women's consciousness" and "permission to reclaim this experience" are from Dagmar Celeste's keynote address to the Fifth Annual Conference of PSI, given June 28, 1991, in Pittsburgh, PA.

84 In a keynote address to the 1991 annual meeting of PSI, Celeste emphasized that "when we get together in self-help environments, we learn to touch each other in ways we never imagined."

85 This information comes from an interview I conducted with Helen Cain Jackson, September 22, 1992, Columbus, OH.

85 Karen Mumford, the only nonavowed feminist of the founders, is probably best characterized as what Kim Dill (1989) terms a "qualified feminist." In an interview I held with Mumford, she said she is "sympathetic" to the aims of the women's movement but avoids the term "feminist" because of its "negative connotations."

86 For the factors that account for the varied relationships between professionals and self-help movements, see Katz 1993 and Chesler and Chesney 1995.

87 This quote is from an interview I conducted with Joe Bound, June 28, 1991, Pittsburgh, PA.

87 On bonds of friendship and tensions and animosities in feminist organizations, see Rupp and Taylor 1987.

88 On the effect on social movements of hostile climates, see Rupp and Taylor 1987; Taylor 1989; Whittier 1995; Sawyers and Meyer unpublished.

88–89 On the role of government in the transformation of the women's movement, see Costain 1992. On the shifting political climate and strategies of the pro-choice movement, see Staggenborg 1991.

89 "Policy domains" are discussed in Burstein 1991; Burstein, Einwohner and Hollander 1995.

89 On the effect of politics on the emergence of social movements, see Jenkins and Klandermans 1995.

89 On nonpolitical social and cultural factors influencing social movements, see Brand 1990; McAdam 1994; Swidler 1995; Gamson and Meyer forthcoming.

89 Karl-Werner Brand (1990) addresses the cultural opportunities that have contributed to the rise of self-help movements. He sees economic recession and the public's awareness of the ecological limits of economic growth as producing significant changes in the political culture of the United States and Western Europe beginning in the 1970s.

89 See Healy 1995 on women's higher rates of health care.

89–90 In reality, the demise of the broad-based mental health care system, created by President Kennedy with the Community Mental Health Centers Act of 1963, started in the 1970s with President Nixon's attempt to impound community mental health care funds. During the decade of increased social services spending in the 1960s, private out-patient care with its emphasis on long-term psychotherapy and short-term crisis intervention had expanded rapidly, bringing about a tremendous increase in in-patient mental health services and swelling the ranks of the mental health professions (Greenley 1990).

90 On the decline in employee health benefits, see Castro 1991.

90 On the federal government's effect on mental health care, see Greenley and Mullen 1990; Katz 1993.

90 Examples of the formal guidelines issued by the NIMH and the NMHCA are the 1988 "Plain Talk about Mutual Help Groups" (NIMH), available from the Office of Scientific Information, Rockville, MD; and "How to Start a Self-Help Advocacy Group," (NMHCA), published in 1987.

90 On self-help clearinghouses around the country, see Katz 1993 and Wuthnow 1994.

90 The paradox is that the conservative agenda to break down the mental health care system produced several policy changes that actually increased the demand for medical care, such as a preference for less costly drug-oriented approaches to treatment over "talk therapy," treating the seriously ill rather than what many consider to be the "worried well," forcing patients into health maintenance organizations, and shifting the burden of in-patient mental health care from state and community hospitals to psychiatric units in private general hospitals, veterans' hospitals, and nursing homes (Brown 1985; Greenley and Mullen 1990).

91 Figures on 1991 health care costs are from Castro 1991.

91 On the domination of the male-centered approach in health care, see Lawrence and Weinhouse 1994; Rosser 1994 and Doyal 1995.

91 Healy 1995 traces the recent developments in women's health programs.

91 Through participating in professional conferences, D.A.D. and PSI maintain connections with groups as diverse as the Marcé Society, the American Psychological Association, the American Psychiatric Association, the American Medical Association, the National Community Mental Health Association, the National Conference on Social Welfare, the American College of Obstetrics and Gynecology, and the National Women's Studies Association. In 1995, D.A.D. added to this list by sending representatives to the annual meetings of the American Society of Psychosomatic Obstetricians and Gynecologists, the March of Dimes Perinatal Nursing Conference, the International Childbirth Education Association, and the International Lamaze Conference.

92 Quotes from Goldstein are from David M. Goldstein "The Psychology of Medication Treatment," *Heartstrings* (Winter/Spring), 1995, pp 3–4.

92 On how the feminist movement has altered women's consciousness of gender oppression, see Mueller 1987.

93 The quote from *Our Bodies, Ourselves* is on pp 112–13.

93 On how feminists redirected their energies in the 1980s, see McCormick 1992; Van Willigen 1993; Steinem 1992b; Levi 199b.

93 On the postpartum depression movement's strategy, see Berchtold and Burrough 1990.

93–94 Polsky 1991 discusses the rise of the therapeutic state which helps us understand the change to a more therapeutic tone taken by the self-help movement.

NOTES TO CHAPTER 4

95 For more on the debate over the value of self-help, see Kaminer 1992; Wolf 1994; Wuthnow 1994.

98 "The culture of solidarity" is from Fantasia 1988.

98 On the strong cultural focus of social movements, see Morris 1984; Johnston 1991; Johnston and Klandermans 1995; Taylor and Whittier 1995; Williams 1995.

98 For the importance in the women's movement of women forming bonds of solidarity, see Smith Rosenberg 1975; Cook 1977; Rupp and Taylor 1987; Kaplan 1992; Rupp 1993.

98 On the creation of the twentieth-century lesbian community, see Kennedy and Davis 1993.

99 On the connection between self-help and community, see Simonds 1992; Simonds and Rothman 1992.

99 On "repertoires of contention" see Tilly 1986; Tarrow 1994; Traugott 1995.

100 McCarthy and Wolfson 1992 discuss "consensus" movements.

100 The quote "women's self-help groups are very threatening . . ." is from Bégin 1989.

100 Van Willigen 1993 looks at the way self-help groups challenge physician authority.

100 On the difficulty consensus movements have mobilizing wide support for their aims, see Lofland 1988; Schwartz and Paul 1992.

101 In denoting self-help a distinctive mode and strategy of collective action, I do not mean to embrace the position of theorists who see sharp contrasts between the presumably more political and economic strategies of earlier nineteenth-century movements and the more cultural and identity-based concerns of what have been termed the "new social movements" of the 1960s and '70s (Melucci 1989). Craig Calhoun (1995) argues convincingly that the distinction between "old" and "new" glosses over the long tradition of personal transformation movements in American society, ranging from Puritanism through nineteenth-century utopian communities. Just as important, such a distinction ignores the political significance of contemporary groups that seek to reform institutions by changing individuals (Whittier 1995). But I do agree with Robert Wuthnow (1994) that the rise of the support group phenomenon represents a turn toward a new form of community building that may be preoccupied with the self at the expense of others.

Scholars writing from a number of different vantage points suggest that we might understand this collective action repertoire as linked to the distinctive history of modernity in the United States and western Europe.

101 On the nature of institutions in late modern societies, see Habermas 1984, 1987; Wuthnow 1994.

101 On the power hierarchies in health and human service agencies, see Walters 1994 and Doyal 1995. For their effects on women's mental health, see Mirkin 1994.

102 On how technical and scientific progress reinforces societal inequities, see Foucault 1980; Habermas 1987; Smith 1990.

102 "The gender subtext . . ." quote is from Smith 1988, 4.

102 On women's codependency, see Haaken 1993.

102 On how the media and other forms of mass communication help create communities see Habermas 1984, 1987; Melucci 1989; Thompson 1990; Gusfield 1994.

102 "Discourses of femininity" is from Smith 1990: 161, which emphasizes the extent to which gender relations are embedded in texts and the interpretive practices of organizations and professions.

103 On how the Internet serves self-help groups, see Kriessierer 1994.

103 On how interactive media in general help facilitate the rise of social movements, see Myers 1994.

103 For a discussion of personalized political strategies in the civil rights movement, see McAdam 1988; in the student new left movement, see Whalen and Flacks 1987; Gitlin 1987 and Flacks 1988; in the antinuclear movement, see Epstein 1992; the feminist movement, see Echols 1989 and Whittier 1995; the gay liberation movement, Adam 1995a; the lesbian feminist movement, Taylor and Whittier 1992; and contemporary gay and lesbian activism, Taylor and Raeburn 1995. The term "spillover" is from Meyer and Whittier 1994.

103 Paul Lichterman (1995, 1996) coined the term "personalized political strategies" to emphasize that the forms of community and the strategies and tactics practiced by groups that follow this newer mode of collective action redefine conventional notions of solidarity, political activity, and success in social movements.

103 On the self-involvement and individualism of middle-class Americans, see Bellah, et al. 1985; Lasch 1979; Riessman 1990; Wuthnow 1994; Lichterman 1994.

103 Study of the support group repertoire can help us to understand how the creation of a positive self-identity, formed by participating in social movement communities, can function as an incentive for individuals to mobilize and organize collectively (Taylor and Whittier 1992). This view of self-help nevertheless contrasts markedly with the interpretation of some writers that the self-help ethos is ultimately nothing more than a collective expression of the kind of self-interest and emphasis on personal success that remains the cornerstone of American ideology (Lasch 1979; Riessman 1950).

104 On the political signifcance of self-help, see Epstein 1996, Katz 1993; Schneider and Stoller 1994; Chesler and Chesney 1996.

104 On the "new" social movements, see Cohen 1985; Klandermans and Tarrow 1988; Melucci 1989; Kriesi et al. 1994; Lichterman 1996.

104 On self-help in the 1960s and 1970s, see Ferree and Hess 1994.

104 On how support groups recruited women to feminism, see Freeman 1975; Cassell 1977.

105 "Prefigurative politics" is discussed in Breines 1982.

105 On the features of feminist organizations, see P. Martin 1990; Leidner 1991; Taylor and Rupp 1993; Ferree and Martin 1995; Sirianni 1993.

106 For an example of men exhorting men to help in the home, see "PPD: A Husband's Experience" in the Spring 1988 issue of the D.A.D. newsletter.

106 For further discussion of male inexpressiveness, see Sattel 1992; Messner and Sabo 1994.

106 Hickman's speech was reprinted as "PPD's Impact on Fathers" in the Summer 1991 issue of *Heartstrings*.

106 D.A.D. distinguishes four support models: self-help mutual aid groups, community-based support groups, educational support groups, and professional therapy groups. For further discussion, see Berchtold and Burrough (1990).

106 The Honikman quote is from McMahon 1993, 6.

107 Even though Postpartum Support International is a separate organization, several of its most active members appear on the D.A.D. list of telephone volunteers.

109 Depression and Anxiety After Delivery in Harrisburg, Pennsylvania, meets at a local women's center, Postpartum Depression Support Group in Burlington, Vermont, gathers in a local coffee house, Mothers Offering Moms Support (MOMS) based in Lodi, California, meets at the facilitator's home, and Postpartum Support in Santa Barbara, California, gets together at local restaurants for breakfast. In Cincinnati, support groups are organized out of the YWCA, whereas Weeding Out the Blues in State College, Pennsylvania, meets in local churches. In Santa Barbara, California, The Emotional You meets to discuss some of the "less joyful" aspects of parenting at the Birth Resource Center, a grassroots organization devoted to providing comprehensive information and support on childbirth and parenting.

112 Research that documents the discrepancy between professional and lay perspectives in self-help movements is found in P. Brown 1992.

113 As early as the late 1970s, women had begun writing to Jane Honikman about their emotional difficulties in response to her 1979 article in the April issue of *American Baby* describing the postpartum education program she was launching in Santa Barbara, CA. And D.A.D. advised Ann Landers, whose 1990 response to readers' questions about postpartum depression helped swell the ranks of the movement by listing the telephone number and address of the national office of Depression After Delivery.

113 *The Cradle Will Fall*, listed in D.A.D.'s literature and recommended to members, tells the story of Michele Remington from Bennington, VT who

killed her six-week-old son in 1987 and then tried to end her own life by shooting herself. Miraculously, Remington survived, the gunshot missing her heart by a mere fraction of an inch; she was declared not guilty by reason of insanity for the murder of her son.

115 The quote from *The Postpartum Survival Guide* is from Dunnewald and Sanford 1994, 5.

115 For the role of early talk shows in feminism, see Wolf 1994; Heaton and Wilson 1994.

115 Gamson 1994 suggests that celebrity-watching serves some of the same functions as survivor narratives. On the attraction of talk shows as a forum that gives voice to silenced groups, see Gamson 1996.

116 The reference to "bibliotherapy" is found in Steinem 1992a. The idea that writing can serve as a form of resistance is not unique to modern self-help. As far back as the nineteenth century, liberals and socialists alike saw the creation of alternative oppositional traditions through cultural production as a political strategy directed at undermining class inequality (Jordan and Weedon 1995).

117 "Alone With My Shame" to Jane Honikman, August 26, 1988, in the personal papers of Jane Honikman, Santa Barbara, CA.

117 The quote about Carol Dix comes from a letter to Nancy Berchtold, April 12, 1990, in the organizational files of Depression After Delivery, Morrisville, PA.

118 "I saw the article on PDD" comes from a letter to Depression After Delivery, April 9, 1991, in the organizational files of Depression After Delivery, Morrisville, PA.

119 The information on the Pontiac woman comes from a letter to Depression After Delivery, June 12, 1991, in the organizational files of Depression After Delivery.

119 The quote from the imprisoned woman comes from a letter to Depression After Delivery, August 13, 1988, in the organizational files of Depression After Delivery.

120 The December 1990 issue of the *Pen Pal Network Newsletter*, in the personal papers of Jane Honikman, discusses linking writers into a single voice.

120 The quote from the Texas woman comes from a letter to Nancy Berchtold, December 19, 1988, in the organizational files of Depression After Delivery.

120 The quote about "life support" comes from *1992 Winter Special Pen Pal Update* in the personal papers of Jane Honikman.

121 The quote about "the best therapy" is reprinted in a letter from Jane Honikman to Friends in the Pen Pal Network, February 25, 1991, in the personal papers of Jane Honikman.

121 The information about the Muncy policy is conveyed in a letter from Jane Honikman to Mary V. Leftridge Byrd, Superintendant, State Correctional Institution at Muncy, January 27, 1991, in the personal papers of Jane Honikman.

121 On the demographics of the feminist movement, see Buechler 1990.

122 For community building in postmodern societies, see Giddens 1991; Etzioni 1993.

122 Bellah, et al. 1985 and Hochschild discuss how self-help is detrimental to community.

123 On rationality and the American ethos, see Jagger 1989.

123 Feminist perspectives on caring and its connections to gender 123are found in Ruddick 1980; Gillian 1982; Tronto 1989.

123 The three forms of consciousness are delineated in Cott 1989.

123 On female consciousness and the gender status quo, see Marshall 1994. On female consciousness as a force for change, see Ladd-Taylor 1994.

124 On communal consciousness, see Shaw 1991; Beckwith unpublished.

NOTES TO CHAPTER 5

125 On the different ways people use crises, see Frank 1993.

125 In his research on Alcoholics Anonymous, Norman Denzin (1987, 1989) shows that alcoholism can serve as an epiphany or existential turning-point, a moment at which individuals connect their personal lives in meaningful ways to larger public issues and institutional structures.

125 See Mills 1959 for more on this discussion.

126 The quote "providing occasions . . ." is from Wuthnow 1994, 213.

126 Collective identity is discussed in Melucci 1989; Taylor 1989; W. Gamson 1992; Taylor and Whittier 1992; Taylor and Raeburn 1994; Calhoun 1994.

126–127 See Goffman 1974; Snow 1987; Snow and Benford 1992; Hunt, Benford, and Snow 1994 for more on framing.

127 On social movement communities as catalysts for societal disintegration, see Touraine 1985; Melucci 1989; Etzioni 1993.

128 Scholars of the women's movement point out that in the type of organizing described here—mainly local and frequently developed out of pre-existing friendships—homogeneity along lines of race, class, and sexual orientation is pervasive (Rothschild-Whitt and Whitt 1986; Acker 1995). As we have seen, the postpartum support group movement is typical of the predominantly white and middle-class organizations that historically have dominated the feminist movement in the United States (Buechler 1990).

128 These 115 individuals represent over half of the telephone support contacts I surveyed. The sample was arrived at in the following way. From D.A.D.'s mailing list of 250 contacts, I excluded the names of organizations and of individuals I had interviewed, which brought the total to 220 individuals. Of the 220 surveys mailed, 15 were returned for lack of a forwarding address. Although a few of the items on the survey were close-ended, most were open-ended and allowed respondents considerable latitude in answering.

128 "Person of the Quarter," *Depression After Delivery Newsletter* (Fall 1989), 8.

128 Joe Bound is a founder and one of the most active members of national D.A.D., having served as a member of the board, as Vice President, and as a facilitator for mixed groups of husbands and wives in the Ocean City, New Jersey area. In addition to providing telephone support out of his home, Bound regularly calls radio and television talk shows featuring maternal

health issues to share what he thinks of as his "own personal experience with postpartum illness."

129 On the demographics of the new social movements, see Offe 1985; Klandermans and Tarrow 1988; Kriesi 1989; Eder 1993.

129 See Bourdieu 1986 and Lichterman 1995 for discussions of "cultural capital."

129 On the numbers of women working outside the home, see Reskin and Padavic 1994, 24.

130 Nancy Berchtold, speech at a Conference on "The Experience and Treatment of Postpartum Depression," October 13, 1990, Children's Hospital, Columbus, OH.

130 On the shifting meaning of feminism, see Whittier 1995.

130–131 Honikman's quote, "We were caught between our mothers . . ." is from Marilyn McMahon "Helping Parents Cope with the Hard Parts," *Santa Barbara News-Press*, Wednesday, October 13, 1993, D6, as is "all new moms. . . ." Honikman's paraphrase of Mead is from a speech given at the First National Conference of PSI, June 26, 1987, Santa Barbara, CA, as are the quotes linking postpartum illness to "the economic future. . . ."

133 Both excerpts are from the letter written to Honikman in June of 1987. "Inwoods" referred to in the second quote is found in Hamilton and Harberger 1992.

133 The quote "much like the spectrum . . ." is from Dunnewald and Sanford 1994, 11.

133 For more on the continuum of postpartum illness, see Dunnewald and Sanford 1994; Kleiman and Raskin 1994; Kirschenbaum 1995.

134 The passage from the *Mothering* magazine article is from Kirschenbaum 1995, 75, as is the quote of "the straw. . . ."

135 For more on the mainstream conceptualization of problems in therapeutic terms, see Polksy 1991.

135 The continuum of feminism is in Goldner and Dill 1995.

136 In response to whether they consider themselves to be feminist, Mansbridge reports that in 1995, between one-quarter and one-third of American women answer "yes" (Mansbridge 1995).

137 The tendency for women to use the disclaimer that they are "not a feminist, but" they believe in equal rights for women has been documented by Schneider 1986; Goldner and Dill 1995. See Faludi 1991 for this backlash phenomenon.

137 Interview with Joe Bound, conducted by Verta Taylor, June 28, 1991, Pittsburgh, PA.

138 On philosophies of feminism in the United States, see Vogel 1993. On scholarly accusations of feminism evoking women's victimization, see Echols 1984; Kaminer 1993.

138 Sociologists and women's historians recently halve found the idea of "maternalism" useful in explaining variations in the political and social activism of women (Skocpol 1992; Allen 1993; Ferree 1993; Gordon 1993; Weiner 1993; Ladd-Taylor 1993).

139 The study of right-wing women is in Klatch 1987.

139 Antifeminists were studied and reported on in Luker 1984; Marshall 1989.

139 The La Leche League is described in Blum 1993; Weiner 1993.

140 For more on mental health models in contemporary feminist self-help groups, see Ferraro 1981; Morgen 1995; Gagne 1996.

140 On how gender enters routine interactions, see West and Zimmerman 1987.

140 Tilly 1978 discusses "repertoire of collective action."

140 Rothman 1989 looks at the patriarchal model of reproduction and parenting.

140 On the use of illness in redefining identities, see Frank 1993; Epstein 1994, 10.

141 On the use of personal narratives in feminism, see Tierney 1982; Staggenborg 1991; Matthews 1994; Levi 1996; Taylor and Van Willigen forthcoming.

141 "Coming out of the closet" with PPD appears in Kleiman and Raskin 1994, 4.

142 The extended quote on society's expectations of mothers' emotions is from Dunnewald and Sanford 1994, 3. Subsequent quotes on the views of motherhood are from ibid., 4.

142 The quote "less socially acceptable . . ." is from Placksin 1994, 8.

143 Dagmar Celeste's quotes are from a speech given at the Fifth Annual Conference of Postpartum Support International, June 28, 1991, Pittsburgh, PA. Celeste's remarks were drawn from "The Myth of Motherhood: Postpartum Illness from a Feminist Mother's Perspective," a presentation at the National Women's Studies Association Conference, June 21, 1990, Akron, OH. I obtained the speech from the personal papers of Dagmar Celeste, Columbus, OH.

144 Nancy Berchtold, "Insights for the 1990s," presentation at the conference, "The Recognition and Treatment of Postpartum Distress," October 13, 1990, Children's Hospital, Columbus, OH.

144 On the expression of anger by women, see Taylor 1994; Taylor and Whittier 1995.

144 In feminist self-help, regaining control of one's life stems from a strong sense of "we-ness," or solidarity among women, that provides the collective strength necessary for women to believe that it is possible to resist and to overcome the structural barriers of gender (Ferree and Hess 1994). In a recent article, Jo Freeman (1995) points out that, although empowerment is one of the few ideas on which feminists of all stripes have agreed almost from the beginning, the goal of feminism is to make things better for women as a group, not just for individual women.

144 Patricia Yancey Martin (1990) writes about empowerment as an individual outcome.

145 On the inequalities exhibited in doctor–patient interactions, see Zola 1972; West 1984; Fisher 1986.

145 On empowerment through confronting medical practitioners, see Scully 1980; Lawrence and Weinhouse 1994.

145 In this respect, the strategies of the postpartum support group movement

continue to reflect the ideals of early women's health activists, who believed that control over reproductive function lays the groundwork for women to gain control over other personal, professional, and political aspects of their lives.

147 Further explanation of these different gender strategies in marital roles can be found in Hochschild 1989.

149 Hochschild 1989 found that most of the couples she studied fell into the transitional category.

149 In her study of feminists who came to the women's movement in the 1960s and early 1970s, Nancy Whittier (1995) describes the tendency of the activists she interviewed to build careers that allow them to sustain their political commitments both in their jobs and in everyday life. And Doug McAdam (1989) has also noted this practice among participants in the civil rights and new left movements, whose personal relationships, marriages, and careers continue to reflect the ideals they took away from their cause.

150 The quote on self-help movements' "stunning disregard for the material barriers to women's liberation" is found in Echols 1989, 279.

150 On the way feminism's preoccupation with the "personal as political" has contributed to the decline of other social movements, see Kauffman 1990, 77.

151 For studies that demonstrate the way women's self-help, despite its emphasis on identity politics and cultural feminism, contributes to social and political change, see Epstein 1991; Stein 1992; Taylor and Rupp 1993; Staggenborg, Eder, and Sudderth 1993/94; Sered 1994; Whittier 1995; and Gagne 1996.

151 The concept of "interpersonal life circle" is discussed in Klandermans 1992, 11.

151 For writings that view collective identity as necessary for the coalescence of all social movements, see W. Gamson 1992; Klandermans 1992; Taylor and Whittier 1992. For analysts who treat the construction of collective identity as social change, see Melucci 1989. The modern lesbian and gay movement that has sought to create a public identity based on sexual orientation is an example of collective identity as an outcome of collective action. For research on social movements that treat identity construction as social change, see Naples 1991; J. Gamson 1992; 1995 and Taylor and Raeburn 1995.

152 On self-help and women's victimization, see Kaminer 1992;; Lehrman 1993; Roiphe 1993; Wolf 1993; Denfeld 1995.

152 The well-being continuum was developed by Mirowsky and Ross 1989.

152 For the correlation between individual's sense of control and their physical and emotional well-being, see Seeman and Seeman 1983; Downey and Moen 1987; Mirowsky and Ross 1986; 1989.

153 On the correlation between social support and health, see Pearlin, Lieberman, Menaghan, and Mullan 1981; Kaplan, Robbins and Martin 1983; Gerstel Riessman, and Rosenfield 1985; Ross, Mirowsky, and Goldsteen 1990.

153 Link and Cullen 1990 summarized the evidence for and against labeling theory.

153–154 The quote "conspiracy of silence . . ." is from a speech given by Diane Fashinpaur, R.N., at a conference on April 23, 1990, at the governor's residence in Columbus, OH.

154 Van Willigen 1993 discusses the background of the three tactics.

154 On the La Leche League, see Blum and Vandewater 1993; on Momazons, see McCormick 1992.

154 The tendency for self-help groups to take vastly different approaches to medical and scientific knowledge is well documented in the sociological literature (Starr 1982; Hoffman 1989; P. Brown 1992). Scholars who have studied self-help movements emphasize that the relationships between professionals and self-help groups are at best strained, at worst openly antagonistic (Katz 1991; Chesler and Chesney 1996). Feminist groups, in particular, have tended both to accommodate and resist the pressures of organized medicine (Morgen 1986; 1988).

154 On self-help's characteristic ambivalence toward medicine, see Gagné 1993.

155 Susan T. Misner, MS., Review in *Heartstrings* 4, No. 4 (Winter 1994), 6.

155 "D.A.D. In the News," *Heartstrings* 5, No. 2 (Summer 1993), 3.

156 Dr. Wisner is Director of Women's Services at the Mood Disorders Program of University Hospitals of Cleveland, OH, and a faculty member at Case Western Reserve University School of Medicine. Dr. Sichel is director of the Postpartum Mood Disorder Program at Newton Wellesley Hospital in Newton, MA.

156 Dr. Wisner recounted her initial contact with D.A.D. at the conference on Improving Women's Health in Ohio held September 21, 1994, in Columbus, OH.

156 For more on their recommendations, see "D.A.D. at Presidential Commission on Health Reform," *Heartstrings* 4, No. 2 (Summer 1993), 3.

156–157 The quote on the limitations of the DSMD III in portraying postpartum illness is from DeBofsky 1992, 296. On getting full insurance coverage, see ibid., 297.

157 The Fall 1991 issue of *Heartstrings* trumpeted Dr. Stowe's grand rounds and provided the laudatory quotes.

157 On this AIDS-pioneered strategy, see S. Epstein 1996.

157 The quote on "investigative approaches" is from Hamilton and Sichel 1992, 220.

157 Hamilton 1977 reviews estrogen treatments; Dalton 1980 examines progesterone injections.

158 In 1993, Depression After Delivery joined forces with the Mental Health Association in a nine-month-long national campaign that featured television, radio, and newspaper advertisements and community education events designed to increase public awareness about clinical depression and its treatment.

158 This unit is described in "Person of the Quarter," *Heartstrings* 4, No. 3 (Fall 1993), 3.

159 For further discussion of the decision to exclude postpartum conditions, see Daniel Purdy, A.B. and Ellen Frank, Ph.D., "Should Postpartum Mood Disorders Be Given A More Prominent or Distinct Place in the DSM–IV?" Published in the Proceedings of the Fifth Annual Conference of Postpartum Support International, June 27–30, 1991, Pittsburgh, PA, 1–26.

159 Activists lobbying of psychiatrists is reported in "News from APA," *Heartstrings* 4, No. 3 (Fall 1993), 7.

160 For more on the Thompsons' story, see Ann Japenga, "The Tragic Ordeal of Postpartum Psychosis." *Los Angeles Times*, February 1, 1991, Part VI, 11.

160 The Pennsylvania campaign is described in "Chief of Police Fights Ignorance," *Heartstrings* 5, No. 1 (Spring 1994), 6.

161 This campaign was laid out in a letter from Kate Carpenter to D.A.D. and PSI Members, published in *Depression After Delivery Newsletter* (June 1989), 4–5.

162 On the distinctions between strategic and identity-oriented movements, see Jenkins 1983; Giddens 1991; Cohen 1985.

NOTES TO CHAPTER 6

164 For a clinical discussion of Margery Kempe's condition, see Drucker 1972; Hamilton, Harberger, and Takins 1992.

165 On the structural, cultural and interactional basis of gender, see Smith 1987; West and Zimmerman 1987; Collins 1990; Reskin and Padavic 1994.

165 Joan Acker (1990) has argued that gender is an organizing principle throughout all groups in society.

166 A mere glance at writings by R. W. Connell, Dorothy Smith, Barrie Thorne, Patricia Hill Collins, Judith Butler, Judith Lorber, Candace West and Sarah Fenstermaker and others I have referred to throughout this book suggests that most of the major theorists have yet to discover the rich body of scholarship on social movements.

166 For one gender scholar who does attend to social movement theory, see Chafetz 1990. Chafetz does not, however, address the gendered nature of social movements and focuses almost exclusively on the structural dimensions and outcomes of collective action. Recent gender theory focuses on processes of change in the gender order.

167 On the effects of the political and cultural context on social moments, see McAdam 1994; Tarrow 1994; Jenkins and Klandermans 1995; Gamson and Meyer forthcoming.

167 On feminists' adoption of personalized political strategies in response to the antifeminist backlash, see Whittier 1995.

167 The Pat Robertson quote is from his 1992 fundraising letter for the Iowa Committee to Stop ERA.

167 Vogel 1995 deals with the acceptance of the sameness strategy.

168 Wertz and Wertz 1977 documents how medicine's hegemony shaped the history of childbirth in the U.S.

168 The quote "that a woman can either react . . ." is from Healy 1994, 12. Bernadine Healy is the first woman director of the National Institutes of Health.

169 On self-contained policy domains, see Burstein 1991.

169 "Gender regime" is from Connell 1987, 99.

169 On small interpersonal networks as the basis for social movements, see Freeman 1975; Morris 1984; Melucci 1989; McAdam 1992; Marwell and Oliver 1993.

169 On women's lack of power in the early civil rights movement, see McAdam 1992; Barnett 1993 and Robnett 1996.

169 On gender and mobilization of the toxic waste movement, see Brown and Ferguson 1995.

170 On gendered patterns of mobilization in the urban squatter movement in Brazil, see Neuhouser 1995.

170 The quote "not political in the classical sense" is from Naples 1991, 485.

170 Examples of works by sociologists of emotions include Hochschild 1983; Cancian 1987; Hochschild and Machung 1989.

170 Cancian and Gordon 1988 trace the roots of the self-help industry in women's emotion work.

170 The place of emotions in feminist resistance is covered in Taylor 1995; Taylor and Whittier 1995.

170 For more on "caring work" see Abel and Nelson 1990.

171 For more on the way the breast cancer movement challenges gender codes, see Taylor and Van Willigen 1996.

171 On the gendering of the Nazi movement, see Koonz 1987; Theweleit 1987. On how gender determines people's participation in strikes, see Fonow 1994, 3.

171 On "gendering" in social movement discourse, see Ferree and Gamson 1995.

172 For more on the Buffalo lesbian community, see Kennedy and Davis 1993.

172 The peace movement is observed in Epstein 1991; Meyer and Whittier 1994.

172 On the effectiveness of formal organizations, see W. Gamson 1975, 1990; McCarthy and Zald 1977; Staggenborg 1989.

173 On movements as "communities of discourse" see Wuthnow, 89.

173 See Katzenstein 1995 for more on feminists in the Catholic Church.

173 Blee 1991 examines women in the Ku Klux Klan.

173 For a gender analysis of Lancashire Women Against Pit Closures, see Beckwith unpublished.

173 On women's communities, see Taylor and Rupp 1993.

174 Arlie Hochschild (1990) coined the term "emotion cultures."

174 The internal conflict in self-help organizations is discussed in Freeman 1972/73; Ryan 1992.

NOTES TO CHAPTER 6

174 Adrienne Rich (1980) conceptualizes societal proscriptions against female bonding as "compulsory heterosexuality."

174 The quote "It is as thrilling . . ." is from Rupp and Taylor 1987, 97

174 Krouse 1993; Schmidt 1993; Taylor 1994; Taylor and Whittier 1995 analyze emotion as a social movement strategy.

175 Sisters of the Yam is described in hooks 1993.

175 On strategies of the antirape movement, see Matthews 1994.

175 On how women's self-help writings challenge emotion norms, see Cancian and Gordon 1988.

175 The quote on "the good of self . . ." is from Ferree 1992, 37.

175 For the Kanter quote, see 250.

175 On the gendered nature of modern organizations, see Acker 1990.

176 For more on the AIDS movement, see Gorman 1992 and Adam 1995b.

176 On the significance of multiple statuses in social movements, see Morris 1992.

176 Gender dynamics in movements are discussed in J. Gamson 1994; Roscigno and Anderson 1995.

176 Whittier 1995 conceptualizes social movement actors as social movement communities that share a collective identity, rather than as formal organizations connected by common strategic actions.

177 The works reviewed by Staggenborg 1995 included W. Gamson 1975; Mueller 1987; Burstein, Einwohner, and Hollander 1994.

177 The quote "to construct women . . . " is from Lorber 1994, 35.

177 Nineteenth-century women's hysteria is described in Smith-Rosenberg 1974.

177 For "All women to need to be mothers . . ." see Oakley 1974, 186.

177 Collins 1990 reviews the delineations between "good" and "bad" mothers.

178 J. Gamson 1995 contains his argument referenced here.

178 The importance of the distinction between "public" and "private" spheres for the organization of gender is covered in Osmond and Thorne 1993.

178 Gloria Steinem (1992b, 26) uses the term "truth-telling" to draw a parallel between the "testifying" of the civil rights movement and the "speaking bitterness" meetings of the Chinese Cultural Revolution.

179 The Steinem quote is from 1992b, 28.

REFERENCES

Abel, Emily K., and Margaret K. Nelsen, eds. 1990. *Circles of Care: Work and Identity in Women's Lives*. Albany: SUNY Press.

Acker, Joan. 1990. "Hierarchies, Jobs, Bodies: A Theory of Gendered Organizations." *Gender and Society* 4:139–58.

———. 1995. "Feminist Goals and Organizing Processes." In *Feminist Organizations: Harvest of the New Women's Movement*, edited by Myra Marx Ferree and Patricia Yancey Martin, 137–44. Philadelphia: Temple University Press.

Adam, Barry D. 1995a. *The Rise of a Gay and Lesbian Movement*. 2d ed. Boston: Twayne.

———. 1995b. "AIDS and the Formation of Community." Paper presented at the Annual Meetings of the American Sociological Association, Washington, DC, August 1995.

Adams, Alice. 1995. "Maternal Bonds: Recent Literature on Mothering." *Signs: Journal of Women in Culture and Society* 20:414–427.

Aguirre, B.E., E.L. Quarantelli, and J.L. Mendoza. 1988. "The Collective Behavior of Fads: The Characteristics, Effects, and Career of Streaking." *American Sociological Review* 53:569–584.

Albi, Linda, Donna Florien Deurloo, Deborah Johnson, Debra Catlin, and Sheryll Greatwood. 1993. *Mothering Twins: From Hearing the News to Beyond the Terrible Twos.* New York: Simon & Schuster.

Allen, Ann Taylor. 1993. "Maternalism in German Feminist Movements." *Journal of Women's History.* 5:99–103.

Allen, Hilary. 1986. "Psychiatry and the Construction of the Feminine." In *The Power of Psychiatry*, edited by Peter Miller and Nikolas Rose, 85–111. Cambridge, UK: Polity Press.

American Psychiatric Association. 1952; 1968; 1980; 1987; 1994. *Diagnostic and Statistical Manual of Disorders*, 1st ed., 2d ed., 3rd ed., 3rd ed., rev., 4th ed. Washington, DC: American Psychiatric Association.

Atkinson, A. Kathleen, and Annette U. Rickel. 1984a. "Depression in Women: The Postpartum Depression Experience." In *Social and Psychological Problems of Women*, edited by A. Rickel, M. Gerrard, and I. Iscoe, 197–218. Washington, DC: Hemisphere.

———. 1984b. "Postpartum Depression in Primiparous Parents." *Journal of Abnormal Psychology* 93:115–119.

Arney, William Ray. 1980. "Maternal-Infant Bonding: The Politics of Falling in Love With Your Child." *Feminist Studies* 6:547–570.

Ball, Jean A. 1987. *Reactions to Motherhood: The Role of Postnatal Care.* Cambridge: Cambridge University Press.

Barnett, Bernice McNair. 1993. "Invisible Southern Black Women Leaders in the Civil Rights Movement: The Triple Constraints of Gender, Race, and Class." *Gender and Society* 7:162–182.

Bassin, Donna, Margaret Honey, and Meryle Mahrer Kaplan, eds. 1994. *Representations of Motherhood.* New Haven, CT: Yale University Press.

Beattie, Melody. 1987. *Codependent No More.* New York: Harper and Row.

Bebb, Deborah. 1995. "Moms Helping Moms Beat Postpartum Blues." *Family Circle* September 1:19–20.

Beck, Cheryl Tatano. 1992. "The Lived Experience of Postpartum Depression: A Phenomenological Study." *Nursing Research* 41:166–170.

———. 1993. "Teetering on the Edge: A Substantive Theory of Postpartum Depression." *Nursing Research* 42:42–48.

Beckwith, B. 1985. "Boston Women's Health Book Collective: Women Empowering Women." *Women and Health* 10:1.

Beckwith, Karen. Unpublished paper. "Lancashire Women Against Pit Closures: Women's Standing in a Men's Movement."

Bégin, Monique. 1989. "Redesigning Health Care for Women." In Canadian Research Institute for the Advancement of Women Conference Proceedings, 34–35, Ottawa, Canada.

Bellah, Robert N., Richard Madsen, William M. Sullivan, Ann Swidler, and Steven M. Tipton. 1985. *Habits of the Heart*. Los Angeles: University of California Press.

Berchtold, Nancy, and Melanie Burrough. 1990. "Reaching Out: Depression After Delivery Support Group Network." *NAACOG's Clinical Issues in Perinatal and Women's Health Nursing: Psychological Aspects of Pregnancy and Postpartum Depression* 1:385–394.

Berry, Mary Frances. 1993. *The Politics of Parenthood: Child Care, Women's Rights, and the Myth of the Good Mother*. New York: Viking Penguin.

Bing, Elisabeth, and Libby Coleman. 1980. *Having a Baby After 30*. New York: Bantam.

Birns, Beverly, and Dale F. Hay, eds. 1988. *The Different Faces of Motherhood*. New York: Plenum.

Blee, Kathleen M. 1991. *Women of the Klan: Racism and Gender in the 1920s*. Berkeley: University of California Press.

Blum, Linda M. 1993. "Mothers, Babies, and Breastfeeding in Late Capitalist America: The Shifting Contexts of Feminist Theory." *Feminist Studies* 19:291–311.

Blum, Linda M., and Elizabeth A. Vandewater. 1993. "Mother to Mother: A Maternalist Organization in Late Capitalist America." *Social Problems* 40: 285–300.

Blumer, Herbert. 1969. *Symbolic Interactionism: Perspective and Method*. Englewood Cliffs, NJ: Prentice-Hall.

Boggs, Carl. 1986. *Social Movements and Political Power*. Philadelphia: Temple University Press.

Bourdieu, Pierre. 1986. "The Forms of Capital." In *Handbook of Theory and Research for the Sociology of Education*, edited by J.G. Richardson, New York: Greenwood.

Boston Women's Health Book Collective. 1971. *Our Bodies, Ourselves—A Course By and For Women*. Boston: New England Free Press.

Brand, Karl-Werner. 1990. "Cyclical Changes in the Cultural Climate as a Context Variable for Social Movement Development." Paper presented at workshop on Social Movements: Framing Processes and Opportunity Structures, Berlin, July.

Breines, Wini. 1982. *Community and Organization in the New Left, 1962–1968: The Great Refusal*. South Hadley, MA: Praeger.

———. 1992. *Young, White, and Miserable: Growing Up Female in the Fifties*. Boston: Beacon.

Brody, Jane. 1994. "Personal Health: New Research on Postpartum Depression Holds Hope for Mothers Caught in its Grip." *New York Times*, October 26: 37.

Broom, Dorothy H. 1991. *Damned If We Do: Contradictions in Women's Health Care*. North Sidney: Allen & Unwin.

Broverman, I.K., D. Broverman, F.E. Clarkson, P. Rosenkrantz, and S. Vogel. 1970. "Sex Role Stereotypes and Clinical Judgments of Mental Health." *Journal of Consulting and Clinical Psychology* 34:1–7.

Brown, Elaine. 1992. *A Taste of Power: A Black Woman's Story*. New York: Pantheon.

Brown, Phil. 1985. *The Transfer of Care: Psychiatric Deinstitutionalization and its Aftermath*. London: Routledge.

―――. 1992. "Popular Epidemiology and Toxic Waste Contamination: Lay and Professional Ways of Knowing." *Journal of Health and Social Behavior* 33:267–281.

Brown, Phil, and Faith I.T. Ferguson. 1995. "'Making a Big Stink': Women's Work, Women's Relationships, and Toxic Waste Activism." *Gender and Society* 9:145–172.

Brumberg, Joan Jacobs. 1988. *Fasting Girls: The History of Anorexia Nervosa.* Cambridge, MA: Plume.

Buechler, Steven M. 1990. *Women's Movements in the United States: Woman Suffrage, Equal Rights, and Beyond.* New Brunswick, NJ: Rutgers University Press.

Burak, Carl S., and Michele G. Remington. 1994. *The Cradle Will Fall.* New York: Donald L. Fine.

Burstein, Paul. 1991. "Legal Mobilization as a Social Movement Tactic: The Struggle for Equal Employment Opportunity." *American Journal of Sociology* 96:1201–1225.

Burstein, Paul, Rachel L. Einwohner, and Jocelyn A. Hollander. 1995. "The Success of Political Movements: A Bargaining Perspective." In *The Politics of Social Protest: Comparative Perspectives on States and Social Movements,* edited by J. Craig Jenkins and Bert Klandermans, 275–295. Minneapolis: University of Minnesota Press.

Butler, Judith. 1990. *Gender Trouble: Feminism and the Subversion of Identity.* New York: Routledge.

Calhoun, Craig. 1995. "'New Social Movements' of the Early Nineteenth Century." In *Repertoires and Cycles of Collective Action,* edited by Mark Traugott, 173–215. Durham, NC: Duke University Press.

Cancian, Francesca M. 1987. *Love in America.* Cambridge: Cambridge University Press.

―――. 1992. "Feminist Science: Methodologies that Challenge Inequality." *Gender and Society* 6:623–642.

Cancian, Francesca M., and Steven Gordon. 1988. "Changing Emotion Norms in Marriage: Love and Anger in U.S. Women's Magazines Since 1900." *Gender and Society* 2:308–342.

Cassell, Joan. 1977. *A Group Called Women: Sisterhood and Symbolism in the Feminist Movement.* New York: David McKay.

Castro, Janice. 1991. "Condition Critical." *Time,* November 25: 32–42.

Chafetz, Janet. 1990. *Gender Equity: An Integrated Theory of Stability and Change.* Beverly Hills, CA: Sage.

Cherry, Sheldon H., Richard L. Burkowitz, and Nathan G. Kase. 1985. *Medical, Surgical, and Gynecologic Complications of Pregnancy.* 3d ed. Baltimore, MD: Williams and Wilkins.

Chesler, Mark A., and Barbara K. Chesney. 1995. *Cancer and Self-Help: Bridging the Troubled Waters of Childhood Illness.* Madison: University of Wisconsin Press.

Chesler, Phyllis. 1972. *Women and Madness.* New York: Avon.

Chesney, Barbara K., and Mark A. Chesler. 1993. "Activism Through Self-Help Group Membership: Reported Life Changes of Parents of Children With Cancer." *Small Group Research* 24:258–273.

Chodorow, Nancy. 1978. *The Reproduction of Mothering: Psychoanalysis and the Sociology of Gender.* Berkeley: University of California Press.

————. 1995. "Gender as a Personal and Cultural Construction." *Signs: Journal of Women in Culture and Society* 20:516–544.

Cohen, Jean L. 1985. "Strategy or Identity: New Theoretical Paradigms and Contemporary Social Movements." *Social Research* 4:663–716.

Collins, Patricia Hill. 1989. "A Comparison of Two Works on Black Family Life." *Signs: Journal of Women in Culture and Society* 14:875–884.

————. 1990. *Black Feminist Thought: Knowledge, Consciousness, and the Politics of Empowerment*. New York: Routledge.

————. 1994. "Shifting the Center: Race, Class, and Feminist Theorizing About Motherhood." In *Mothering: Ideology, Experience, and Agency*, edited by Evelyn Nakano Glenn, Grace Chang, and Linda Rennie Forcey, 45–65. New York: Routledge.

Commins, Dorothy Berliner. 1941. *Lullabies of Many Lands*. New York: Harper and Brothers.

Connell, R.W. 1987. *Gender and Power: Society, The Person, and Sexual Politics*. Sidney: Allen & Unwin.

Conrad, Peter, and Joseph Schneider. 1980. *Deviance and Medicalization*. St. Louis, MO: C.V. Mosby.

Cook, Blanche Wiesen. 1977. "Female Support Networks and Political Activism: Lillian Wald, Crystal Eastman, and Emma Goldman." *Chrysalis* 3:43–61.

Costain, Anne. 1992. *Inviting Women's Rebellion: A Political Process Interpretation of the Women's Movement*. Baltimore: John Hopkins University Press.

Cott, Nancy F. 1989. "What's in a Name? The Limits of 'Social Feminism'; or, Expanding the Vocabulary of Women's History." *Journal of American History* 76:809–829.

Cunningham, F. Gary, Paul C. MacDonald, Norman F. Grant, Kenneth J. Leveno, and Larry C. Gilstrap III, eds. 1993. *Williams Obstetrics*, 19th edition. Norwalk, CT: Appleton & Lang.

Dalton, Katharina. 1980. *Depression After Childbirth*. New York: Oxford University Press.

Danforth, David N. 1982. *Obstetrics and Gynecology: Fifth Edition*. New York: Harper & Row.

Davis, Flora. 1991. *Moving the Mountain: The Women's Movement in America Since 1960*. New York: Simon & Schuster.

DeBofsky, Mark D. 1992. "Medical Insurance Litigation Problems of Postpartum Patients." In *Postpartum Psychiatric Illness: A Picture Puzzle*, edited by James Alexander Hamilton and Patricia Neel Harberger, 296–304. Philadelphia: University of Pennsylvania Press.

DeLyser, Femmy. 1989. *Jane Fonda's New Pregnancy Workout and Total Birth Program*. New York: Simon & Schuster.

Denfeld, Rene. 1995. *The New Victorians: A Young Woman's Challenge to the Old Feminist Order*. New York: Warner Books.

Denzin, Norman K. 1987. *The Alcoholic Self*. Beverly Hills, CA: Sage.

————. 1989. *Interpretive Interactionism*. Newbury Park, CA: Sage.

Dill, Kim. 1989. "'Qualified Feminism' and its Influence on Identification with the Women's Movement." Undergraduate honors thesis, Ohio State University.

Dix, Carol. 1985. *The New Mother Syndrome: Coping with Postpartum Stress and Depression*. New York: Doubleday.

Dixon, Jo, Cynthia Gordon, and Tasnim Khomusi. 1995. "Sexual Symmetry in Psychiatric Diagnosis." *Social Problems* 42:429–448.

Dowling, Colette. 1981. *The Cinderella Complex*. New York: Pocket Books.

Downey, Geraldine, and Phyllis Moen. 1987. "Personal Efficacy, Income, and Family Transitions: A Longitudinal Study of Women Heading Households." *Journal of Health and Social Behavior* 28:320–333.

Doyal, Lesley. 1995. *What Makes Women Sick: Gender and the Political Economy of Health*. New Brunswick, NJ: Rutgers University Press.

Driscoll, Jeanne. 1992. "My Personal Journey." Tape-recorded speech, Postpartum Support International Conference, San Diego, CA. June 27, 1992.

Drucker, T. 1972. "Malaise of Margery Kempe." *New York State Journal of Medicine* 72:2911–2917.

Dunnewald, Ann, and Diane G. Sanford. 1994. *The Postpartum Survival Guide: It Wasn't Supposed To Be Like This*. Oakland, CA: New Harbinger Publications.

Echols, Alice. 1984. "The Taming of the Id: Feminist Sexual Politics, 1968–83." In *Pleasure and Danger: Exploring Female Sexuality*, edited by Carole S. Vance, 50–72. London: Routledge and Kegan Paul.

———. 1989. *Daring to Be Bad: Radical Feminism in America 1967–1975*. Minneapolis: University of Minnesota Press.

Eder, Klaus. 1993. *The New Politics of Class: Social Movements and Cultural Dynamics in Advanced Societies*. London: Sage.

Ehrenreich, Barbara, and Deirdre English. 1973. *Witches, Midwives, and Nurses*. Old Westbury: SUNY Press.

———. 1979. *For Her Own Good*. Garden City, NY: Anchor Press/Doubleday.

Eisenberg, Arlene, Heidi Eisenberg Murkoff, and Sandee Eisenberg Hathaway. 1989. *What To Eat When You're Expecting*. New York: Workman.

———. 1991. *What to Expect When You're Expecting*. New York: Workman.

Eisenstein, Hester. 1991. *Gender Shock: Practicing Feminism on Two Continents*. Boston: Beacon.

Etzioni, Amitai. 1993. The Spirit of Community: *The Reinvention of American Society*. New York: Columbia University Press.

Emirbayer, Mustafa, and Jeff Goodwin. 1994. "Network Analysis, Culture, and the Problem of Agency." *American Journal of Sociology* 99:1411–1454.

Epstein, Barbara Leslie. 1981. *The Politics of Domesticity: Women, Evangelism, and Temperance in 19th Century America*. Middletown, CT: Wesleyan University Press.

Epstein, Barbara. 1991. *Political Protest and Cultural Revolution: Nonviolent Direct Action in the 1970s and 1980s*. Berkeley: University of California Press.

Epstein, Steven. 1996. *Impure Science: AIDS, Activism, and the Politics of Knowledge*. Berkeley: University of California Press.

Eyer, Diane E. 1992. *Mother-Infant Bonding: A Scientific Fiction*. New Haven, CT: Yale University Press.

Faludi, Susan. 1991. *Backlash: The Undeclared War Against American Women*. New York: Anchor.

Fantasia, Rick. 1988. *Cultures of Solidarity: Consciousness, Action, and Contemporary American Workers*. Berkeley: University of California Press.

Ferraro, Kathleen. 1981. "Processing Battered Women." *Journal of Family Issues* 2:415–438.

Ferree, Myra Marx. 1992. "The Political Context of Rationality: Rational Choice Theory and Resource Mobilization." In *Frontiers in Social Movement Theory*, edited by Aldon D. Morris and Carol McClurg Mueller, 29–52. New Haven, CT: Yale University Press.

―――. 1993. "The Rise and Fall of 'Mommy Politics': Feminism and Unification in (East) Germany." *Feminist Studies* 19:89–115.

―――. 1994. "'The Time of Chaos Was the Best': Feminist Mobilization and Demobilization in East Germany." *Gender and Society* 8:597–623.

Ferree, Myra Marx, and William A. Gamson. 1995. "Cross-National Influence of the Women's Movement in Framing the Abortion Issue." Paper presented at the International Conference on Cross National Influences and Social Movement Research, Mont-Pelerin, Switzerland.

Ferree, Myra Marx, William A. Gamson, and Beth B. Hess. 1994. *Controversy and Coalition: The New Feminist Movement Across Three Decades of Change*, Revised Edition. New York: Twayne.

Ferree, Myra Marx, and Patricia Yancey Martin, eds. 1995. *Feminist Organizations: Harvest of the New Women's Movement*. Philadelphia: Temple University Press.

Firestone, Shulamith. 1970. *The Dialectics of Sex*. New York: Bantam.

Fisher, Sue. 1986. *In the Patient's Best Interest: Women and the Politics of Medical Decisions*. New Brunswick, NJ: Rutgers University Press.

Flacks, Richard. 1988. *Making History: The American Left and the American Mind*. New York: Columbia University Press.

Fonow, Mary Margaret. 1994. "Protest Engendered: The Participation of Women Steelworkers in the Wheeling, Pittsburgh Steel Strike of 1985." Unpublished paper.

Fonow, Mary Margaret, and Judith A. Cook, eds. 1991. *Beyond Methodology: Feminist Scholarship as Lived Research*. Bloomington: Indiana University Press.

Foucault, Michel. 1973. *The Birth of the Clinic*. London: Tavistock.

―――. 1979. *Discipline and Punish*. London: Allen Lane.

―――. 1980. *The History of Sexuality, Volume One, An Introduction*. New York: Vintage.

―――. 1986. *The History of Sexuality, Volume Two, The Use of Pleasure*. Harmondsworth, UK: Pelican.

Frank, Arthur W. 1993. "The Rhetoric of Self-Change: Illness Experience as Narrative." *Sociological Quarterly* 34:39–52.

Frankenberg, Ruth. 1993. *White Women, Race Matters: The Social Construction of Whiteness*. Minneapolis: University of Minnesota Press.

Freedman, Estelle. 1979. "Separatism as Strategy: Female Institution Building and American Feminism, 1870–1930." *Feminist Studies* 5:512–529.

Freeman, Jo. 1972/73. "The Tyranny of Structurelessness." *Berkeley Journal of Sociology* 17:151–164.

―――. 1975. *The Politics of Women's Liberation*. New York: David McKay.

―――. 1995. "From Seed to Harvest: Transformations of Feminist Organizations and Scholarship." In *Feminist Organizations: Harvest of the New Women's Movement*, edited by Myra Marx Ferree and Patricia Yancey Martin, 1. Philadelphia: Temple University Press.

Friederich, Mary Anna. 1982. "Emotional Aspects of Pregnancy." In *Current Obstetric and Gynecological Diagnosis and Treatment*, 4th ed., edited by Ralph C. Benson, 972–983. Los Altos, CA: Lange Medical Publications.

Frye, Marilyn. 1983. *The Politics of Reality: Essays in Feminist Theory*. Trumansburg, NY: The Crossing Press.

Gabbe, Steven G., Jennifer R. Niebyl, and Joe Leigh Simpson, eds. 1991. *Obstetrics: Normal and Problem Pregnancies*, 2d ed. New York: Churchill Livingstone.

Gagné, Patricia. 1993. "The Battered Women's Movement in the 'Postfeminist' Era: New Social Movement Strategies and the Celeste Clemencies." Ph.D. dissertation, Ohio State University.

———. 1996. "Identity, Strategy, and Feminist Politics: Clemency for Battered Women Who Kill." *Social Problems*. 43:77–93.

Gamson, Joshua. 1989. "Silence, Death, and the Invisible Enemy: AIDS Activism and Social Movement 'Newness.'" *Social Problems* 36:351–367.

———. 1994. *Claims to Fame: Celebrity in Contemporary America*. Berkeley: University of California Press.

———. 1995. "Must Identity Movements Self-Destruct? A Queer Dilemma." *Social Problems* 42:390–407.

———. 1996. "Do Ask, Do Tell." *Utne Reader* January–February: 78–83.

Gamson, William A. 1975. *The Strategy of Social Protest*. Homewood, IL.: Dorsey Press.

———. 1990. *The Strategy of Social Protest*. 2d ed. Belmont, CA: Wadsworth.

———. 1992. "The Social Psychology of Collective Action." In *Frontiers in Social Movement Theory*, edited by Aldon D. Morris and Carol McClurg Mueller, 53–76. New Haven, CT: Yale University Press.

———. 1995. "Hiroshima, the Holocaust, and the Politics of Exclusion: 1994 Presidential Address." *American Sociological Review*, 60:1–20.

Gamson, William A., and David S. Meyer. Forthcoming. "Framing Political Opportunity." In *Opportunities, Mobilizing Structures, and Framing: Comparative Applications of Social Movement Theory*. New York: Cambridge University Press.

Gamson, William A., and Andre Modigliani. 1987. "The Changing Culture of Affirmative Action." In *Research in Political Sociology*, edited by Richard D. Braungart, 137–177. Greenwich, CT: JAI.

Gelb, Joyce, and Marian Lief Palley. 1982. *Women and Public Policies*. Princeton, NJ: Princeton University Press.

Gerstel, Naomi, Catherine K. Riessman, and Sarah Rosenfield. 1985. "Explaining the Symptomatology of Separated and Divorced Women and Men: The Role of Material Conditions and Social Networks." *Social Forces* 64:84–101.

Giddens, Anthony. 1991. *Modernity and Self-Identity: Self and Society in the Late Modern Age*. Stanford, CA: Stanford University Press.

Gilkes, Cheryl Townsend. 1983. "Going Up for the Oppressed: Career Mobility of Black Women Community Workers." *Journal of Social Issues* 39:115–139.

Gilligan, Carol. 1982. *In a Different Voice: Psychological Theory and Women's Development.* Cambridge: Harvard University Press.

Gilman, Charlotte Perkins. 1973. *The Yellow Wallpaper.* Old Westbury, NY: The Feminist Press.

Gitlin, Michael J., and Robert O. Pasnau. 1989. "Psychiatric Syndromes Linked to Reproductive Function in Women: A Review of Current Knowledge." *American Journal of Psychiatry* 146:1413–1422.

Gitlin, Todd. 1987. *The Sixties: Years of Hope, Days of Rage.* New York: Bantam.

Gleicher, Norbert. 1985. *Principles of Medical Therapy in Pregnancy.* New York: Plenum Medical.

Glenn, Evelyn Nakano. 1994. "Social Constructions of Mothering: A Thematic Overview." In *Mothering: Ideology, Experience, and Agency,* edited by Evelyn Nakano Glenn, Grace Chang, and Linda Rennie Forcey, 1–29. New York: Routledge.

Glenn, Evelyn Nakano, Grace Chang, and Linda Rennie Forcey, eds. 1994. *Mothering: Ideology, Experience, and Agency.* New York: Routledge.

Goffman, Erving. 1974. *Frame Analysis.* Cambridge: Harvard University Press.

Goldner, Melinda, and Kim Dill. 1995. "Explaining Postfeminism: A Continuum of Responses to the Contemporary Women's Movement." Unpublished paper.

Goldstein, Robert L. 1989. "The Psychiatrist's Guide to Right and Wrong: Part III. Postpartum Depression and the 'Appreciation' of Wrongfulness." *Bulletin of the American Academy of Psychiatry and the Law* 17:121–128.

Gordon, Linda. 1993. *Putting Children First: Women, Maternalism, and Welfare in the Twentieth Century.* Madison: University of Wisconsin Press.

———. 1994. *Pitied but Not Entitled: Single Mothers and the History of Welfare, 1890–1935.* New York: Free Press.

Gorman, Phyllis. 1992. "The Ohio AIDS Movement: Competition and Cooperation between Grassroots Activists and Professionally Sponsored Organizations." Ph.D. dissertation, Ohio State University.

Gove, Walter, ed. 1975. *Labeling Deviant Behavior: Evaluating a Perspective.* New York: Sage/Halsted.

———. 1980. "Labelling and Mental Illness: A Critique." In *The Labelling of Deviance,* 2d ed., edited by Walter R. Gove, 53–99. Beverly Hills: Sage.

Gove, Walter R., and Michael R. Geerken. 1977. "The Effect of Children and Employment on the Mental Health of Married Men and Women." *Social Forces* 56:66–76.

Gove, Walter R., and Jeannette F. Tudor. 1973. "Adult Sex Roles and Mental Illness." *American Journal of Sociology* 78:812–835.

Greenley, James R. 1990. "Mental Illness as a Social Problem." In *Research in Community and Mental Health,* vol. 6, 7–40. Greenwich, CT: JAI.

Greenley, James R., and Julia A. Mullen. 1990. "Help Seeking and the Use of Mental Health Services." In *Research in Community and Mental Health,* vol. 6, 325–350. Greenwich, CT: JAI.

Gusfield, Joseph. 1981. "Social Movements and Social Change: Perspectives of

Linearity and Fluidity." In *Research in Social Movements, Conflict, and Change*, edited by Louis Kriesberg, 317–339. Greenwich, CT: JAI.

———. 1989. "Constructing the Ownership of Public Problems." *Social Problems* 36:431–441.

———. 1994. "The Reflexivity of Social Movements: Collective Behavior and Mass Society Theory Revisited." In *New Social Movements: From Ideology to Identity*, edited by Enrique Laraña, Hank Johnston, and Joseph R. Gusfield, 58–78. Philadelphia: Temple University Press.

Haaken, Janice. 1993. "From Al-Anon to ACOA: Codependence and the Reconstruction of Caregiving." *Signs: Journal of Women in Culture and Society* 18:321–345.

Habermas, Jürgen. 1984. *Reason and the Rationalization of Society*, vol. 1 of *The Theory of Communicative Action*. Boston: Beacon Press.

———. 1987. *Lifeworld and System: A Critique of Functionalist Reason*, vol. 2 of *The Theory of Communicative Action*. Boston: Beacon Press.

Hamilton, James Alexander. 1962. *Postpartum Psychiatric Problems*. St. Louis, MO: C.V. Mosby.

———. 1977. "Puerpural Psychoses." In *Gynecology and Obstetrics*, edited by J. Sciarra. New York: Harper and Row.

———. 1984. "Psychobiology in Context: Reproductive-related Events in Men's and Women's Lives." *Contemporary Psychiatry* 3:12–16.

———. 1992a. "The Issue of Unique Qualities." In *Postpartum Psychiatric Illness: A Picture Puzzle*, edited by James Alexander Hamilton and Patricia Neel Harberger, 15–32. Philadelphia: University of Pennsylvania Press.

———. 1992b. "Patterns of Postpartum Illness." In *Postpartum Psychiatric Illness: A Picture Puzzle*, edited by James Alexander Hamilton and Patricia Neel Harberger, 5–14. Philadelphia: University of Pennsylvania Press.

Hamilton, James Alexander, and Patricia Neel Harberger, eds. 1992. *Postpartum Psychiatric Illness: A Picture Puzzle*. Philadelphia: University of Pennsylvania Press.

Hamilton, James Alexander, Patricia Neel Harberger, and Robert M. Atkins. 1992. "Information and Its Applications." In *Postpartum Psychiatric Illness: A Picture Puzzle*, edited by James Alexander Hamilton and Patricia Neel Harberger, 313–323. Philadelphia: University of Pennsylvania Press.

Hamilton, James Alexander, and Deborah A. Sichel. 1992. "Prophylactic Measures." In *Postpartum Psychiatric Illness: A Picture Puzzle*, edited by James Alexander Hamilton and Patricia Neel Harberger, 219–234. Philadelphia: University of Pennsylvania Press.

Hamilton, James Alexander, and B.L. Parry, and S.J. Blumenthal. 1988. "The Menstrual Cycle in Context: I. Affective Syndromes Associated with Reproductive Hormonal Changes." *Journal of Clinical Psychiatry* 49:471–480.

Hankin, Janet R. 1990. "Gender and Mental Illness." In *Research in Community and Mental Health*, vol. 6, 183–201. Greenwich, CT: JAI.

Harberger, Patricia Neel, Nancy Gleason Berchtold, and Jane Israel Honikman. 1992. "Cries for Help." In *Postpartum Psychiatric Illness: A Picture Puzzle*, edited by James Alexander Hamilton and Patricia Neel Harberger, 41–60. Philadelphia: University of Pennsylvania Press.

219

Healy, Bernadine. 1995. *A New Prescription for Women's Health: Getting the Best Medical Care in a Man's World*. New York: Viking.

Heaton, Jeanne Albronda. 1995. *Tuning in Trouble: Talk TV's Destructive Impact on Mental Health*. San Francisco: Jossey-Bass.

Heaton, Jeanne Albronda, and Nona Leigh Wilson. 1995. "Tuning in to Trouble." *Ms.* (Sept./Oct.):44–51.

Hickman, Robert. "PPD's Impact on Fathers—Starting Support Groups for Men." *Heartstrings* 2 (Summer 1991).

Hine, Darlene, and Kate Wittenstein. 1981. "Female Slave Resistance: The Economics of Sex." In *Feminist Frontiers III*, edited by Laurel Richardson and Verta Taylor, 431–436. New York: McGraw Hill.

Hock, Ellen, and Debra K. DeMeis. 1990. "Depression in Mothers of Infants: The Role of Maternal Employment." *Developmental Psychology* 26:285–291.

Hochschild, Arlie. 1983. *The Managed Heart*. Berkeley: University of California Press.

———, with Anne Machung. 1989. *The Second Shift: Working Parents and the Revolution at Home*. New York: Viking.

———. 1990. "Ideology and Emotion Management: A Perspective and Path for Future Research." In *Research Agendas in the Sociology of Emotions*, edited by Theodore D. Kemper, 117–142. Albany: SUNY Press.

———. 1994. "The Commercial Spirit of Intimate Life and the Abduction of Feminism: Signs from Women's Advice Books." *Theory, Culture & Society* 11:1–24.

Hoffman, Lily. 1989. *The Politics of Knowledge: Activist Movements in Medicine and Planning*. Albany: SUNY Press.

hooks, bell. 1993. *Sisters of the Yam: Black Women and Self-Recovery*. Boston: South End Press.

Hotchner, Tracy. 1984. *Pregnancy and Childbirth: The Complete Guide for a New Life*. New York: Avon.

Huber, Joan. 1976. "Toward a Sociotechnological Theory of the Women's Movement." *Social Problems* 23:371–388.

Huber, Joan, and Glenna Spitze. 1983. *Sex Stratification: Children, Housework, and Jobs*. New York: Academic.

Hunt, Scott A., Robert D. Benford, and David A. Snow. 1994. "Identity Fields: Framing Processes and the Social Construction of Movement Identities." In *New Social Movements: From Ideology to Identity*, edited by Enrique Laraña, Hank Johnston, and Joseph R. Gusfield, 185–208. Philadelphia: Temple University Press.

Ireland, Mardy S. 1993. *Reconceiving Women: Separating Motherhood from Female Identity*. New York: Guilford.

Jack, Dana Crowley. 1991. *Silencing the Self: Women and Depression*. Cambridge: Harvard University Press.

Jaggar, Alison M. 1989. "Love and Knowledge: Emotion in Feminist Epistemology." In *Gender/Body/Knowledge: Feminist Reconstructions of Being and Knowing*, edited by Alison M. Jaggar and Susan R. Bordo, 145–171. New Brunswick, NJ: Rutgers University Press.

Japenga, Ann. 1991. "The Tragic Ordeal of Postpartum Psychosis." *Los Angeles Times*, Feb. 1, Part VI, 11.

Jenkins, J. Craig. 1983. "Resource Mobilization Theory and the Study of Social Movements." *Annual Review of Sociology* 9:527:53.

Jenkins, J. Craig, and Bert Klandermans, eds. 1995. "The Politics of Social Protest." In *The Politics of Social Protest: Comparative Perspectives on States and Social Movements*, edited by J. Craig Jenkins and Bert Klandermans, 3–13. Minneapolis: University of Minnesota Press.

Jenness, Valerie. 1995. "Social Movement Growth, Domain Expansion, and Framing Processes: The Gay/Lesbian Movement and Violence Against Gays and Lesbians as a Social Problem." *Social Problems* 42:145–170.

Joeres, Ruth-Ellen B., and Barbara Laslett. 1995. "Maternity and Motherhood: Recent Feminist Scholarship." *Signs: Journal of Women in Culture and Society* 20:395–396.

Johnston, Hank. 1991. *Tales of Nationalism: Catalonia, 1939–1979*. New Brunswick, NJ: Rutgers University Press.

Johnston, Hank, and Bert Klandermans, eds. 1995. *Social Movements and Culture*. Minneapolis: University of Minnesota Press.

Jones, Jacqueline. 1985. *Labor of Love, Labor of Sorrow*. New York: Vintage

Jordan, Glenn, and Chris Weedon. 1995. *Cultural Politics: Class, Gender, Race, and the Postmodern World*. Cambridge: Basil Blackwell.

Kaminer, Wendy. 1992. *I'm Dysfunctional, You're Dysfunctional: The Recovery Movement and Other Self-Help Fashions*. Reading, MA: Addison-Wesley.

———. 1993. "Feminism's Identity Crisis." Atlantic Monthly (October):51–68.

Kanter, Rosabeth Moss. 1977. *Men and Women of the Corporation*. New York: Basic Books.

Kaplan, Howard B., Cynthia Robbins, and Steven S. Martin. 1983. "Toward the Testing of a General Theory of Deviant Behavior in Longitudinal Perspective: Patterns of Psychopathology." *Research in Community and Mental Health* 3:27–65.

Kaplan, Marcie. 1983. "A Woman's View of DSM-III." *American Psychologist* 38: 786–792.

Kaplan, Meryle Mahrer. 1992. *Mother's Images of Motherhood: Case Studies of Twelve Mothers*. London: Routledge.

Katz, Alfred H. 1981. "Self-Help and Mutual Aid: An Emerging Social Movement?" *Annual Review of Sociology* 7:129–155.

———. 1993. *Self-Help in America: A Social Movement Perspective*. New York: Twayne.

Katzenstein, Mary Fainsod. 1995. "Discursive Politics and Feminist Activism in the Catholic Church." In *Feminist Organizations: Harvest of the New Women's Movement*, edited by Myra Marx Ferree and Patricia Yancey Martin, 35–52. Philadelphia: Temple University Press.

Kauffman, L.A. 1990. "The Anti-Politics of Identity." *Socialist Review* 20:66–79.

Kempe, Margery. 1985. *The Book of Margery Kempe*. New York: Penguin.

Kemper, Theodore. 1978. *A Social Interactional Theory of Emotions*. New York: Wiley.

———. 1987. "How Many Emotions Are There? Wedding the Social and Autonomic Components." *American Journal of Sociology* 93:263–289.

221

Kennedy, Elizabeth Lapovsky, and Madeline D. Davis. 1993. *Boots of Leather, Slippers of Gold: The History of a Lesbian Community*. New York: Routledge.

Kessler, Suzanne J., and Wendy McKenna. 1978. *Gender: An Ethnomethodological Approach*. Chicago: University of Chicago Press.

Kirschenbaum, Sara. 1995. "More Than Blue." *Mothering Spring*:73–78.

Kirk, Stuart A., and Herb Kutchins. 1992. *The Selling of DSM: The Rhetoric of Science in Psychiatry*. New York: Aldine de Gruyter.

Kitzinger, Celia, and Rachel Perkins. 1993. *Changing Our Minds: Lesbian Feminism and Psychology*. New York: New York University Press.

Klandermans, Bert. 1992. "The Social Construction of Protest and Multiorganizational Fields." In *Frontiers in Social Movement Theory*, edited by Aldon D. Morris and Carol McClurg Mueller, 77–103. New Haven, CT: Yale University Press.

————. 1988. "The Formation and Mobilization of Consensus." In *From Structure to Action: Comparing Movement Participation across Cultures*, vol. 1, International Social Movement Research, edited by Bert Klandermans, Hanspeter Kriesi, and Sidney Tarrow. Greeenwich, CT: JAI.

Klandermans, Bert, and Sidney Tarrow. 1988. "Mobilization into Social Movements: Synthesizing European and American Approaches." *International Social Movement Research* 1:1–38.

Klatch, Rebecca. 1987. *Women of the New Right*. Philadephia: Temple University Press.

Kleiman, Karen R., and Valerie D. Raskin. 1994. *This Isn't What I Expected*. New York: Bantam.

Koonz, Claudia. 1987. *Mothers in the Fatherland*. New York: St. Martin's.

Korte, Diana, and Roberta Scaer. 1984. *A Good Birth, A Safe Birth*. New York: Bantam.

Kressierer, Dana Katherine. 1994. "Adoptees and Adoptive Families: An Exploration of the Formation of the Legal Family, the Stigma of Adoption, and the Decision to Search." Master's thesis, Virginia Polytechnic Institute and State University.

Krieger, Susan. 1991. *Social Science and the Self*. New Brunswick, NJ: Rutgers University Press.

Kriesi, Hanspeter. 1989. "New Social Movements and the New Class in the Netherlands." *American Journal of Sociology* 94:1078–1116.

Kriesi, Hanspeter, Ruud Koopmans, Jan Willem Duyvendak, and Marco G. Giugni. 1995. *New Social Movements in Western Europe: A Comparative Analysis*. Minneapolis: University of Minnesota Press.

Krouse, Mary Beth. 1993. "Gift-Giving and Social Transformation: The AIDS Memorial Quilt as Social Movement Culture." Ph.D. dissertation, Ohio State University.

Kumar, R., and Maureen Marks. 1992. "Infanticide and the Law in England and Wales." In *Postpartum Psychiatric Illness: A Picture Puzzle*, edited by James Alexander Hamilton and Patricia Neel Harberger, 257–274. Philadelphia: University of Pennsylvania Press.

Ladd-Taylor, Molly. 1993. "Toward Defining Maternalism in U.S. History." *Journal of Women's History* 5:110–113.

————. 1994. *Mother-Work: Women, Child Welfare, and the State, 1890–1930*. Urbana: University of Illinois Press.

Laraña, Enrique. 1994. "Continuity and Unity in New Forms of Collective Action: A Comparative Analysis of Student Movements." In *New Social Movements: From Ideology to Identity*, edited by Enrique Laraña, Hank Johnston, and Joseph R. Gusfield, 209–233. Philadelphia: Temple University Press.

Laraña, Enrique, Hank Johnston, and Joseph R. Gusfield, eds. 1994. *New Social Movements: From Ideology to Identity*. Philadelphia: Temple University Press.

Lasch, Christopher. 1979. *The Culture of Narcissism: American Life in an Age of Diminishing Expectations*. New York: Warner.

Laurence, Leslie, and Beth Weinhouse. 1994. *Outrageous Practices: The Alarming Truth about How Medicine Mistreats Women*. New York: Fawcett Columbine.

Leahy, Terry. 1994. "Taking Up a Position: Discourses of Femininity and Adolescence in the Context of Man/Girl Relationships." *Gender and Society* 8:48–72.

Leavitt, Judith Walzer. 1986. *Brought to Bed: Childbearing in America, 1750–1950*. New York: Oxford University Press.

Lehrman, Karen. 1993. "Off Course." *Mother Jones* (September/October):44–51, 64–68.

Leidner, Robin. 1991. "Stretching the Boundaries of Liberalism: Democratic Innovation in a Feminist Organization." *Signs: Journal of Women in Culture and Society* 16:263–289.

Levi, Andre. 1996. "Feminist Reconstructions of Identity in a Self-Help Program: A Study of Two Social Movement Organizations for Incest Survivors." Ph.D. dissertation, Ohio State University.

Lewin, Barbara. "The Moon and the Mythbegotten: Distortions About PPD." *Heartstrings* 3 (Winter/Spring 1992).

Lewin, Ellen. 1994. "Negotiating Lesbian Motherhood: The Dialectics of Resistance and Accommodation." In *Mothering: Ideology, Experience, and Agency*, edited by Evelyn Nakano Glenn, Grace Chang, and Linda Rennie Forcey, 333–353. New York: Routledge.

Lichterman, Paul. 1995. "Piecing Together Multicultural Community: Cultural Differences in Community-Building among Grass-roots Environmentalists." *Social Problems* 42:701–723.

————. 1996. *The Search for Political Community: American Activists Reinventing Commitment*. New York: Cambridge University Press.

Link, Bruce G., and Francis T. Cullen. 1990. "The Labeling Theory of Mental Disorders: A Review of the Evidence." In *Research in Community and Mental Health*, vol. 6, 75–105. Greenwich, CT: JAI.

Lofland, John. 1985. *Protest: Studies of Collective Behavior and Social Movements*. New Brunswick, NJ: Transaction Books.

————. 1989. "Consensus Movements: City Twinning and Derailed Dissent in the American Eighties." *Research in Social Movements: Conflicts and Change* 11:163–196.

Lorber, Judith. 1984. *Women Physicians: Careers, Status, and Power*. New York: Tavistock.

————. 1994. *Paradoxes of Gender*. New Haven, CT: Yale University Press.

Loscocco, Laurie. 1987. "Depression 'Cures' Disputed: Celeste, a Victim Herself, Says Drugs Alone Aren't Answer." Columbus *Dispatch*, November 4.

Luker, Kristin. 1984. *Abortion and the Politics of Motherhood*. Berkeley: University of California Press.

Lunbeck, Elizabeth. 1994. *The Psychiatric Persuasion: Knowledge, Gender, and Power in Modern America*. Princeton, NJ: Princeton University Press.

MacPherson, Karen. "Books for Parents-to-Be." *Dispatch*, July 30, 1990, p. 2D.

Mansbridge, Jane. 1986. *Why We Lost the ERA*. Chicago: University of Chicago Press.

———. 1995. "What Is the Feminist Movement?" In *Feminist Organizations: Harvest of the New Women's Movement*, edited by Myra Marx Ferree and Patricia Yancey Martin, 27–34. Philadelphia: Temple University Press.

Marshall, Susan. 1989. "Keep Us on a Pedestal: Women against Feminism in Twentieth-Century America." In *Women: A Feminist Perspective*, 4th ed., edited by Jo Freeman, 567–580. Mountainview, CA: Mayfield.

———. 1995. "Confrontation and Cooptation in Antifeminist Organizations." In *Feminist Organizations: Harvest of the New Women's Movement*, edited by Myra Marx Ferree and Patricia Yancey Martin, 323–335. Philadelphia: Temple University Press.

Martin, Emily. 1987. *The Woman in the Body: A Cultural Analysis of Reproduction*. Boston: Beacon.

Martin, Patricia Yancey. 1990. "Rethinking Feminist Organizations." *Gender and Society* 4:182–206.

Marwell, Gerald, and Pam Oliver. 1993. *The Critical Mass in Collective Action: A Micro-Social Theory*. New York: Cambridge University Press.

Matthews, Nancy A. 1994. *Confronting Rape: The Feminist Anti-Rape Movement and the State*. London: Routledge.

McAdam, Doug. 1982. *Political Process and the Development of Black Insurgency, 1930–1970*. Chicago: University of Chicago Press.

———. 1988. *Freedom Summer*. New York: Oxford University Press.

———. 1989. "The Biographical Consequences of Activism." *American Sociological Review* 54:744–760.

———. 1992. "Gender as a Mediator of the Activist Experience: The Case of Freedom Summer." *American Journal of Sociology* 97:1211–1249.

———. 1994. "Culture and Social Movments." In *New Social Movments: From Ideology to Identity*, edited by Enrique Laraña, Hank Johnston, and Joseph R. Gusfield, 36–57. Philadelphia: Temple University Press.

———. 1995. "'Initiator' and 'Spin-off' Movements: Diffusion Processes in Protest Cycles." In *Repertoires and Cycles of Collective Action*, edited by Mark Traugott, 217–239. Durham, NC: Duke University Press.

———. John D. McCarthy, and Mayer N. Zald. 1988. "Social Movements." In *Handbook of Sociology*, edited by Neil Smelser, 695–737. Newbury Park, CA: Sage.

McCarthy, John D., and Mayer N. Zald. 1973. *The Trend of Social Movements in America: Professionalization and Resource Mobilization*. Morristown, NJ: General Learning Press.

———. 1977. "Resource Mobilization and Social Movements: A Partial Theory." *American Journal of Sociology* 82:1212–1241.

————. 1987. "The Trend in Social Movements in America: Professionalization and Resource Mobilization." In *Social Movements in an Organizational Society: Collected Essays*, edited by Mayer N. Zald and John D. McCarthy, 337–391. New Brunswick, NJ: Transaction Books.

McCarthy, John D., and Mark Wolfson. 1992. "Consensus Movements, Conflict Movements, and the Cooptation of Civic and State Infrastructures." In *Frontiers in Social Movement Theory*, edited by Aldon D. Morris and Carol McClurg Mueller, 273–297. New Haven, CT: Yale University Press.

McCormick, Kelly. 1992. "Moms Without Dads: Women Choosing Children." Ph.D. dissertation, Ohio State University.

McGrath, Ellen, Gwendolyn Puryear Keita, Bonnie R. Strickland, and Nancy Felipe Russo. 1990. *Women and Depression: Risk Factors and Treatment Implications*. Washington, DC: American Psychological Association.

McMahon, Marilyn. 1993. "Helping Parents Cope with the Hard Parts." *Santa Barbara News-Press*, October 13.

Melucci, Alberto. 1989. *Nomads of the Present: Social Movements and Individual Needs in Contemporary Society*. Philadelphia: Temple University Press.

————. 1994. "A Strange Kind of Newness: What's 'New' in New Social Movements." In *New Social Movements: From Ideology to Identity*, edited by Enrique Laraña, Hank Johnston, and Joseph R. Gusfield, 101–130. Philadelphia: Temple University Press.

————. 1995. "The Process of Collective Identity." In *Social Movements and Culture*, edited by Hank Johnston and Bert Klandermans, 41–63. Minneapolis: University of Minnesota Press.

Menaghan, Elizabeth G. 1989. "Role Changes and Psychological Well-Being: Variations in Effects by Gender and Role Repertoire." *Social Forces* 67:693–714.

————. 1990. "Social Stress and Individual Distress." In *Research in Community and Mental Health*, vol. 6, 107–141. Greenwich, CT: JAI.

Messner, Michael A., and Don F. Sabo. 1994. *Sex, Violence, and Power in Sports: Rethinking Masculinity*. Freedom, CA: Crossing Press.

Meyer, David S., and Nancy Whittier. 1994. "Social Movement Spillover." *Social Problems* 41:277–298.

Michaelson, Marc. 1994. "Wangari Maathai and Kenya's Green Belt Movement: Exploring the Evolution and Potentialities of Consensus Movement Mobilization." *Social Problems* 41:540–561.

Mies, Maria. 1991. "Women's Research or Feminist Research? The Debate Surrounding Feminist Science and Methodology." In *Beyond Methodology: Feminist Scholarship as Lived Research*, edited by Mary Margaret Fonow and Judith A. Cook, 60–84. Bloomington: Indiana University Press.

Miles, Agnes. 1988. *The Neurotic Woman: The Role of Gender in Psychiatric Illness*. New York: New York University Press.

Mills, C. Wright. 1959. *The Sociological Imagination*. New York: Oxford University Press.

Mirkin, Marsha Pravder, ed. 1994. *Women in Context: Toward a Feminist Reconstruction of Psychotherapy*. New York: Guilford.

Mirowsky, John, and Catherine E. Ross. 1986. "Social Patterns of Distress." *Annual Review of Sociology* 12:23–45.

———. 1989. *Social Causes of Psychological Distress*. New York: Aldine de Gruyter.

———. 1995. "Sex Differences in Distress: Real or Artifact?" *American Sociological Review* 60:449–468.

Moen, Phyllis. 1992. *Women's Two Roles: A Contemporary Dilemma*. New York: Auburn House.

Morgan, Marabel. 1973. *The Total Woman*. Old Tappan, NJ: F.H. Revell.

Morgen, Sandra. 1986. "The Dynamics of Cooptation in a Feminist Health Clinic." *Social Science and Medicine* 23:201–210.

———. 1988. "The Dream of Diversity, the Dilemmas of Difference: Race and Class Contradictions in a Feminist Health Clinic." In *Anthropology for the Nineties*, edited by J. Cole, 370–380. New York: Free Press.

———. 1995. "'It Was the Best of Times, It Was the Worst of Times': Emotional Discourse in the Work Cultures of Feminist Health Clinics." In *Feminist Organizations: Harvest of the New Women's Movement*, edited by Myra Marx Ferree and Patricia Yancey Martin, 234–247. Philadelphia: Temple University Press.

Morris, Aldon D. 1984. *The Origins of the Civil Rights Movement: Black Communities Organizing for Change*. New York: Free Press.

———. 1992. "Political Consciousness and Collective Action." In *Frontiers in Social Movement Theory*, edited by Aldon D. Morris and Carol McClurg Mueller, 351–373. New Haven, CT: Yale University Press.

Morris, Aldon D., and Carol McClurg Mueller, eds. 1992. *Frontiers in Social Movement Theory*. New Haven, CT: Yale University Press.

Mueller, Carol McClurg. 1987. "Collective Consciousness, Identity Transformation, and the Rise of Women in Public Office in the United States." In *The Women's Movements of the U.S. and Western Europe: Consciousness, Political Opportunity, and Public Policy*, edited by M.F. Katzenstein and C.M. Mueller, 89–108. Philadelphia: Temple University Press.

———. 1992. "Building Social Movement Theory." In *Frontiers in Social Movement Theory*, edited by Aldon D. Morris and Carol McClurg Mueller, 3–25. New Haven, CT: Yale University Press.

Myers, Daniel J. 1994. "Communication Technology and Social Movements: Contributions of Computer Networks to Activism." *Social Science Computer Review* 12:250–260.

Naples, Nancy A. 1991. "'Just What Needed to Be Done': The Political Practice of Women Community Workers in Low-Income Neighborhoods." *Gender and Society* 5:478–494.

Neuhouser, Kevin. 1995. "'Worse Than Men': Gendered Mobilization in an Urban Brazilian Squatter Settlement." *Gender and Society* 9:38–59.

Nixon, Deborah. 1985. "The Etiology and Treatment of Postpartum Depressive Disorders." *International Journal of Women's Studies* 8:140–148.

Nock, Steven L. 1987. "The Symbolic Meaning of Childbearing." *Journal of Family Issues* 8:373–393.

Norwood, Robin. 1985. *Women Who Love Too Much*. New York: Basic Books.

Oakley, Ann. 1974. *Woman's Work: The Housewife, Past and Present*. New York: Pantheon Books.

———. 1979a. "A Case of Maternity: Paradigms of Women as Maternity Cases." *Signs: Journal of Women in Culture and Society* 4:607–631.

———. 1979b. "The Baby Blues." *New Society* (April):11–12.

———. 1981. "Interviewing Women: A Contradiction in Terms." In *Doing Feminist Research*, edited by Helen Roberts, 30–61. London: Routledge and Kegan Paul.

———. 1986. "Feminism, Motherhood, and Medicine—Who Cares?" In *What is Feminism?* edited by Juliet Mitchell and Ann Oakley, 125–150. Oxford: Basil Blackwell.

Oberschall, Anthony. 1973. *Social Conflict and Social Movements*. Englewood Cliffs, NJ: Prentice-Hall.

Offe, Claus. 1985. "New Social Movements: Challenging the Boundaries of Institutional Politics." *Social Research* 52:817–868.

Osmond, Marie Withers, and Barrie Thorne. 1993. "Feminist Theories: The Social Construction of Gender in Families and Society." In *Sourcebook of Family Theories and Methods: A Contextual Approach*, edited by P.G. Boss, W.J. Doherty, R. LaRossa, W.R. Schumm, and S.K. Steinmetz. 591–625. New York: Plenum.

O'Meara, Therese. "Out of the Darkness . . . Into the Light." *Heartstrings* (Summer/Fall 1992).

Pearlin, Leonard I., and Morton A. Lieberman. 1979. "Social Sources of Emotional Distress." In *Research in Community and Mental Health*, vol. 1, edited by Roberta G. Simmons, 217–248. Greenwich, CT: JAI.

Pearlin, Leonard I., Morton A. Lieberman, Elizabeth G. Menaghan, and Joseph T. Mullan. 1981. "The Stress Process." *Journal of Health and Social Behavior* 22:337–356.

Philipson, Ilene. 1993. *On the Shoulders of Women: The Feminization of Psychotherapy*. New York: Guilford.

Piercy, Marge. 1980. *The Moon Is Always Female*. New York: Alfred A. Knopf.

Placksin, Sally. 1994. *Mothering the New Mother: Your Postpartum Resource Companion*. New York: Newmarket.

Plotke, David. 1990. "What's So New About New Social Movements?" *Socialist Review* 20:81–102.

Polsky, Andrew J. 1991. *The Rise of the Therapeutic State*. Princeton, NJ: Princeton University Press.

Ransdell, Lisa. 1990. "Postpartum Depression and the Medicalization of Motherhood." Ph.D. dissertation, Ohio State University.

Reinharz, Shulamit, with Lynn Davidman. 1992. *Feminist Methods in Social Research*. New York: Oxford University Press.

Reskin, Barbara F. 1988. "Bringing the Men Back In: Sex Differentiation and the Devaluation of Women's Work." *Gender and Society* 2:58–81.

Reskin, Barbara F., and Irene Padavic. 1994. *Women and Men at Work*. Thousand Oaks, CA: Pine Forge.

Resnick, Phillip J., M.D. 1969. "Child Murder by Patients: A Psychiatric Review of Filicide." *American Journal of Psychiatry* 126:325–333.

Rich, Adrienne. 1976. *Of Woman Born: Motherhood as Experience and Institution*. New York: W.W. Norton.

————. 1980. "Compulsory Heterosexuality and Lesbian Existence." *Signs: Journal of Women in Culture and Society* 5:631–660.

Riessman, Frank. 1990. "The New Self-Help Backlash." *Social Policy* (Summer):42–48.

Roberts, Dorothy E. 1995. "Motherhood and Crime." *Social Text* 42:99–123.

Robnett, Belinda. 1996. "African American Women in the Civil Rights Movement, 1954–1965: Gender, Leadership, and Micromobilization." *American Journal of Sociology* 101: 1661-1693.

Roiphe, Katie. 1993. *The Morning After: Sex, Fear, and Feminism on Campus*. Boston: Little, Brown.

Romito, Patrizia. 1989. "Unhappiness after Childbirth." In *Effective Care in Pregnancy and Childbirth*, edited by Iain Chalmus, Murray Emkin, and Marc Keirse, 1433–1446. New York: Oxford University Press.

————. 1990. "Postpartum Depression and the Experience of Motherhood." *Acta Obstetricia et Gynecologica Scandinavica* 69 Suppl. 154:5.

Roscigno, Vincent J. and Cynthia D. Anderson. 1995. "Subordination and Struggle: Social Movement Dynamics and Processes of Inequality." In *Perspectives on Social Problems*, vol. 7, 249–274. Greenwich, CT: JAI.

Ross, Catherine E., John Mirowsky, and Karen Goldsteen. 1990. "The Impact of the Family on Health: The Decade in Review." *Journal of Marriage and the Family* 52:1059–1078.

Ross, Catherine E., John Mirowsky, and Joan Huber. 1983. "Dividing Work, Sharing Work, and In-Between: Marriage Patterns and Depression." *American Sociological Review* 48:809–823.

Ross, Catherine E., and Marieke Van Willigen. 1995. "Activism, Personal Control, and Well-Being among Women with Breast Cancer." Unpublished paper.

Ross, Ellen. 1995. "New Thoughts on 'the Oldest Vocation': Mothers and Motherhood in Recent Feminist Scholarship." *Signs: Journal of Women in Culture and Society* 20:397–413.

Rosser, Sue V. 1994. *Women's Health—Missing from U.S. Medicine*. Bloomington: Indiana University Press.

Rossi, Alice. 1984. "Gender and Parenthood: An Evolutionary Perspective." *American Sociological Review* 49:1–19.

Rothman, Barbara Katz. 1989. *Recreating Motherhood: Ideology and Technology in a Patriarchal Society*. New York: W.W. Norton.

Rothschild-Whitt, Joyce, and J.A. Whitt. 1986. *The Cooperative Workplace*. Cambridge: Cambridge University Press.

Ruddick, Sara. 1980. "Maternal Thinking." *Feminist Studies* 6:342–367.

————. 1989. *Maternal Thinking: Toward a Politics of Peace*. New York: Ballantine.

Rupp, Leila J. 1993. "'Imagine My Surprise': Women's Relationships in Mid-Twentieth-Century America." In *Feminist Frontiers III*, edited by Laurel Richardson and Verta Taylor, 301–315. New York: McGraw-Hill.

————. 1994. "Constructing Internationalism: The Case of Transnational Women's Organizations, 1888–1945." *American Historical Review* 99:1571–1600.

Rupp, Leila J., and Verta Taylor. 1986. "The Women's Movement Since 1960: Structure, Strategies, and New Directions." In *American Choices: Social Dilemmas and Public Policy Since 1960*, edited by Robert H. Bremner, Gary W. Reichard, and Richard J. Hopkins, 75–104. Columbus: Ohio State University Press.

————. 1987. *Survival in the Doldrums: The American Women's Rights Movement, 1945 to the 1960s*. New York: Oxford University Press.

Ruzek, Sheryl. 1978. *The Women's Health Movement: Feminist Alternatives to Medical Control*. New York: Praeger.

Ryan, Barbara. 1992. *Feminism and the Women's Movement: Dynamics of Change in Social Movement Ideology and Activism*. New York: Routledge.

Saks, B., J. Frank, T. Lowe, W. Berman, F. Naftolin, D. Phil, and D. Cohen. 1985. "Depressed Mood During Pregnancy and the Puerperium: Clinical Recognition and Implications for Clinical Practice." *American Journal of Psychiatry* 142:728–731.

Sattel, Jack W. 1992. "The Inexpressive Male: Tragedy or Sexual Politics?" In *Men's Lives*, 2d edition, edited by Michael S. Kimmel and Michael A. Messner, 350–358. New York: Macmillan.

Sawyers, Traci, and David Meyer. "Missed Opportunities: Social Movement Abeyance and Public Policy." Unpublished paper.

Schecter, S. 1982. *Women and Male Violence: The Visions and Struggles of the Battered Women's Movement*. London: Pluto.

Scheff, Thomas J. 1966. *Being Mentally Ill*. Chicago: Aldine.

————. 1990. *Microsociology: Discourse, Emotion, and Social Structure*. Chicago: University of Chicago.

Schmidt, Martha. 1993. "Emotion, Identity, and Social Movements: The Effects of Jeffrey Dahmer's Serial Killings on Milwaukee's Lesbian and Gay Community." Ph.D. dissertation, Ohio State University.

Schneider, Beth E. 1986. "Feminist Disclaimers, Stigma, and the Contemporary Women's Movement." Paper presented at the Annual Meetings of the American Sociological Association, New York City.

Schneider, Beth. 1988. "Political Generations in the Contemporary Women's Movement." *Sociological Inquiry* 58:4–21.

Schneider, Beth E., and Nancy E. Stoller, eds. 1995. *Women Resisting AIDS: Feminist Strategies of Empowerment*. Philadelphia: Temple University Press.

Schur, Edwin. 1984. *Labeling Women Deviant*. New York: Random House.

Schwartz, Michael, and Shuva Paul. 1992. "Resource Mobilization versus the Mobilization of People: Why Consensus Movements Cannot Be Instruments of Social Change." In *Frontiers in Social Movement Theory*, edited by Aldon D. Morris and Carol McClurg Mueller, 205–223. New Haven, CT: Yale University Press.

Sciarra, John J., ed. 1989. *Gynecology and Obstetrics*. Philadelphia: Lippincott.

Scott, Anne Firor. 1992. *Natural Allies: Women's Associations in American History*. Urbana: University of Illinois Press.

Scott, Joan Wallach. 1988. *Gender and the Politics of History*. New York: Columbia University Press.

Scully, Diana. 1980. *Men Who Control Women's Health: The Miseducation of Obstetrician-Gynecologists*. Boston: Houghton Mifflin.

Seeman, M. and T.E. Seeman. 1983. "Health Behavior and Personal Autonomy: A Longitudinal Study of the Sense of Control in Illness." *Journal of Health and Social Behavior* 24:144–159.

Segura, Denise A., and Jennifer L. Pierce. 1993. "Chicana/o Family Structure and Gender Personality: Chodorow, Familism, and Psychoanalytic Sociology Revisited." *Signs: Journal of Women in Culture and Society* 19: 62–91.

Sered, Susan Starr. 1994. "Ideology, Autonomy, and Sisterhood: An Analysis of the Secular Consequences of Women's Religions." *Gender and Society* 8:486–506.

Shaw, Stephanie J. 1991. "Black Club Women and the Creation of the National Association of Colored Women." *Journal of Women's History* 3:10–25.

Shin, Gi Wook. 1994. "The Historical Making of Collective Action: The Korean Peasant Uprisings of 1946." *American Journal of Sociology* 99:1596–1624.

Simonds, Wendy. 1992. *Women and Self-Help Culture: Reading Between the Lines*. New Brunswick, NJ: Rutgers University Press.

Simonds, Wendy, and Barbara Katz Rothman. 1992. *Centuries of Solace: Expressions of Maternal Grief in Popular Literature*. Philadelphia: Temple University Press.

Sirianni, Carmen. 1993. "Learning Pluralism: Democracy and Diversity in Feminist Organizations." In *Democratic Community: NOMOS XXXV*, edited by John Chapman and Ian Shapiro, 283–312. New York: New York University Press.

Skocpol, Theda. 1992. *Protecting Soldiers and Mothers: The Political Origins of Social Policy in the United States*. Cambridge: Belknap Press of Harvard University Press.

Smith, Dorothy E. 1979. "A Sociology for Women." In *The Prism of Sex: Essays in the Sociology of Knowledge*, edited by Julia Sherman and Evelyn Beck, 135–187. Madison: University of Wisconsin Press.

———. 1987. *Everyday World as Problematic: A Feminist Sociology*. Boston: Northeastern University Press.

———. 1988. "Femininity as Discourse." In *Becoming Feminine: The Politics of Popular Culture*, edited by L.G. Roman et al. London: Falmer.

———. 1990. *Texts, Facts, and Femininity: Exploring the Relations of Ruling*. New York: Routledge.

Smith-Rosenberg, Carroll. 1972. "The Hysterical Woman: Sex Roles and Role Conflict in Nineteenth-Century America." *Social Research* 39:652–678.

Smith-Rosenberg, Carroll, and Charles Rosenberg. 1973. "The Female Animal: Medical and Biological Views of Woman and Her Role in Nineteenth-Century America." *Journal of American History* 60:332–356.

Snitow, Ann. 1990. "A Gender Diary." In *Conflicts in Feminism*, edited by Marianne Hirsch and Evelyn Fox Keller, 9–43. New York: Routledge.

Snow, David A. 1987. "Organization, Ideology, and Mobilization: The Case of Nichiren Shoshu of America." In *The Future of New Religious Movements*, edited by D.G. Bromley and P.E. Hammond, 153–172. Macon, GA: Mercer University Press.

Snow David A., and Robert D. Benford. 1992. "Master Frames and Cycles of

Protest." In *Frontiers in Social Movement Theory*, edited by Aldon D. Morris and Carol McClurg Mueller, 133–155. New Haven, CT: Yale University Press.

Snow, David A., and Pamela E. Oliver. 1995. "Social Movements and Collective Behavior: Social Psychological Dimensions and Considerations." In *Sociological Perspectives on Social Psychology*, edited by Karen S. Cook, Gary Alan Fine, and James S. House, 571–599. Boston: Allyn and Bacon.

Snow, David, A., E. Burke Rochford, Jr., Steven K. Worden, and Robert D. Benford. 1986. "Frame Alignment, Micromobilization, and Movement Participation." *American Sociological Review* 51:464–481.

Solinger, Rickie. 1992. *Wake Up Little Susie: Single Pregnancy and Race Before Roe v. Wade*. New York: Routledge.

Stacey, Judith. 1987. "Sexism by a Subtler Name? Postindustrial Conditions and Postfeminist Consciousness in the Silicon Valley." *Socialist Review* 17:7–28.

———. 1991. *Brave New Families: Stories of Domestic Upheaval in Late Twentieth Century America*. New York: Basic Books.

Stacey, Judith, and Barrie Thorne. 1985. "The Missing Feminist Revolution in Sociology." *Social Problems* 32:301–316.

Stack, Carol B., and Linda M. Burton. 1994. "Kinscripts: Reflections on Family, Generation, and Culture." In *Mothering: Ideology, Experience, and Agency*, edited by Evelyn Nakano Glenn, Grace Chang, and Linda Rennie Forcey, 33–44. New York: Routledge.

Staggenborg, Suzanne. 1989. "Stability and Innovation in the Women's Movement: A Comparison of Two Movement Organizations." *Social Problems* 36:75–92.

———. 1991. *The Pro-Choice Movement: Organization and Activism in the Abortion Conflict*. New York: Oxford University Press.

———. 1995. "Can Feminist Organizations Be Effective?" In *Feminist Organizations: Harvest of the New Women's Movment*, edited by Myra Marx Ferree and Patricia Yancey Martin, 339–355. Philadelphia: Temple University Press.

Staggenborg, Suzanne, Donna Eder, and Lori Sudderth. 1993/94. "Women's Culture and Social Change: Evidence from the National Women's Music Festival." *Berkeley Journal of Sociology* 38:31–56.

Stanley, Liz, and Sue Wise. 1983. *Breaking Out: Feminist Consciousness and Feminist Research*. London: Routledge and Kegan Paul.

Starr, P. 1982. *The Social Transformation of American Medicine*. New York: Basic Books.

Stein, Arlene. 1992. "Sisters and Queers: The Decentering of Lesbian Feminism." *Socialist Review* 22:33–55.

Steinem, Gloria. 1992a. *Revolution From Within: A Book of Self-Esteem*. Boston: Little, Brown.

———. 1992b. "Helping Ourselves to Revolution." *Ms.* (November/December):24–29.

Stern, Gwen, and Laurence Kruckman. 1983. "Multi-disciplinary Perspectives on Post-Partum Depression: An Anthropological Critique." *Social Science and Medicine* 17:1027–1041.

Strong, P.M. 1979. "Sociological Imperialism and the Profession of Medicine: A Critical Examination of the Thesis of Medical Imperialism." *Social Science and Medicine* 13:199–215.

Styron, William. 1990. *Darkness Visible*. New York: Random House.

Swidler, Ann. 1986. "Culture in Action: Symbols and Strategies." *American Sociological Review* 51:273–286.

———. 1995. "Cultural Power and Social Movements." In *Social Movements and Culture*, edited by Hank Johnston and Bert Klandermans, 25–40. Minneapolis: University of Minnesota Press.

Tarrow, Sidney. 1989. *Democracy and Disorder: Protest and Politics in Italy, 1965–1975*. Oxford: Clarendon.

———. 1994. *Power in Movement: Social Movements, Collective Action, and Mass Politics in the Modern State*. New York: Cambridge University Press.

Tauber, Ben-Zion. 1984. *Manual of Gynecologic and Obstetric Emergencies*. 2d ed. Philadelphia: W.B. Saunders.

Tavris, Carol. 1993. "Beware the Incest Survivor Machine." *New York Times Book Review*, January 3:1, 16–17.

Taylor, Verta. 1987. "Breaking the Emotional Rules of Motherhood: The Experience and Treatment of Postpartum Depression." Final Report to the Ohio Department of Mental Health, Columbus, OH.

———. 1989. "Sources of Continuity in Social Movements: The Women's Movement in Abeyance." *American Sociological Review* 54:761–775.

———. 1995. "Self-Labeling and Women's Mental Health: Postpartum Illness and the Reconstruction of Motherhood." *Sociological Focus* 28:23–47.

Taylor, Verta, and Nicole C. Raeburn. 1995. "Identity Politics as High-Risk Activism: Career Consequences for Lesbian, Gay, and Bisexual Sociologists." *Social Problems* 42:252–273.

Taylor, Verta, and Leila J. Rupp. 1991. "Researching the Women's Movement: We Make Our Own History, But Not Just as We Please." In *Beyond Methodology: Feminist Scholarship as Lived Research*, edited by Mary Margaret Fonow and Judith A. Cook, 119–132. Bloomington: Indiana University Press.

———. 1993. "Women's Culture and Lesbian Feminist Activism: A Reconsideration of Cultural Feminism." *Signs: Journal of Women in Culture and Society* 19:32–61.

Taylor, Verta, and Marieke Van Willigen. 1996. "Women's Self-Help and the Reconstruction of Gender: The Postpartum Support and Breast Cancer Movements." *Mobilization: An International Journal* 1: 122–144.

———. 1995. "Analytical Approaches to Social Movement Culture: The Culture of the Women's Movement." In *Social Movements and Culture*, edited by Hank Johnston and Bert Klandermans, 163–187. Minneapolis: University of Minnesota Press.

Taylor, Verta, and Nancy E. Whittier. 1992. "Collective Identity in Social Movement Communities: Lesbian Feminist Mobilization." In *Frontiers in Social Movement Theory*, edited by Aldon D. Morris and Carol Mueller, 104–29. New Haven, CT: Yale University Press.

———. 1993. "The New Feminist Movement." In *Feminist Frontiers III*, edited by Laurel Richardson and Verta Taylor, 533–548. New York: McGraw Hill.

Theriot, Nancy M. 1990. "Diagnosing Unnatural Motherhood: Nineteenth Century Physicians and 'Puerperal Insanity.'" *American Studies* 26:69–88.

———. 1993. "Women's Voices in Nineteenth-Century Medical Discourse: A Step toward Deconstructing Science." *Signs: Journal of Women in Culture and Society* 19:1–31.

Theweleit, Klaus. 1987. *Male Fantasies*, vol. 1. Minneapolis: Minnesota.

Thoits, Peggy A. 1983. "Multiple Identities and Psychological Well-Being: A Reformulation and Test of the Social Isolation Hypothesis." *American Sociological Review* 48:174–187.

———. 1985. "Self-Labeling Processes in Mental Illness: The Role of Emotional Deviance." *American Journal of Sociology* 91:221–249.

Thompson, John B. 1990. *Ideology and Modern Culture*. Oxford: Polity.

Thorne, Barrie. 1993. *Gender Play: Girls and Boys in School*. New Brunswick, NJ: Rutgers University Press.

Thorne, Barrie, with Marilyn Yalom. 1992. *Rethinking the Family: Some Feminist Questions*. Boston: Northeastern University Press.

Thurer, Shari L. 1994. *The Myths of Motherhood: How Culture Reinvents the Good Mother*. Boston: Houghton Mifflin.

Tierney, K.J. 1982. "The Battered Women Movement and the Creation of the Wife Beating Problem." *Social Problems* 29:207–220.

Tilly, Charles. 1978. *From Mobilization to Revolution*. Reading, MA: Addison-Wesley.

———. 1984. "Social Movements and National Politics." In *Statemaking and Social Movements: Essays in History and Theory*, edited by Charles Bright and Susan Harding, 297–317. Ann Arbor: University of Michigan Press.

———. 1986. *The Contentious French*. Cambridge: Harvard University Press.

Touraine, Alain. 1981. *The Voice and the Eye: An Analysis of Social Movements*. New York: Cambridge University Press.

———. 1985. "An Introduction to the Study of Social Movements." *Social Research* 52:749–787.

———. 1988. *A Return of the Actor: Social Theory in Post-Industrial Society*. Minneapolis: University of Minnesota Press.

———. 1992. "Beyond Social Movements." *Theory, Culture, and Society* 9:125–145.

Traugott, Mark, ed. 1995. *Repertoires and Cycles of Collective Action*. Durham, NC: Duke University Press.

Trebilcot, Joyce, ed. 1984. *Mothering: Essays in Feminist Theory*. Lanham, MD: Rowman and Littlefield.

Tronto, Joan C. 1989. "Women and Caring: What Can Feminists Learn about Morality from Caring?" In *Gender/Body/Knowledge: Feminist Reconstructions of Being and Knowing*, edited by Alison M. Jaggar and Susan R. Bordo, 172–187. New Brunswick, NJ: Rutgers University Press.

Tudor, William, Jeannette F. Tudor, and Walter R. Gove. 1977. "The Effect of Sex Role Differences on the Social Control of Mental Illness." *Journal of Health and Social Behavior* 18:98–112.

Turner, Ralph, and Lewis Killian. 1987. *Collective Behavior*, 3rd ed. Englewood Cliffs, NJ: Prentice-Hall.

Van Willigen, Marieke. 1993. "Collective Identity and Activist Strategies in the Breast Cancer Movement." Master's thesis, Ohio State University.

Vogel, Lisa. 1993. *Mothers on the Job: Maternity Policy in the U.S. Workplace*. New Brunswick, NJ: Rutgers University Press.

———. 1995. *Woman Questions: Essays for a Materialist Feminism*. New York: Routledge.

Walters, Marianne. 1994. "Service Delivery Systems and Women: The Construction of Conflict." In *Women in Context: Toward a Feminist Reconstruction of Psychotherapy*, edited by Marsha Pravder Mirkin, 9–24. New York: Guilford.

Weedon, Chris. 1987. *Feminist Practice and Poststructuralist Theory*. Cambridge: Blackwell.

Weigand, Kathleen. 1995. "Vanguards of Women's Liberation: The Old Left and the Continuity of the Women's Movement in the United States, 1945–1970s." Ph.D. dissertation, Ohio State University.

Weiner, Lynn Y. 1993. "Maternalism as a Paradigm: Defining the Issues." *Journal of Women's History* 5:96–98.

———. 1994. "Reconstructing Motherhood: The La Leche League in Postwar America." *Journal of American History* 80:1357–1381.

Weissman, Myrna M., and Eugene S. Paykel. 1974. *The Depressed Woman*. Chicago: University of Chicago Press.

Welburn, V. 1980. *Postnatal Depression*. Glasgow: William/Collins Sons.

Wertz, Richard W., and Dorothy C. Wertz. 1977. *Lying-In: A History of Childbirth in America*. New Haven, CT: Yale University Press.

West, C. 1984. *Routine Complications: Troubles with Talk between Doctors and Patients*. Bloomington: Indiana University Press.

West, Candace, and Sarah Fenstermaker. 1995. "Doing Difference." *Gender and Society* 9:8–37.

West, Candace, and Don Zimmerman. 1987. "Doing Gender." *Gender and Society* 1:125–151.

West, Guida, and Rhoda Lois Blumberg, eds. 1990. *Women and Social Protest*. New York: Oxford University Press.

Whalen, Jack, and Richard Flacks. 1987. *Beyond the Barricades: The Sixties Generation Grows Up*. Philadelphia: Temple University Press.

Whittier, Nancy E. 1995. *Feminist Generations: The Persistence of the Radical Women's Movement*. Philadelphia: Temple University Press.

Williams, Rhys H. 1995. "Constructing the Public Good: Social Movements and Cultural Resources." *Social Problems* 42:124–144.

Wolf, Naomi. 1994. *Fire with Fire: The New Female Power and How It Will Change the 21st Century*. New York: Random House.

Wuthnow, Robert. 1989. *Communities of Discourse: Ideology and Social Structure in the Reformation, the Enlightenment, and European Socialism*. Cambridge: Harvard University Press.

———. 1994. *Sharing the Journey: Support Groups and America's New Quest for Community*. New York: Free Press.

Yee, Shirley J. 1992. *Black Women Abolitionists: A Study of Activism, 1828–1860.* Knoxville: University of Tennessee Press.

Zald, Mayer N., and John D. McCarthy. 1987. *Social Movements in an Organizational Society.* New Brunswick, NJ: Transaction Books.

Zimmerman, Mary K. 1987. "The Women's Health Movement: A Critique of Medical Enterprise and the Position of Women." In *Analyzing Gender: A Handbook of Social Science*, edited by Beth B. Hess and Myra Marx Ferree, 442–472. Newbury Park, CA: Sage.

Zola, Irving. 1972. "Medicine as an Institution of Social Control." *Sociological Review* 20: 487–504.

———. 1991. "Bringing Our Bodies and Ourselves Back In: Reflections on a Past, Present, and Future 'Medical Sociology.'" *Journal of Health and Social Behavior* 32:1–16.

INDEX

INDEX